Performance and Cognition

Cognitive scientists working in neuroscience, psychology, linguistics, philosophy, and other fields have made rapid strides in the past 20 years in understanding perception, empathy, spatiality, emotions, meaning-making, and many other cognitive areas that are crucial to producing, enacting, and responding to performances on stage. Surprisingly, however, scholars in theatre and performance studies are just beginning to apply these findings to their field. This book invites theatre and performance scholars to incorporate many of the insights of cognitive science into their work and to begin considering all of their research projects from the perspective of cognitive studies.

As well as including a comprehensive introduction to the challenges of cognitive studies for theatre and performance scholarship, the volume features essays in all of the major areas of theatre and performance. Several of the essays use cognitive studies to challenge some of the key scholarly and practical orientations in theatre and performance studies. The experimentally based insights of cognitive science are shown to be at odds with Saussurean semiotics, psychoanalysis, and aspects of deconstruction, New Historicism, and Foucauldian discourse theory. The contributors also apply ideas from cognitive studies to open up the possible meanings of plays to readers, and to illuminate the process of acting through the work of the cognitive neuroscientist Antonio Damasio. Theatrical response is examined with an essay focusing on the general dynamics of perception, and another explaining the riots that greeted the 1907 production of *The Playboy of the Western World* through cognitive stereotyping.

Performance and Cognition opens up fresh perspectives on theatre studies – with applications for dramatic criticism, performance analysis, acting practice, audience response, theatre history, and other important areas – and sets the agenda for future work, helping to map the emergence of this new approach.

Bruce McConachie is Professor of Theatre at the University of Pittsburgh, USA, and specializes in theatre history, theatre historiography and cognitive approaches to theatre. **F. Elizabeth Hart** is Associate Professor of English at the University of Connecticut, Storrs, USA, where she teaches Renaissance studies, Shakespeare, and cognitive approaches to literature.

Routledge advances in theatre and performance studies

Performance and Cognition

Theatre studies and the cognitive turn

Edited by Bruce McConachie and
F. Elizabeth Hart

LIS LIBRARY

Date	Fund
23/6/15	d-che

Order No
2628211

| University of Chester |

Routledge
Taylor & Francis Group

LONDON AND NEW YORK

First published 2006
by Routledge
2 Park Square, Milton Park, Abingdon, Oxon, OX14 4RN

Simultaneously published in the USA and Canada
by Routledge
270 Madison Ave, New York NY 10016

Routledge is an imprint of the Taylor & Francis Group, an informa business

Transferred to Digital Printing 2010

© 2006 Editorial matter and selection, Bruce McConachie and
F. Elizabeth Hart; individual chapters, the contributors

Typeset in Garamond by Wearset Ltd, Boldon, Tyne and Wear

All rights reserved. No part of this book may be reprinted or
reproduced or utilized in any form or by any electronic, mechanical,
or other means, now known or hereafter invented, including
photocopying and recording, or in any information storage or
retrieval system, without permission in writing from the publishers.

British Library Cataloguing in Publication Data
A catalogue record for this book is available from the British Library

Library of Congress Cataloging in Publication Data
A catalog record for this book has been requested

ISBN10: 0-415-76384-3 (hbk
ISBN10: 0-415-58339-X (pbk)
ISBN10: 0-203-96656-2 (ebk)

ISBN13: 978-0-415-76384-4 (hbk)
ISBN13: 978-0-415-58339-8 (pbk)
ISBN13: 978-0-203-96656-3 (ebk)

Contents

Contributors

Rhonda Blair, Professor of Theatre at Southern Methodist University, has been acting and directing for the past 35 years and doing original performances for the past 20. She publishes primarily in performance pedagogy and feminism and performance, and has done translations of Chekhov for university productions.

F. Elizabeth Hart is Associate Professor of English at the University of Connecticut, Storrs, where she teaches Renaissance studies and Shakespeare. She has published articles on cognitive approaches to literary theory and Shakespeare.

John Lutterbie is an Associate Professor who holds a joint appointment in the Department of Theatre Arts and the Department of Art at Stony Brook University, where he is also the Associate Director of the Humanities Institute.

Bruce McConachie is Professor of Theatre at the University of Pittsburgh. He has published widely on American theatre history and theatre historiography, including *American Theatre in the Culture of the Cold War* (2003), which uses Lakoff and Johnson's "embodied realism" to understand the containment culture of the era.

Howard Mancing is Professor of Spanish at Purdue University. He has been primarily a Cervantes specialist; his *Cervantes Encyclopedia* (2 vols, 2004) is his major work. He has been working with cognitive science and literary theory since the early 1990s.

Tobin Nellhaus is the Librarian for Drama, Film, and Theatre Studies at Yale University. He has published on theatre history and historiography, performance theory, critical realism, social theory, community-based performance, and humanities in the digital environment.

Jennifer Ewing Pierce is a Ph.D. candidate at the University of Pittsburgh, a freelance playwright and director, and a Visiting Lecturer at Bridgewater State College. She has published on aesthetics and classical cognitivism in the journal *Consciousness and the Arts and Literature*.

Her article "Emotional Lifeworlds: A Paradigm Shift for Acting Theory" will soon be translated and published in Croatia and will also appear in a volume published by Cambridge University Press.

Naomi Rokotnitz graduated from Cambridge University with a double first and is now completing her Ph.D. at Bar Ilan University, writing a dissertation on "Trusting Plays: Dramatic Genres of Response to Skepticism."

Neal Swettenham lectures in drama at Loughborough University. His research into the role and status of narrative in contemporary theatre has looked at both traditional story-based drama and avant-garde performance work and especially the theatre of Richard Foreman.

Lisa Zunshine teaches at the University of Kentucky. She is the author of *Bastards and Foundlings: Illegitimacy in Eighteenth-Century England* and *Why We Read Fiction: Theory of Mind and the Novel*; she is also editor of *Philanthropy and Fiction, 1698–1818* and *Nabokov at the Limits*, as well as co-editor of *Approaches to Teaching the Novels of Samuel Richardson*.

Preface

Bruce McConachie

Our general goals for *Performance and Cognition* are to invite theatre and performance scholars to incorporate many of the insights of cognitive science into their work and to begin considering all of their research projects from the perspective of cognitive studies. These goals rest on a loose distinction between cognitive science and the more general category of cognitive studies. Cognitive scientists in psychology, linguistics, neuroscience, and other areas do empirically based tests to advance our knowledge of the mind/brain. The field of cognitive studies includes such scientific investigation but also encompasses philosophers, anthropologists, humanists, and other scholars who base many of their ideas and theories on cognitive science.

Among its several tasks, *Performance and Cognition* will demonstrate that cognitive studies provides a valid framework for understanding the potential truth value of many theories and practices that we presently deploy in theatre and performance studies. Indeed, the insights of cognitive science challenge some of the theoretical approaches now widely practiced, including Saussurean semiotics, Lacanian psychoanalysis, and aspects of deconstruction, New Historicism, and Foucauldian discourse theory. While notions of the "embodied mind," the "cognitive unconscious," "empathetic projection," "basic-level categories," "primary metaphors," and other foundational concepts at play in cognitive studies share some common ground with phenomenology, post-structuralist anthropology, and Marxist materialism, they also depart from several of the assumptions and methods of these approaches and bear the potential to qualify them productively. Similarly, these same cognitive concepts underlie several physically based performance techniques, challenge Brechtian ideas, and can enrich Stanislavskian approaches to acting. In general, cognitive studies finds substantial common ground between "theatre" and "performance," as they are usually defined. For this reason, the cognitive turn may help to heal our institutional divisions.

Why should we turn to cognitive studies for epistemological justification? Isn't this framework just as good as any other as a road to truth? We argue that it is better. The validity of cognitive studies rests on the empirical assumptions and self-correcting procedures of cognitive science. Like other sciences, the sciences of the mind and brain offer conclusions that are based on years of experimentation and research. Indeed, many cognitive scientists have changed their initial assumptions about how the mind/brain works. First-generation cognitive science generally assumed that the digital computer provided a good model for the mind/brain. For the past 25 years, as we will see in more detail, a "connectionist" model, which understands mental processing more analogically as a web of possible neuronal connections, has gained many adherents. (Francisco Varela and others have already posited a third major paradigm, which he terms "enactive" cognitive science (Varela *et al.* 1991: 207–13).) As this ongoing controversy demonstrates, no science produces final truth, and cognitive science, like biology and chemistry, remains open to future revision. Nonetheless, much is already known about the mind/brain that will very likely remain valid knowledge regardless of future models and modifications.

Cognitive science can offer empirically tested insights that are directly relevant to many of the abiding concerns of theatre and performance studies, including theatricality, audience reception, meaning making, identity formation, the construction of culture, and processes of historical change. The key terms here – and ones that differentiate *Performance and Cognition* from nearly all other books about theory and practice in our field – are "science" and "empirically tested." We recognize that theatre and performance artists and scholars, like most academics in other humanities departments, have not usually turned to the empirical sciences for help with their research and practice. At least since the 1940s, when C.P. Snow deplored the existence of "two cultures" in the academy, many humanists and scientists have tended to regard their academic "Other" with a mixture of bewilderment, skepticism, and scorn. To this cauldron of misperception must be added the envy of many humanists, because, as we all know, the two-cultures division has never been an equal one in prestige and funding. Envy aside, however, humanists have many reasons to question the practices of Big Science in the academy – socializing students to link their research to corporate expectations, isolating their methods and procedures from ethical concerns, arranging contracts that tie their innovations at public universities to private profits, and using their cultural authority to inhibit the democratic regulation of scientific "progress," to name just a few. Many individual scientists deplore these practices, of course, as do we.

These institutional problems, however, do not necessarily compromise the truth claims of academic science and of cognitive science in particular. Perhaps the biggest difficulty in this regard – and one immediately relevant to humanists eager for an exchange of knowledge with scientists – is scientific objectivism. If scientists come to the table with the certainty that their methods ensure objective knowledge, humanists have little incentive to take a seat and begin the conversation. In his essay "The Challenge of Science," Andrew Ross seconds the conclusions of other cultural studies scholars on the vexed question of objectivity: "[These] studies, identifying the role played by social interests in every aspect of research, demonstrated that scientific research is not given by the natural world but is produced or constructed through social interactions between/among scientists and their instruments . . ." (Ross 1999: 296). Ross approvingly quotes science critic Donna Haraway for pushing scientists to abandon their usual objectivist, God's-eye-view of the natural world and adopt instead a position of "situated knowledge" based on "embodied" perspectives of nature (Ibid.: 303). Similarly, in *Hermes: Literature, Science, Philosophy*, Michel Serres has noted that the problematics of human observation provide a "rare and narrow passage" that can link the sciences and the humanities (Serres 1982: 18).[1] The conviction among many scientists that they can achieve objective knowledge cuts short the possibility of a productive conversation between scientists and humanists.

Although no current poll indicates the percentage of cognitive scientists who hold strong positions on the question of scientific objectivity, significant members of this scientific community and others in cognitive studies have retreated from this claim. Cognitive linguist George Lakoff and cognitive philosopher Mark Johnson, for example, adopt an epistemological position of "embodied realism" close indeed to the "embodied" perspective called for by Haraway. In this, they reject both objectivist and relativist epistemologies for a qualified form of realism. Recognizing that the structures and operations of the mind/brain shape all human conclusions about nature, Lakoff and Johnson hold cognitive science to the same limitation. This renders a God's-eye-view of nature fundamentally impossible. Nor do Lakoff and Johnson accept the objectivist procedures of classical empiricism; for Lakoff and Johnson, assumption-free observations are not possible, and there is no one logic that will guarantee the correct construction of scientific laws from observable data. This does not mean, they insist, "that there is no reliable or stable science at all and that there can be no lasting scientific results. . . . Much of what we have learned about the brain and the mind is now stable knowledge" (Lakoff and Johnson 1999: 87).[2] They base their confidence on the wide variety of experiments conducted over the past 30 years and on the mutually reinforcing conclusions that have emerged from different approaches to the subject. Grounded in an impressive amount of convergent evidence over time, the knowledge of cognitive science cannot be dismissed as simply another theoretical narrative with no more legitimate claim to truth than other points of view. As Lakoff and Johnson explain, embodied realism is an "empirically responsible" philosophy (Ibid.: 79).

Can the same be said of theatre and performance studies? This is not to require that we begin arranging for empirical tests to validate all of our insights. But it would mean altering many of our assumptions about perception, creativity, imagination, identity, representation, and a host of other processes that scientists, philosophers, and others in cognitive studies have been redefining in empirically responsible ways for several decades. To put it another way, can we continue to rely on our business-as-usual theories and orientations for responsible epistemologies? The foundational shortcomings of formalist aesthetics, structuralism, psychoanalysis, and totalizing Marxisms have been exposed as partial and/or misleading, and analytic philosophy (along with cognitive studies) continues to undermine the credibility of deconstruction and other derivatives of the Continental philosophical tradition. Further, as we will see, the conclusions of many in cognitive studies significantly qualify the relativism at the heart of historicism and place empirical limits on the kinds of insights to be gleaned from phenomenology.

In the past, the academy viewed several of our current approaches to knowledge as scientific. Psychologists spoke confidently of the science of Freudian psychoanalysis in the 1950s, and many European semioticians indebted to Saussure referred to their trade as scientific in the 1970s. (Despite the two-cultures divide, we have often depended on the science of strangers.) While these and other questionable methods may still yield some valuable insights, we believe it is time to recognize that psychoanalysis and semiology are both based in scientifically outmoded assumptions.

Several of the essays in this volume will demonstrate that many of the current truth claims of theatre and performance scholarship are built upon unstable foundations. This does not make them wrong, necessarily, but it will render them vulnerable to irrelevance in the coming decades. Recognizing the shallowness of our epistemological grounding is especially crucial because, like many of our colleagues in the rest of the field, we believe that many theatre and performance events have had, and will continue to reflect and embody, profound political and ethical ramifications for the many people whose lives they shape. Performance matters, and cognitive studies can help to show how and why this is so. It is clear, however, that scholarship oriented toward a politics and ethics based on untenable assumptions about the nature and efficacy of theatre and performance can only lead to foolish dreams or cynical despair.

In light of the epistemological difficulties of the field, cognitive studies offers a breath of fresh air. Further, the modest claims of scientists and others committed to embodied realism and similar positions offer humanists an opening for genuine conversation. Indeed, it should come as no surprise that several humanists and cognitive scientists have been working together toward a variety of common goals for over a decade. Pursuing their mutual interest in metaphorical thinking, Lakoff published a book with literary studies professor Mark Turner in 1989, *More Than Cool Reason: A Field Guide to Poetic Metaphor*. Turner published several outstanding books on his own (most notably, perhaps, *The Literary Mind* (1996)) and went on to work with cognitive scientist Gilles Fauconnier. Both developed "conceptual blending" theory, a model of thought processes that many neuroscientists find useful, which they recently summarized in *The Way We Think: Conceptual Blending and the Mind's Hidden Complexities* (2002). *The Way We Think* uses theatrical production as a key example to understand mental processing. Several other cognitive scientists and philosophers rely on examples from performance to explain and expand their findings. These include Gerald Edelman, who speaks of "scenes" of mental representation; Robert M. Gordon, who writes persuasively on the ubiquity of empathy in social interaction and knowledge formation; Antonio Damasio, who has several books on human emotion; Owen Flanagan, who is interested in the importance of narrative processing for ethical understanding; and Raymond Gibbs, who (like Lakoff) emphasizes the metaphorical creativity of conceptualization and language.

Among social scientists and humanists, academics in anthropology, economics, film studies, philosophy, history, music, literary studies, and several other fields have already joined in this interdisciplinary conversation. These include Joseph D. Anderson, *The Reality of Illusion: An Ecological Approach to Cognitive Film Theory* (1996); Roy D'Andrade, *The Development of Cognitive Anthropology* (1995); Gregory Currie, *Image and Mind: Film, Philosophy and Cognitive Science* (1995); Susan Feagin, *Reading with Feeling: The Aesthetics of Appreciation* (1996); and Bradd Shore, *Culture in Mind: Cognition, Culture, and the Problem of Meaning* (1996). Two recent books point to significant breakthroughs in cooperation between literary and cognitive scholars: *Narrative and Consciousness: Literature, Psychology, and the Brain*, edited by Gary D. Fireman, Ted E. McVay, and Owen Flanagan (2003) and *On Our Mind: Salience, Context, and Figurative Language* (2003), by Rachel Giora. Our colleagues in the Modern Language Association have put together a Discussion Group on Cognitive Approaches to Literature (www2.bc.edu/~richarad/lcb/fea/pet.html) that has organized many conference sessions and helped to launch several books in the past six years.

A few scholars in dramatic literature, theatre, and performance studies are also encouraging this scholarly exchange. In *Shakespeare's Brain: Reading with Cognitive Theory* (2000), Mary Thomas Crane has identified significant cognitive traces of Shakespearean authorship in his plays that alter the usual scholarly emphasis on cultural and historical construction. My co-author F. Elizabeth Hart, in addition to her several essays on cognition and materialism, has taken a new look at the theory of genre as it applies to Shakespearean tragedy. To judge from several recent books and articles, some practitioners are beginning to apply cognitive science to problems of teaching and training actors. These include Elly Konijin, Phillip Zarrilli, and John Emigh. Jennifer Pierce and Rhonda Blair, represented in our anthology, have demonstrated the usefulness of the physical actor on stage to rethink cognitive notions of representation (Pierce), and of cognitive conceptions of emotion for reconsidering many of the practices of Stanislavsky-based acting (Blair). Howard Mancing, also in this book, has two recent essays proposing cognitive science as an alternative to Lacanian theory and Saussurian semiotics. For over a decade, Tobin Nellhaus, published here too, has underlined the many epistemological advantages of a philosophy of critical realism, which will allow theatre and performance historians to synthesize relevant communication and cognitive theory for understanding theatre history. I have authored several articles on theatre history and cognitive studies and recently published a book on Cold War American theatre that uses the ideas of Lakoff and Johnson to probe the culture of containment.

Although the conversation between humanists and cognitive scientists has been going on for a couple of decades now, there are advantages for theatre and performance academics in our joining this discussion late. Many of our colleagues in other fields have already benefited from the conclusions of cognitive studies to establish a better epistemological grounding for their truth claims and to explore new areas of their disciplines. We can learn from their mistakes and borrow productively from their successes. Theatre and performance scholars have always been magpies, stealing from others to build their own nests of theory and method. Knowing what approaches and conclusions from cognitive science have worked in other fields will enable us to become more efficient borrowers.

This does not mean, of course, that we must turn ourselves into cognitive scientists. While the goal of science is reliable and generalizable prediction, our goal will necessarily remain the interpretation and explanation of relatively unique events – acting a role, producing a play, responding to a performance, etc. Science can help us to define what performance is and to describe the cognitive systems that allow for certain kinds of artistry to flourish, but it cannot predict the emergence of discrete performances – there will always be too many variables. Dialogue with the scientists of brain and mind, moreover, will also enable significant numbers in our field to join the loose coalition of scholars working in the interdisciplinary field of cognitive studies. Several of us, as noted above, are already a part of this widening field.

Although the conversation between theatre and performance academics and cognitive scientists is just beginning, we have high hopes for its future. Short term, we believe that the immediate problem for our field is not the science of cognitive studies, *per se*, but the application of its major conclusions to the scholarly concerns of our work. If other fields are any guide in this regard, it is unlikely that there will ever be a single method that will guarantee the direct and smooth application of conclusions in cognitive neuroscience, linguistics, and psychology to understanding acting, spectatorship, theatre history, performance in everyday life, and the other areas that interest us. The essays in this anthology, however, make a good start at exploring methods for this transfer of knowledge to occur. Long term, it is already clear that theatre and performance scholars will not always be magpies in this relationship. A few cognitive scientists already recognize that performance as a phenomenon offers a rich body of evidence with which to test and elaborate their theories. More scientists and many more in the general field of cognitive studies will follow. Our goal is a friendly symbiosis with cognitive science, and consequently the incorporation of many areas of theatre and performance scholarship within the expanding field of cognitive studies.

Notes

1 See also the issue on "Postmodern Science" in Smith and Froemke (2004).
2 For their full discussion of embodied realism, see Lakoff and Johnson 1999: 74–117.

References

Anderson, J.D. (1996) *The Reality of Illusion: An Ecological Approach to Film Theory*, Carbondale, IL: Southern Illinois University Press.

Crane, M.T. (2001) *Shakespeare's Brain: Reading with Cognitive Theory*, Princeton, NJ: Princeton University Press.

Currie, G. (1995) *Image and Mind: Film, Philosophy and Cognitive Science*, Cambridge: Cambridge University Press.

D'Andrade, R. (1995) *The Development of Cognitive Anthropology*, Cambridge: Cambridge University Press.

Fauconnier, G. and Turner, M. (2002) *The Way We Think: Conceptual Blending and the Mind's Hidden Complexities*, New York: Basic Books.

Feagin, S. (1996) *Reading with Feeling: The Aesthetics of Appreciation*, Ithaca, NY and London: Cornell University Press.

Fireman, G.D., McVay, T.E., and Flanagan, O. (eds) (2003) *Narrative and Consciousness: Literature, Psychology, and the Brain*, Oxford: Oxford University Press.

Giora, R. (2003) *On Our Mind: Salience, Context, and Figurative Language*, Oxford: Oxford University Press.

Lakoff, G. and Johnson, M. (1999) *Philosophy in the Flesh: The Embodied Mind and Its Challenge to Western Thought*, New York: Basic Books.

Lakoff, G. and Turner, M. (1989) *More Than Cool Reason: A Field Guide to Poetic Metaphor*, Chicago, IL: University of Chicago Press.

Ross, A. (1999) "The Challenge of Science," in During, S. (ed.) *The Cultural Studies Reader*, 2nd edn, London and New York: Routledge.

Serres, M. (1982) *Hermes: Literature, Science, Philosophy*, Baltimore, MD: Johns Hopkins University Press.

Shore, B. (1996) *Culture in Mind: Cognition, Culture, and the Problem of Meaning*, New York: Oxford University Press.

Smith, C.J. and Froemke, R. (eds) (2004) "Special topic: postmodern science," *Reconstruction: Studies in Contemporary Culture*, 4: 4.

Turner, M. (1996) *The Literary Mind*, New York: Oxford University Press.

Varela, F.J., Thompson, E., and Rosch, E. (1991) *The Embodied Mind: Cognitive Science and Human Experience*, Cambridge, MA: MIT Press.

Acknowledgments

The editors would like to thank a variety of people who have helped make this volume possible in a variety of ways. Both would like to thank – first and foremost – our talented contributors whose professionalism and endurance have sustained this project from inception to completion. Bruce McConachie is grateful to the graduate students in his "Seminar on Cognitive Studies and Performance" for their curiosity, insight, and patience; and he thanks Stephanie McConachie for her encouragement and knowledge of cognitive science and education. F. Elizabeth Hart extends gratitude and affection to friends at the International Office, City University, London, for their companionship and support; and offers thanks as well to Geoffrey Meigs and James Parks of the University of Connecticut Computer Support Group. Hart also thanks Shelly Reno for last-minute life-support and Cameron Vickers for being the patient child of an academic mom.

Introduction

Bruce McConachie and F. Elizabeth Hart

We have divided our Introduction into three parts. The first part, which picks up where our Preface left off, introduces the major challenges that the cognitive turn poses for several of our current approaches to the study of theatre and performance. We will also discuss those theoretical orientations that are generally congruent with the conclusions of cognitive science. While we hope that this section will provide a "dramatic hook" for most of our readers, we also recognize that it will be frustrating for some because we will not pause for extensive explanation of the cognitive neuroscience, psychology, and linguistics that underlie this overview. More detail concerning the cognitive side of these comparisons and contrasts will be available in several of the essays. In the second section, we will discuss the organization of our anthology, introduce the essays that follow, and suggest the relevance of the essays to the challenges and congruencies we have already noted. The third and final section examines several recent scientific investigations that hold significant promise for the future interdisciplinary mix of cognitive studies and theatre and performance scholarship.

We must emphasize at the outset, however, that this Introduction (and indeed the anthology as a whole) can only provide readers with an initial look at this new field. *Performance and Cognition* is intended to open a door to cognitive studies for theatre and performance scholars who are largely ignorant of the garden of possibilities that awaits them on the other side. We cannot fully describe the many plants and animals that populate this garden; nor can we take you down all of the paths that will allow you to explore its entirety. Further (to continue the metaphor), this garden is evolving quickly; new species and short cuts will soon invite fresh investigations. We do hope, however, that your initial stroll will arouse your curiosity and prompt return visits.

The challenges of cognitive science for theatre and performance studies

Many cognitive scientists begin with some concept of mind/brain embodiment. It is clear that the mind/brain evolved to help the body survive and that the operations of minding with regard to performance are necessarily linked to what our bodies do every day. According to the "embodied realism" of George Lakoff and Mark Johnson, for example, mental concepts arise, fundamentally, from the experience of the body in the world. As "neural beings," humans must make meaning within certain "spatial-relations" and "bodily action" schemas along with other mental constructs arising from the interplay of experience and patterning in the brain. "Primary metaphors" flesh out the skeletal possibilities of many of these foundational schemas. Regarding spatial-relations concepts, for instance, the "source–path–goal" schema, which humans learn at an early age by crawling from a starting point to an end point, undergirds numerous metaphors that organize certain events in our lives as narratives with a beginning, a middle, and an end. "Balance," a bodily action schema, provides many metaphors for mental health, ethical behavior, and public justice. For Lakoff and Johnson, these primary metaphors are "creative" in the sense that they create an analogy linking two phenomena through similarity. The cognitive linguists do not assume that humans can recognize an inherent, objective similarity between two phenomena, however, because embodied realism (like other philosophical realisms) argues that such objective knowledge is humanly impossible (see Lakoff and Johnson 1999: 16–60).

According to Lakoff and Johnson, these submerged schemas and their metaphorical extensions are nearly universal to human experience: "Much of a person's conceptual system is either universal or widespread across lan-guages and cultures. Our conceptual systems are not totally relative and not merely a matter of historical contingency, even though a degree of concep-tual relativity does exist and even though historical contingency does matter very much" (Ibid.: 6). Within embodied realism, cultural relativity and the historicity of experience occur in two ways. Lakoff and Johnson note that cultures typically differ in their "worldviews," which they define as a "con-sistent constellation" of foundational concepts and primary metaphors over one or more cultural domains, such as politics, morality, psychology, etc." (Ibid.: 511). Certain basic schemas and metaphors, in other words, organize significant areas of a culture. Secondly, new "complex metaphors and other conceptual blends" can arise that facilitate shifts in thinking and historical change (Ibid.: 97). The complex metaphor *time is money*, for instance, helped to structure the rise of capitalism in the West – a metaphor largely absent from cultures with less quantifiable conceptions of time.

Metaphors also structure our sense of selves. In *Philosophy in the Flesh*, Lakoff and Johnson describe four primary metaphors that construct how "subjects" understand their "selves" – the physical object self, the locational self, the social self, and the multiple-selves metaphor. These notions of the self are largely unconscious but may be brought to the surface by reflection and analysis. The cognitive unconscious for Lakoff and Johnson is not the Freudian home of sexual desire and repression but simply the level of mind/brain operations that usually works below conscious awareness.

Nonetheless, nearly all human behavior, including rational thought, derives from this level. "It is the rule of thumb among cognitive scientists that unconscious thought is 95 percent of all thought – and that may be a serious underestimate," state Lakoff and Johnson (Ibid.: 13).

Saussurian semiotics ignores the link between language use and the cognitive unconscious. Ferdinand de Saussure developed his conception of language, which forms the basis of most semiotics and much of deconstruction, before the First World War, when science knew very little about the relation between cognition and linguistics. Saussure believed that "our thought – apart from its expression in words – is only a shapeless and indistinct mass" and that "there are no pre-existing ideas, and nothing is distinct before the appearance of language" (de Saussure 1974: 111–12). This belief flatly contradicts the findings of cognitive neuroscience and linguistics over the past 30 years and calls into question approaches to theatre and performance studies that are based primarily on Saussurian semiotics. This is not to deny that semiotic critics can analyze performances on the basis of signs and sign systems; indeed, cognitive linguists can tell semioticians how the mind/brain is able to do this. But it is to conclude that semiotic theories of human meaning-making are seriously awry. Most cognitive scientists would agree that language has a role to play in the construction of thought, but its role derives from the embeddedness of language in the workings of the mind/brain, which is not at all "shapeless and indistinct" when it comes to making meaning. Cognitive scientist Jean Mandler joins Lakoff, Johnson, and others in identifying "image schemas" as processes in the mind/brain that are prior to language (Mandler 1992: 587–604). In addition, the psychologist Eleanor Rosch has identified "basic-level categories" as the default level of generalizability at which the mind/brain operates with regard to objects – a level widely accepted by other scientists (Rosch and Lloyd 1978).[1] These images and categories in the mind/brain are not available directly as language, but they do underlie and motivate the production of all human sign systems, including language.

Predating cognitive linguistics, Jacques Derrida turned the structuralism of Saussurian semiotics against itself to propose the free play of signification, the inevitable slippage of meaning, and a notion of textuality that pervades all human behavior. From a cognitive point of view, it is probably fair to say that Derridean deconstruction argued from incorrect premises to arrive at some insightful conclusions. Regarding his assumptions, Lakoff and Johnson note that the following claims about the nature of language are "empirically incorrect":

> (1) The complete arbitrariness of the sign; that is, the utter arbitrariness of the pairing between signifiers (signs) and signifieds (concepts); (2) the locus of meanings in systems of binary oppositions among free-floating signifiers (*différance*); (3) the purely historical contingency of meaning; [and] (4) the strong relativity of concepts.
>
> (Lakoff and Johnson 1999: 463–4)[2]

Cognitive science undercuts the major assumptions upon which Derrida built deconstruction. Ironically, though, most cognitive scientists would agree with conclusions deriving from modifications of Derrida's insights. While the attribution of meaning to a text or performance is not cognitively free, the enormous flexibility of the mind/brain does make it impossible for even a single reader or spectator to pin down any fixed or final meaning. Further, Derrida's idea of "arche-writing" coupled with his (in)famous belief that "there is nothing outside the text" may sound eerily familiar to cognitive scientists and philosophers interested in the evolution of cognition and the limits of human knowledge. Substitute "cognition" for "text" in Derrida's claim, and we arrive at a point of view about the biological basis of epistemology that has affinities with the "qualified realism" espoused by neuroscientists Gerald Edelman and Guilio Tononi. According to them, humans can only know what their "concepts" in the mind/brain will allow them to know. As they explain, "concepts are not propositions in a language (the common usage of this term); rather, they are constructs the brain develops by mapping its own responses prior to language.... Concepts, in our view, precede language, which develops by epigenetic means to further enhance our conceptual and emotional exchanges" (Edelman and Tononi 2000: 215–16).[3] Edelman and Tononi's "concepts" are akin to Derrida's "arche-writing," except that these neuroscientists can generalize about all human cognition to arrive at an epistemology of qualified realism which improves upon Derrida's language-limited relativism.

Skinnerian and Freudian notions of psychology also run counter to most cognitive science. Cognitive approaches to psychology began to replace Skinnerian ones in the 1950s because it was clear that humans had meta-cognitive abilities lacking in maze-trained rats. For all of its philosophical subtlety, the understanding of behavior at the root of Judith Butler's notion of "performativity" is finally closer to Skinnerian conditioned response – i.e., reward people for playing certain roles and they will continue to perform them – than to conceptions of behavior based in cognitive research. Butler also bases some of her thinking on a Lacanian notion of the unconscious that derives from Freud. Although Freudian psychology had a significant impact on Western science early in the twentieth century, cognitive psychologists have largely rejected the Freudian model, in part because it is untestable by empirical means (Bucci 1997: 9–10). Not only does Lacanian psychoanalysis suffer from the same difficulty, it also relies on a notion of language that derives from semiology. Plus, it builds upon a binary of Self and Other to understand identity, mental processing, and a person's relation to the world. Most cognitive psychology, like Lakoff and Johnson's understanding of the several "selves" inherent in our self-conceptions, involves a more fluid sense of identity than Freudian or Lacanian theory allows. Further, instead of a monolithic Other, cognitivists have found a variety of embodied and contextualized others in our lives.

Notions of the spectator as reader, which generally derive from language-based theories of performance, have limited our understanding of audience response. Cognitive science suggests that empathy and emotional response are more crucial to a spectator's experience than the kind of decoding that most semioticians imagine. Recent psychological and philosophical investigations have altered and broadened the conventional definition of empathy. Although empathy still involves seeing the world "through another person's eyes," many in cognitive studies have decoupled empathic projection from emotional identification to craft a Theory of Mind (ToM) approach to epistemology. ToM advocates now understand simulation, the basic psychological mechanism that deploys empathy, as the major means of interpreting and predicting human behavior and as more important than rational approaches to understanding others. Anthropologist Georg Vielmetter, for example, recommends that we hone our natural ability to empathize with others into "empathetic observation" to gather information and form tentative conclusions about the emotions, behaviors, and beliefs of cultural others (Vielmetter 2000: 95). Vielmetter bases his assumptions on the work of cognitive philosopher Robert Gordon, who uses the conclusions of cognitive psychology to argue that empathy can move spectators beyond the problematics of "othering" those who are looked at (Gordon 1996a: 62–82; 1996b: 165–80). Following Gordon and Vielmetter, it is evident that most spectators engage in empathetic observation as soon as a performance begins, watching facial expressions and body language in human exchanges to figure out what is going on. This is not the same as reading the body as a sign. Rather, it is a mode of cognitive engagement involving mirror neurons in the mind/brain that allow spectators to replicate the emotions of a performer's physical state without experiencing that physical state directly.

Indeed, ToM is also helping us to understand how our unconscious propensity to ascribe feelings, intentions, calculations, etc., to others governs the ways in which readers can interpret the "minds" of fictional characters in print. Lisa Zunshine, for example, has applied ToM to textual representations of fictional consciousness. In an essay on Samuel Richardson's *Clarissa*, Zunshine extends this investigation by asking, "How do different cultural-historical milieux encourage different literary explorations of this capacity?" (Zunshine 2004: 128). Work by other literary critics and historians, including Alan Palmer (2004) and Blakey Vermule (in progress), is also exploring the intersection of ToM and readers' perceptions. Ongoing experiments in the cognitive sciences underlying ToM will likely continue to provide literary and performance scholars with new insights about the experiences of reading and spectating.

Empathizing often leads to emotional involvement, and cognitive psychologists affirm that our emotions are central to the construction of meaning, not just a welcome or intrusive addition to theatre- and performance-going. Cognitive philosopher Daniel Dennett and psychologist Antonio Damasio have demonstrated that the old Cartesian separation of mind and body is empirically invalid (Dennett 1991; Damasio 1999 and

2003). Because the mind/brain is a part of the body – and because emotions and feelings (which are emotions brought into consciousness) produce physio-chemical responses – affective responses become an ongoing part of the feedback loop of spectating. In effect, the body's pro-active biochemistry shapes each percept and "tells" the mind/brain what is important, enabling the spectator to "pay more attention" to moments in a performance that are more emotionally charged than others. Spectating is not an unusual human activity in this regard. Damasio makes it clear that emotional engagement is even a part of solving a math problem. Moreover, perceptions of beauty, humor, and general aesthetic as well as cognitive enjoyment may depend on what cognitive philosopher Paul Thagard calls "emotional coherence" (Thagard 2000: 165–221).

With its emphasis on empathic and emotional engagement, a cognitive approach to spectating and the making of meaning have much in common with phenomenology. If, as Maurice Merleau-Ponty writes, perception involves "lived bodiliness" and that "to perceive is to render oneself present to something through the body," then phenomenology and a cognitive approach to human minding begin at much the same place (quoted in Garner 1994: 27, 28). They also share a mutual interest in intentionality, memory, the gestalt nature of perception, and the human ability to bracket off some phenomena to better understand others. However, when critic and theorist Stanton Garner notes that the phenomenological orientation "offers both a return of experience and subjectivity (the cornerstones of givenness) to the theoretical field" (Ibid.: 13), cognitivists would be likely to take him up on only half of his offer. Epistemologically, cognitive science tends toward realism; like other sciences, it has no use for an epistemology of total subjectivism and/or relativism. Compared to empirical research, the phenomenologist's attentiveness to consciousness is ill equipped to reveal the operations of the cognitive *unconscious*. Nonetheless, phenomenological insights, impressionistic though they are, can open up important questions for a rigorous cognitive approach to performance.

Theatre and performance cognitivists also have much in common with philosophical materialists owing to the fact, of course, that cognitive science is itself materialist. It begins with a brain in a body – both material substances – and tries to understand how the embodied mind of this brain responds to the world, which includes other material human bodies with minds/brains and the rest of material existence.

Secondarily, at the cultural-historical level, cognitive studies examines the material results of the projections of minds/brains – which includes texts and performances – and the material responses of other minds/brains to those material projections. Cognitive materialism, however, has a broader understanding of agency than those Marxists who tend to reduce agency to resisting dominant practices and ideologies. Unlike many Marxists, cognitivists define agency as an image schema in the mind that allows a subject to intend and cause a material change in the world. In this sense, both lifting a bag of groceries and running for president involve agency. As these examples suggest, cognitive science does not attempt to predict a relationship between individual or collective agents and the course of history. Cognitive studies has nothing to say about modes of production, class relations, or economic determination "in the last instance." There is no single theory of history or practice of historiography that necessarily follows from cognitive materialism. This open-ended quality will no doubt appear limiting to some materialists and liberating to others.

The absence of determinism aside, the conclusions of cognitive studies suggest some productive modifications of several cultural and historical materialist approaches. If the material results of certain image schemas and other specific mental processes distinguish one culture from another, materialist anthropology can use cognitive science to describe the conditions of consciousness and behavior that structure a culture. Anthropologist Roy D'Andrade and others have been practicing this approach to anthropology for several years (D'Andrade 1995).[4] Deploying an understanding of culture that includes human cognition, the theorist may redefine Raymond Williams' concept of a "dominant culture" as the material manifestations of the primary image schemas and their accompanying metaphors that legitimate the power of certain groups and classes.[5] Similarly, Pierre Bourdieu's "habitus," the aptitudes, routines, and body language of a social group, can be grounded in the mind/brain. Edward Said's "Orientalism," too, may be linked to certain mental operations and primary metaphors dominant in the West during the centuries of imperialism. Close attention to the cultural "circulation" of certain tropes and metaphors, a concern of Stephen Greenblatt and other New Historicists, is also generally congruent with cognitive understandings of culture and history.

As a general approach to historical knowledge, however, New Historicism is open to the charge of relativism. Following J.G. Herder, the founder of historicism, and Nietzsche, New Historicists generally agree that the historian can never fully escape from her or his historical past to make valid judgments about the history of another people with different values and traditions. For many historicists, culturally specific mentalities share too few common qualities upon which to ground a comparison; they are incommensurable. Cognitivists, however, must disagree. Most people, it is true, are conditioned to arrive at a very narrow conception of other cultures and other times. But cognitive science has found nothing in the mind/brain that makes this inevitable. Rather, the comparativist work of cognitive linguistics has concluded that people in all cultures probably use many of the same image schemas and basic-level categories to structure their languages.[6] Because the human species shares minds/brains that are fundamentally alike, different belief systems are not incommensurable; historians can assume some common mental processes for all people over time when they generate cultural-historical knowledge. This is good news for historians of performance, of course, but it does pose a problem for New Historicism.

Much of the approach and epistemology of New Historicism derives from the work of Michel Foucault. Distrusting origins, Foucault famously reduced authorship to a function of discourse. As Renaissance scholar and cognitive literary critic Mary Thomas Crane has pointed out, however, this epistemological strategy is problematic for cognitive materialists because it effectively removes the body and the mind/brain of the writer from discussion and exploration. In *Shakespeare's Brain*, Crane disagrees with the materialists who have followed Foucault down this path because it occludes "Shakespeare's material existence in time and space" (Crane 2001: 4). The general failure of materialists to think about the brain, says Crane, "prevents most contemporary accounts of subject formation in the body from noting that just as surely as discourse shapes bodily experience and social interactions shape the material structures of the brain, the embodied brain shapes discourse" (Ibid.: 7). Note that Crane, following other cognitivists, grants substantial power to discursive practices; yet she also insists that authorship be recognized for the cognitive traces it leaves as well as for its manifestation of institutional power.

Foucauldian notions of the power of discourse have provided crucial epistemological support for several theories of post-colonialism and queer studies (e.g., Homi Bhabha, Trinh T. Minh-Ha, Marjorie Garber, Jonathan Goldberg). It remains to be seen how these theories will fare when the embodied minds/brains of imperialized and queer bodies are figured into their economies of discourse. For theatre and performance theorists and historians, of course, these concerns are relevant to understanding every step in the ongoing circuitry of production and reception, from playwriting through directing, design, and acting, to spectatorship and the cultural feedback loop that this process serves.

The organization of the anthology

The three essays that comprise our first section explore the theoretical underpinnings of a cognitive approach to theatre and performance. The essays by Hart, McConachie, and Nellhaus invest similarly in the cognitive concept of "mind-embodiment," the idea that many if not most of the mind's structures for thought and expression arise through the embeddedness of the brain within the human body, a body that, in turn, is embedded within deterministic physical and social environments. The biological and thus transhistorical condition of having a human body guarantees that people's minds will produce a certain number of unchanging, cross-cultural, perhaps even universal structures. However, the varying historical contingencies that situate all human bodies within specific contexts ensure that the structures of people's minds *also* reflect the culturally specific conditions of their given moments and places. Thus, mind-embodiment operates as a kind of mediator between essentialist and relativistic ontologies and epistemologies, revealing that philosophical questions about being and knowing *must* take into account the mind–brain–body nexus. In fact, the important epistemological position that mind-embodiment gives rise to has been labeled "embodied realism" and is a key perspective adopted by the three essayists in our first section, particularly McConachie and Nellhaus.

F. Elizabeth Hart's essay "Performance, Phenomenology, and the Cognitive Turn" explores one aspect of the origins of mind-embodiment theory within the philosophy of Maurice Merleau-Ponty. Merleau-Ponty's phenomenology of the "embodied consciousness" has been suggested by theatre and performance critics in the recent past as an antidote to the abstractions of semiotics as a basis for criticism. Hart supports this turn toward Merleau-Ponty and further demonstrates the relevance of his ideas to contemporary cognitive science. But she also encourages a shift in the terms of debate toward a view that finds common ground – literally, within the human body – between phenomenological and semiotic approaches, insofar as the "semiotic" is restricted to language rather than encompassing all other modes of theatrical communication (i.e., criticism has tended to reduce all language to the play of signs). If, as cognitive linguists assert, language emerges from structures within the embodied mind, taking its forms from the constraints of the mind–brain–body nexus, then what we are really looking at are not philosophical opposites but two aspects of the same set of determinants. This reconfiguration bears implications for performance theories, Hart argues, such as Butler's concept of "performativity," which misleadingly credits the realm of the discursive with sole powers of embodiment. To demonstrate a more complex, inclusive model of theatrical embodiment – one that takes mind-embodiment as a ground for theatrical reception – Hart examines the cognitive-discursive dynamics of the performance space within two examples: Shakespeare's opening Chorus of *Henry V* and a performance of the contemporary British play *After Mrs. Rochester*.

The next two essays in this section extend the epistemology of mind-embodiment and its corollary, embodied realism, into theatre history, recognizing that historical methodologies are dependent on valid epistemologies and finding in embodied realism the most "robust" (as McConachie phrases it) among the various options and particularly as compared with psychoanalysis. In his "Cognitive Studies and Epistemic Competence in Cultural History: Moving Beyond Freud and Lacan," Bruce McConachie examines both Freudian and Lacanian forms of psychoanalysis in light of recent philosophers' and historiographers' mandates regarding epistemological guidelines for historical theory, arguing that psychoanalysis has failed to meet these guidelines. The better paradigm, McConachie asserts, is cognitive studies, which, owing to the mediating effects of embodied realism, meets such standards as empirical falsifiability, historical specificity, methodological diversity (e.g., the use of speculation and simulation), and less dependence on its own models and more on actual data gained from empirical evidence. To demonstrate both how psychoanalysis fails to meet the standards of a "robust" epistemology and how a cognitive critique more effectively does, McConachie takes a look at the historically specific "wench act" performed by blacked-up, white male actors, cross-dressing as women. This genre of performance was the subject of Eric Lott's psychoanalytic treatment in *Love and Theft: Blackface Minstrelsy and the American Working Class* (1993), a study that gives McConachie a basis for a comparative analysis using the tools of simulation theory (Theory of Mind) and the ideas of Lakoff and Johnson. At the foundations of cognitive linguistics lies the epistemology of embodied realism that, as McConachie argues, renders "the paradigm of cognitive studies . . . more empirically responsible [and historically inclusive] than versions of psychoanalysis" (p. 70).

Tobin Nellhaus similarly appeals to the epistemological flexibility of embodied realism in his contribution, "Performance Strategies, Image Schemas, and Communication Frameworks." Nellhaus advances these concerns a step further, however, by appealing to the similar but more broad-ranging epistemology of "critical realism." Critical realism recognizes the key role of embodied knowledge as a foundation for people's knowledge of the world; but it also points to the enormous amount of knowledge people necessarily gain secondhand via discursive practices: "Few people travel around the world to learn if it is spherical, conduct the experiments necessary to discover that we need to breathe oxygen and not neon, or dig up bones to convince themselves of the theory of evolution. Instead, we listen to other people, read books, watch television, tune in to the radio; and conversely, to provide knowledge to others, we rely on speaking, writing, drawing, and the like" (p. 82). Embodied cognitive "schemas" or metaphors both give rise to and are recursively influenced by culturally specific "communication frameworks," which are themselves indexed to the various technologies of communication (e.g., speech, writing, printing, electronics) that have emerged over time and will continue to emerge. Nellhaus appeals to these interconnections to generate a theory of how strategies of theatrical performance have arisen throughout the history of the theatre in response to changing communication frameworks, to the cognitive metaphors those frameworks select for, and to the epistemological and ontological "assumptions" inherent in these dominant cognitive metaphors. Such assumptions are "re-embodied" in theatrical practices and in dramatic texts, Nellhaus argues, "establish[ing] the foundations of the performance strategies of [a given] period" (p. 83). An example that Nellhaus explores at some depth is the relationship between the eighteenth-century sentimental theatre, the cognitive metaphors governing bodily gestures and texts as expressions of emotional interiority, and the period's key innovation of regular periodical distribution – obviously indebted to the earlier invention of printing – which helped to generate, as never before, a wide-based community of readers. Knowledge, particularly self-knowledge, became equated with texts; and in the theatre this metaphor manifested itself in the fetishizing of the gesture as the corporeal equivalent of the written sign, both evoking from their "readers" emotional, even confessional, self-evaluations. Nellhaus' vision – the most far ranging of any in this section and perhaps this volume – demonstrates the potential for a cognitive approach to performance both to acknowledge the myriad complexities of theatre and to illuminate the dynamics behind that complexity.

Our second section on cognitive approaches to drama maintains an awareness of the ontological and epistemological issues, but these are subordinated to more specific discussions about the efficacy of cognitive models as tools for interpreting dramatic texts. We begin to see, in both essays from this section, how many and varied are the models that fall under the heading "cognitive studies" and, equally, how wide-ranging are their potential applications. These essays treat drama to the extent that they consider play texts within their specific literary and philosophical traditions; however, both are also quite invested in understanding the unique status of performance and the role that cognition plays in defining the difference that performance makes. In particular, both authors explore the transitions that narratives exemplify in moving from literary form to the stage – for instance, the cohabitation of the same story in both novel and dramatic forms (Zunshine), or the evolution of a tale from prose romance to tragicomedy (Rokotnitz) – with a keen eye toward the differences that such transitions demand in terms of cognitive apparatus and response (e.g., What distinguishes the cognitive experience of a narrative's performance from the cognitive experience of reading that same narrative?). To address such questions, these two essayists call on diverse empirical analyses within cognitive studies, expanding the repertoire of cognitive resources from that offered by this volume's first three essayists.

Lisa Zunshine's "Essentialism and Comedy: a Cognitive Reading of the Motif of Mislaid Identity in Dryden's *Amphitryon* (1690)" explores the literary and dramatic theme of the lost self, particularly its comic renditions in the use of stage twins. Finding in these representations an enduring fascination with situations that challenge people's tendency to essentialize, Zunshine appeals to cognitive-evolutionary studies of essentialism that seek to explain this tendency as an adaptive – if not always socially desirable – attribute. Zunshine cites a wide range of literary and play texts, including a twenty-first-century novel by Mexican writer Ignacio Padilla (*Shadow Without a Name*, 2002), an untitled twentieth-century children's poem by the Polish poet Yulian Tuvim, Dryden's seventeenth-century play *Amphitryon; or the Two Sosias*, Shakespeare's sixteenth-century *The Comedy of Errors*, and Plautus' 200 BC *Amphitruo*, in order to demonstrate not just the longevity of the twin theme but its obvious cross-cultural salience. What interests her is the unexpectedly complex cognition underlying this salience – the mystery behind the reader's/audience's "knowing" laughter at characters like Plautus' Sosia, who naïvely assume that their very selves have been mislaid when confronted by someone who appears to be their twin. What is it, in fact, that readers and audiences *know*, Zunshine asks, that makes these characters naïve and funny? And why is such knowledge accessible to so many different kinds of people? In addition to cognitive-evolutionary theory, Zunshine also appeals to the "conceptual blending" theory of Mark Turner and Gilles Fauconnier to help describe the unconscious ease with which readers and audiences perform "domain-crossing attributions" (p. 105), those feats of anthropomorphization that enable us to credit inanimate objects, animals, and fictional characters with having human traits, including essential selfhood. After registering the similarities between novelistic and stage uses of the twin motif, Zunshine turns to a discussion of their crucial differences, arguing that the inferential possibilities opened up by the embodied performance of twins adds "a level of engagement with such biases [as the tendency to essentialize] that is in principle unavailable to the readers of the novel" (p. 118). She concludes: "Different genres and different media thus appear to engage the same cognitive propensities in markedly different ways, satisfying and creating highly nuanced cognitive needs" (Ibid.).

Naomi Rokotnitz brings similar concerns about the cognitive distinctiveness of performance to her essay " 'It is required/You do awake your faith': Learning to Trust the Body Through Performing *The Winter's Tale*." Although primarily a reading of the patterns of skepticism in Shakespeare's late romance (and one that adds important nuances to extant interpretations), this essay is also keen to establish that the art of performance uniquely possesses the power to close the gap between logic and more embodied forms of knowledge. Focusing on the rise of skepticism during the late sixteenth and early seventeenth centuries, Rokotnitz credits nonrational mental experiences, such as emotion, intuition, memory, and desire, with bearing strong correlations to "the body" (i.e., the embodied mind) and as such providing the "supplemental" forms of understanding that are necessary to stave off the despair of a "radical" or unmitigated skepticism. Supplemental or embodied knowledge is more accessible through art than through philosophical inquiry, Rokotnitz argues; hence, Shakespeare's representation of the power of art in the form of Hermione's living statue, whose awakening culminates and thaws the long winter of Leontes' despair. Leontes' original madness, according to Rokotnitz, had stemmed from his over-reliance on logic at the expense of intuition and his memories of a long and loving marriage with Hermione. The second phase of his suffering, however, after his loss of wife and children, takes the form of the darkness of uncertainty, with no hope for the recovery of – much less a different kind of – knowledge to fill the void. As is typical in Shakespeare, the missing element of embodied knowledge arrives in feminine form, indeed, in the stage embodiment of the fetishized female saint. This feminized supplement evolves in the play through the conventions of the pastoral genre that inform its third and fourth acts, conventions associated with the regenerative "green world" and that world's edifying effects on tainted society. Appealing to cognitive studies of simulation or Theory of Mind, Rokotnitz develops an application of empathy to the experience of an audience watching Hermione's performance: Our capacity for empathy allows us to respond to the near-real-life stimulation that performance offers in a conjoining of embodiment by both performers and audience. Performance is thus a visceral source of knowledge that exceeds and transcends the "logic" of logic.

The two essays in Section 3 on cognitive approaches to acting also complement each other in important ways. Both adopt a quasi-empirical strategy with which to explore the creative processes actors deploy in preparing for their roles, featuring interviews with actors about their experiences in rehearsal and performance. Then, using the concepts and especially the metaphorical frameworks that emerge from these interviews, both essayists highlight the tension between the intellect and emotions, a dichotomy assumed by modern theories of acting but no longer supported by cognitive science. While the two base their scientific claims on a varied assortment of studies, one source in particular offers a starting point for both: the work of the cognitive neuroscientist Antonio Damasio. In three books published over the past ten years, *Descartes' Error* (1994), *The Feeling of What Happens* (1999), and *Looking for Spinoza* (2003), Damasio has argued persuasively against the traditional binaries of mind vs. brain and mind vs. body, emphasizing instead the fluid relations among the three within a complex system of integration. Cognition is an ever-unfolding *process*, Damasio argues, in which the mind operates against the conditioning backdrop of embodied and unconscious brain-level functions, which are themselves conditioned by bodily (i.e., biological) states. Within this scenario, emotions, far from being bracketed off from reason, actually frame what we think of as rationality, providing an embodied context to all kinds of mental activity from basic decision-making to our most vaulted reasoning processes. Further, emotions may be understood as distinct from *feelings* insofar as they occur at unconscious brain levels, whereas feelings are what become of emotions when they surface in the conscious mind to be acknowledged and articulated. Developed from Damasio's work with brain-damaged medical patients, this holistic reconfiguration of human mental life bears implications not only for how actors actually create but also for how they themselves *believe* they create; that is, it inspires a fresh look at the various metaphors actors themselves use both to understand and practice their art.

In "Neuroscience and Creativity in the Rehearsal Process," John Lutterbie offers statements from actors, who, despite their very different backgrounds and approaches to acting, employ the same metaphor of the "self as a container" (though unstated *per se*) to describe their rehearsal processes. Noting the relevance of Lakoff and Johnson's work on conceptual metaphors, Lutterbie explores how the repeated motif of the self "emptied" of thought and judgment (and thereby allowing the free flow of feelings) encapsulates actors' understanding both that the self is a container and that the boundaries of the container-self help to maintain the supposed split between intellect and emotion. The presence of such metaphors in the actors' minds, Lutterbie argues, implies that they believe they have conscious control over the modes of their mental processing; when in fact – or so Damasio's research suggests – such control is very likely impossible. Instead, what seems to govern the actor's creative processes, which is an intensified form of a general cognitive capacity, are instances of "lateralization across zones of convergence," also known as synesthesia. Lutterbie cites studies by V.S. Ramachandran and E.M. Hubbard on cross-modality, cognition in which concentrated neural activity reaches across the senses, allowing humans to create and/or recall unexpected associations: for instance, the ability to experience tactility in terms of vision ("seeing" the texture of velvet cloth) or abstraction in terms of concrete sense (visualizing numbers as colors). Taken together, the works of Damasio, Lakoff and Johnson, and Ramachandran and Hubbard all point to a convergence of evidence that "underlining the cen-trality of associative cognition to an understanding of the acting process" (p. 150). Importantly, what is at stake here is *not* whether an actor's process is metaphorical or, for that matter, the fact that actors must use metaphors to describe their processes. Rather, what matters is that "metaphors current in the culture best describe the creative process" (p. 163) since metaphors are by their nature value-laden; and values determine, Lutterbie notes, the practices that govern theatre.

In "Image and Action: Cognitive Neuroscience and Actor-training," Rhonda Blair builds upon Damasio's process model of cognition (the idea that mental life is an ever-unfolding process of connections), applying it, as she phrases it, to what it is that actors *do*. Modern theories of acting have always tended to emphasize capturing the essence of a character, striving to reach a state of imaginary inhabitation in which there resides an objective and authentic *self*, and then working to embody the objective trappings of that self. Yet a process model of cognition denies that such an authentic and objective state of being (and thus of a character) can ever exist. Rather, it emphasizes that even at the neuronal level, human mental life is con-stantly revising itself, adapting to the steady streams of imagery, sensation, emotions and intellectual input that characterize every living moment. Citing not just Damasio but other neuroscientists like Joseph LeDoux and Jerome Kagan, whose work highlights the relationships between neuronal activity and higher-level cognition, Blair explores how even memory has come to be viewed as unstable, subject to neuronal rearrangement by the contexts in which past experiences are recalled. Given the central place of memory in character development, argues Blair, we would do well to appropriate these new insights and direct them toward a more concrete acting method: "If we can view memory as neither an accurately retrievable truth nor an object (in the sense of being a fact) but as a trace, a neuro-chemical reconstruction whose nature is affected by the given moment and context of retrieval, we might more effectively manipulate memory as a tool for the actor" (p. 175). Specifically, Blair suggests, actors and directors might use the technique of visualizing "image streams" to help them inhabit a character's experience, a set of concrete images suggested by a play-text's semantics but made more dynamic as an exercise than mere semantic exploration. The conventional meanings of words differ profoundly from an actor's repertoire of image-streams associated with those same words, image-streams that the actor may now consciously develop as part of the rehearsal process and that can become a material element of the actor's own neuronal make-up. The result, Blair believes, is a degree of character-embodiment that is far more *literal* – in the sense of being more directly experiential – than we normally understand when we talk about embodiment: Embodiment signals an actor's ability to live imaginatively *within the process* of a given character's cognitive unfolding, just as that same actor lives his/her own unfolding during every moment of every day. "The reframing of the actor's process allowed by cognitive neuroscience moves us past some counter-productive historical and cultural conventions ... related to acting. It has nothing to do with a preordained sense of [what a human] 'ought to be,' but rather works with the intertwining of the cultural and biological in a way that acknowledges the contingency and fluidity of ... [being] human ..." (pp. 181–2).

Our fourth and final section on cognition and spectatorship presents two essays that address what, from a cognitive perspective, is extraordinary about the experience of performance. Theatre and performance theorists need little convincing that the reception of performance art differs fundamentally from that of other art forms since, unlike even the visual arts, it requires the immediate and interactive presence – the embodiment – of its performers and receivers. But if performance reception is characterized by this heightened degree of embodiment, what must performance theorists make of the emphasis that cognitive science now places on *mind*-embodiment as an added dimension of embodiment in general? What, in other words, is the exact role that the mind plays in theatre spectatorship? The two essayists approach this question quite differently: the first offers a wide-based theoretical discussion, achieving an impressive synthesis of numerous cognitive resources; while the second applies a narrower range of cognitive theory toward the reconstruction of an historically specific and important theatre event, *The Playboy* riots of 1907. Both essays illustrate the necessity of trying to incorporate an understanding of the mechanics of cognitive processing in spectatorship, recognizing embodied cognition as one aspect of the uniqueness of theatre that must now be considered alongside cultural and historical determinants.

In "See the Play, Read the Book," Howard Mancing takes issue with the poststructualist tendency to collapse all seeing into the "reading" of signs, asserting instead that "seeing and knowing is not the same thing as reading and knowing" (p. 189). In a critique that shares points in common with the first two theoretical essays (Hart and McConachie) in this volume, Mancing takes issue with Saussurean linguistics, deconstruction, and Lacanian psychoanalysis, all of which have had the effect of reducing a wide range of nonlinguistic perception to the very specialized act of symbol processing – that is, the reception of language and its graphic representations through reading. Contrary to these reductive models, writes Mancing, perceiving the world directly through the senses and especially through the visual system involves very different cognitive processes than does the processing of symbols. Citing the works of cognitive scientists Allan Paivio, James J. Gibson, Merlin Donald, Terrence Deacon, and others, Mancing urges us to recognize these differences, noting that the perceptual system and the symbolic system developed at different times during the evolution of human cognition and that in modern brains they continue to perform separate functions while also integrating with each other. Humans can perceive the world without the mediation of symbols; while, in fact, in order to process symbols, humans must first be able to *perceive* those symbols. Thus, while we have to *hear* language or *see* it in its graphic or gestural forms in order to process it, we are able to *see* Niagara Falls *directly* and to understand what we are seeing without the aid of symbols to do so. Such cognitive parameters, when applied to theatre and novel-reading, for instance, reveal that the two activities share some commonalities in that they both involve the perceiving and processing of symbols. But theatre differs from reading in that it allows for the direct perception – by a community of spectators, in irreversible time – of specific sights, sounds, textures, climate, etc. (allowing for some degree of individual difference); and that the range of possible interpretations of a theatre event will therefore be much narrower than that for readers of the same novel whose isolated and almost purely symbol-driven reconstructions of narrative worlds will allow for greater diversity. Mancing's point is not to privilege one form of processing or one art form over another but to celebrate their differences and to circumvent the fallacies that have arisen from their collapse: "If all cognition is considered as reading, then reading is synonymous with perceiving, feeling, knowing, understanding, thinking, and so forth; there thus exists but a single process, and the uniqueness of reading . . . is devalued. . . . Similarly, if all cognition is like the reading of texts, we lose our ability to recognize the life-like, vivid, direct perception of a play on the stage" (pp. 197–8).

Taking a different approach to the cognition of spectatorship, Neal Swettenham's "Categories and Catcalls: Cognitive Dissonance in *The Playboy of the Western World*" focuses on one important theatre event – the riots that broke out at Dublin's Abbey Theatre in response to J.M. Synge's play – and examines it in light of the highly suggestive research into the nature of cognitive categories. As Swettenham notes, there have been numerous attempts by theatre historians to explain the behavior of Synge's Irish audience on that night in January 1907, when the shouts of many in the audience were so loud that Lady Gregory felt compelled to offer a free second-night performance to those who could not hear the play. Swettenham offers a supplementary explanation based on cultural and political premises, asserting that discoveries in the field of cognitive science can offer us significant fresh insight into the causes and can "enhance our understanding in more general

terms of the ways in which audiences will tend to read narrative in performance" (p. 208). Specifically, he points to research by Eleanor Rosch and
George Lakoff on the "prototype" configurations of mental categories, the
embodied (i.e., non-transcendental) origins of these category structures, and
the cultural contingency (owing to their embodiment) of produced meanings, including meanings produced during performances. (We should point
out here that Swettenham is unique among the essayists in this volume in
taking up the research on cognitive categories and that, in spite of the difficulty such research poses for non-specialists, he clearly demonstrates its
untapped potential for performance criticism.) In brief, prototypes are especially salient features of a given category that can stand in for the entire category because they represent fundamental, basic levels of cognitive
understanding. The basic-level category CAT, signifying the common
household pet, is perceived as having some examples that are more salient or
typical than others; for instance, for Americans, the American domestic
short-hair will seem more representative as a type of CAT than will, say, a
Manx or a Japanese Bobtail. The relationship between the prototype (American domestic short-hair) and other members of the category (CAT) is a
matter of its *degree of fitness* and not a simple one-to-one or a transcendental
equation. Such fitness is historically and culturally contingent, something
that changes over time and varies between cultures, thus giving rise to (and
to some extent explaining) both semantic change and cultural difference.
Swettenham first surveys the various kinds of prototypes that have been theorized by Rosch and Lakoff; then, with respect to Synge's play, he delineates
these prototypes in terms of the category IRISHNESS, matching the various
prototypes for IRISHNESS to the range of characters we find in the play.
Swettenham finds in these prototypes "such unflattering portraits" (p. 217)
that it is no wonder the play's first audience shouted, "That's not the West
of Ireland!" to the actors on the stage. By itself, this is an uncontroversial
finding, but Swettenham takes his reading of the play further by stressing
Synge's dramatic strategy with respect to the various "unflattering portraits"
that the play's prototypical characters represent: "Synge did not provide a
rhetorical debate . . . nor an intellectual speculation on idealism in action,
but a 'physical' encounter with a large number of far-from-ideal category
members, any one of which might be taken to represent the category [of
IRISHNESS] as a whole. The narrative force was a direct result of the cognitive dissonance generated by the clash of categories, operating at the
most basic, and therefore most significant, level of knowledge organization"
(p. 220).

Swettenham concludes with an observation that might well summarize
the spirit of all the essays in this volume, devoted as they are to exploring
how a cognitive perspective might illuminate interrelations between the
material and the symbolic exigencies of performance. Noting the different
reactions Synge's characters have to Christy's first and second attempts to
murder his father (the first, accessible only through narration, is considered

an act of heroism, while the second, enacted before their eyes, is deemed a "dirty deed"), Swettenham hones in on the unmediated materiality of theatre itself, asserting that Synge's disruption of idealized Irishness was simply *intolerable* within the context of 1907 Irish cultural consciousness since it was being played out physically and in real time before its audience (a circumstance, recalling Mancing, that bespeaks the processing differences between symbolization and perception). These insights bear implications not only for the aesthetic but also for the *ethical* dimensions of theatre and performance – the power of performance as an instrument for social and political change. As Swettenham writes, "Wherever there is material embodiment, there is also a heightened sense of physical interaction and an increased possibility of category disruption: this is the so-called 'magic' of live performance" (Ibid.).

Possibilities for future research

Some recent publications in cognitive studies suggest several promising new directions for theatre and performance scholarship in the coming years. In this final section, we will survey some of the developments and suggest their possible relevance for theatre and performance studies. One development in particular warrants the extended description we have given it here: the "conceptual-blending" theory of Gilles Fauconnier and Mark Turner. Although not represented in the essays that follow (Zunshine refers to it but briefly in her essay on the essentialism of natural kinds), we believe that conceptual-blending theory bears special promise for future studies in theatre and performance. For instance, conceptual blending, which as a theory is generally compatible with Lakoff and Johnson's embodied realism, offers a material and experiential explanation for the inherent doubleness of theatricality – the fact that performing human beings exist simultaneously in both real and fictitious time-space. Many acting teachers work to diminish this doubleness by helping actors to merge their bodies and voices with their fictitious characters. Some theatre scholars, by contrast, fear the apparent collapse of this doubleness in theatrical realism and celebrate its exploration in productions that favor Brechtian and other overtly theatrical techniques. A similar concern about the conflation of theatrical doubleness occurs in performance studies. There, scholars worry that repeated performances of conventionally gendered and racialized roles may lead people to accept as authentic an identity that compromises their agency and limits their potential for change. Although few cognitive scientists have even considered the problem of theatrical doubleness, interestingly, Fauconnier and Turner draw directly on the puzzle of theatricality to discuss their conclusions (Fauconnier and Turner 2002: 217–67). In brief, Fauconnier and Turner concur with sociologist Erving Goffman that theatricality is a matter of "framing" (Goffman 1974: 157); and they would support but also modify the notion of mimesis as put forward by the aesthetic philosopher Kendall Walton, who has written on the ways in which spectators use actors as "props in games of make-believe" while enjoying theatre (Walton 1990: 292).

Fauconnier and Turner demonstrate that actors can engage in theatrical doubleness and spectators can understand it because of the ability of human beings to do "conceptual blending," the mental synthesizing of concepts from different areas of cognition. This process, ubiquitous in human imagination, generally occurs automatically and for the most part well below the level of awareness. When actors engage in conceptual blending to play a role, then, they share in a cognitive ability possessed by all but do not compromise their inherent, singular identities. Nor do audience members "willingly suspend their disbelief" when they enjoy the actor's doubleness; conscious "willing" may begin the process of spectating, but after spectators have accepted the frame of performance, "willingness" has very little to do with it. Instead, actors and spectators together create a fourth "mental space," which is distinct from the perception of themselves in real time-space or the knowledge that they are playing a game of make-believe. Within this fourth space, information from the juxtaposed "inputs" of actor and spectator along with information from a third "generic" domain (memory containing conventional image-schematic knowledge) are "blended" together to create perceptions that are distinct from all the inputs. While experiencing a dramatic performance, spectators and actors mostly "live in the blend," according to Fauconnier and Turner:

> The spectator will live in the blend only by selective projection: Many aspects of her existence (such as sitting in a seat, next to other people, in the dark), although independently available to her, are not to be projected to the blend.... The actor, meanwhile, is engaged in a different kind of blend, one in which his motor patterns and power of speech come directly into play, but not his free will or his foreknowledge of the [dramatic] outcome. In the blend, he says just what the character says and is surprised night after night by the same events.
>
> (Fauconnier and Turner 2002: 267)

Other selective projections that blend social and make-believe realities shape ongoing spectator–performer interactions. The spectator in the example above hears something amusing on stage, accommodates the laughter of others in a new blend, and begins to laugh herself. The actor hears the laughter, instantly builds a new blend to justify his pause, and then plunges back into the behavior of the character when the laughter subsides. Actors and spectators adjust their blends throughout every performance, interacting to sustain and/or modify their enjoyment of theatrical doubleness. Cognitive blending structures and enables all games of make-believe, from playing with dolls to professional football. As far as cognitive scientists can tell, it is a uniquely human ability; the minds/brains of other animals do not seem to allow for it.

Deriving theatricality from conceptual blending may seem innocuous and even commonsensical, but it hides several bombshells for some theories that theatre and performance scholars rely on to explain it. First, the linkage between conceptual blending and theatricality means that dramatic performance does not directly "imitate" an action or any other reality. Blending involves selective projections and cognitive compressions and places in mental play a whole host of what Fauconnier and Turner call "vital relations": change, identity, space, time, cause–effect, part–whole, representation, role, analogy, dis-anology, property, similarity, category, intentionality, and uniqueness (Ibid.: 92–102). The mind/brain's ability to project and compress information about these relationships into a blend that constitutes a person's mental image of a millisecond of a performance defies the notions of mimesis that our field currently entertains.

The linkage between theatricality and blending also complicates the usual distinctions dividing realistic from overtly theatrical productions and "passive" from "active" spectators. Given cognitive blending, it is clear that all plays on stage involve spectator recognition of theatrical framing. Some productions may invite spectators to move in and out of various blends more than other kinds, but these are differences of degree, not of kind. Consequently, it is unlikely that formal differences in the degree of theatricality have much to do with the political efficacy of certain kinds of theatre. Although Brechtian theatre may indeed pack a certain kind of political punch, it is not due to the so-called "alienation effect." Further, all viewing, even of a television soap opera, involves active cognition; there is no foundational cognitive distinction between "active" and "passive" spectators.

Finally, all cultural performances based in make-believe role-playing involve this kind of cognitive blending. This means, as many scholars in performance studies have argued, that theatre and theatricality are a subset of performance in general. Like role-playing in psychodrama sessions, major-league sporting events, and primitive rituals, theatrical performances involve the mutual recognition by its participants of a make-believe frame and the general goal of sustaining "the blend." Cognitive science thus provides general validation of Richard Schechner's definition of performance as "restored behavior," but it can also assist in sharpening and qualifying Schechner's insight. First, performance is not "behavior," if behavior is understood as conditioned responses to external stimuli. A behaviorist approach to performance denies the conceptual blending that shapes the mind/brain's ability to frame and select from every performance environment. Second, if "living in the blend" (or blends) for performers and spectators is a necessary part of any definition of performance, simply restoring some kind of cultural practice that occurred before does not, by itself, constitute performance. Both parties, spectators and performers, must frame and selectively project those concepts that will sustain the blends that are appropriate for different cultural performances. Without such mental work, all performances, from impressive religious rituals to boys playing at soldiering, simply disintegrate. Cognitive studies, then, would substitute a more modest definition of performance for the inflated claims of some of its advocates.

In particular, theorists have had difficulty in distinguishing between social role-playing and playing roles in situations that are obviously set aside from our everyday roles of mother, student, lover, etc. Without going into the minds of participants, it may be possible to discern behavior that involves the mutual recognition of a performance frame and activities from all participants dedicated to sustaining "the blend" for the duration of the performance, in other words, the "strip" of behavior under restoration in Schechner's terms. This would allow for the recognition of "performance" in everyday life without collapsing all role-playing into a definition that includes social role-playing.[7] The goal-directed performance of social roles, by itself, does not involve the mutual recognition of representation and the intention of sustaining a "what if" game. Dogs and cats learn to play limited kinds of social roles but, as far as the cognitivists can tell, do not engage in make-believe.[8]

Another important development in cognitive science is category theory, a sub-field of both psychology and linguistics. In our anthology, Neal Swettenham draws on psychologist Eleanor Rosch's category theory to supplement historical and cultural explanations for the response of *The Playboy* audience to Synge's comedy; but Swettenham is alone among our contributors in acknowledging category theory's importance. Insights from within this field may be applied to other aspects of theatre as well, including color-blind casting. A recent article on color-blind casting in the United States notes the difficulties that some audiences experience in accepting nonwhite actors in some roles written to be played by white performers (Pao 2001: 389–409). Apparently, many American spectators will more easily accept a nonwhite actor in a "white" Shakespearean role (even when this undercuts family genetics, e.g., white Capulets producing a black Juliet) than in a realist drama such as *Death of a Salesman*. Cognitive category theory suggests a significant reason for this: most spectators see Willy Loman and his family as prototypical Americans, and "the American family," as a category, is racialized as white by the dominant culture. Understanding and applying category theory to this problem might shed some light on its intractability and, not incidentally, help casting directors in the future.

The key idea of salience as an aspect of category theory is also changing linguistics, offering implications for the understanding of playwriting and the reception of language on stage. As Rosch has demonstrated, humans put together cognitive categories on the basis of salience, meaning that they grant precedence to ideas that are familiar and prominent within their own cultures. In her recent book, psycholinguist Rachel Giora (2003) brings together several years' worth of research among English and Hebrew speakers on the salience of certain words and phrases that play a more important role in the users' constructions of meaning than do contextual factors and literal denotative meanings. More so than others, good playwrights are especially sensitive to degrees of salience in the words they give their actors to utter. Giora is interested as well in the mechanisms of mental processing and in the time it takes for listeners to process such linguistic constructions as irony, metaphor, and joking, all of which depend on salience. These issues, of course, are directly relevant to understanding how audiences follow and comprehend dialogue, from the everyday speech of realist dramas to the poetic plays of W.B. Yeats.

Another development in cognitive science involves its forays into the domain of moral philosophy. The ethics of theatre and performance is an emerging area in our own practice and scholarship, and scholars in cognitive studies have made contributions here as well. If mutual cognitive framing and shared responsibility for sustaining "the blend" are key discernible attributes of all performance events, then phenomenologist Bruce Wilshire's ethical concern that all para-theatrical situations must be carefully separated from situations that entail direct moral responsibility gains added force (Wilshire 1990: 177–8). For example, Wilshire would object to the practice of Augusto Boal's "invisible theatre," which involves a troupe of actors "invisibly" performing roles in a public space for the purpose of inciting controversy among spectators who do not know that the scenario they are watching is a "show." Since invisible theatre does not involve a mutual interest in framing and make-believe, Wilshire might fuse a cognitive perspective to his ethical beliefs to deny that "invisible theatre" is, by definition, theatre at all. This does not rule out the possibility of performances raising significant ethical implications, of course. It simply contains those implications within the make-believe of "the blend." Much as people cast themselves and others to run "what if" conjectures in their imaginations to weigh moral options, they may use a play or ritual performance for the same purpose.

Many moral philosophers have been in conversation with cognitive psychologists and neuroscientists for more than a decade to gain a better understanding of moral reasoning. Moral naturalist Owen Flanagan, for example, uses cognitive science to acknowledge the constraints that the mind/brain places on moral reasoning so as to better understand how people make "good" moral judgments. Flanagan urges moral philosophers to "make sure when constructing a moral theory or projecting a moral ideal that the character, decision processing, and behavior prescribed are possible, or perceived to be possible, for creatures like us" (Flanagan 1991: 32).[9] While Flanagan and other moral naturalists are careful not to reduce moral claims to psychological norms, they do argue that ethicists can make their best case for moral action by understanding its cognitive possibilities and limitations. Also at the intersection of moral philosophy and cognitive science are questions about moral education and the role of empathy in moral thought. All of these ethical issues, of course, are fundamental for producers, directors, theorists, and historians of performance.

While conceptual blending, category theory, and the intersections of cognitive science and moral philosophy have significant implications for our understandings of theatre and performance, these recent developments in cognitive science (and the more widely interdisciplinary cognitive studies) are only the tip of the iceberg. Invoking this hoary metaphor at the close of our Introduction may appear to be a rhetorical slip into mindless conventionality, but we do it intentionally. The cognitive turn in humanistic scholarship has filled our business-as-usual channels toward valid truth claims in theatre and performance studies with chunks of ice. We can continue to plow the same seas in chilly isolation, sinking into irrelevance, or we can join the interdisciplinary trek toward more temperate and liberating insights.

Notes

1 See also Taylor (1995).
2 Regarding the basis of Derridean theory (and that of Lacan and Foucault) in Saussurean semiotics, see Silverman (1983). For a critique of Saussure's formalism and its influence on Derrida, see Hart (1998).
3 See also Edelman (2004).
4 See also Shore (1996) for an explanation of the relations among cognitive models in the mind and cultural models of the world.
5 See McConachie (2003: 15–16) for an explanation of Williams' concepts of "dominant," "residual," and "emergent" culture in cognitive terms.
6 See Lakoff and Johnson (1999: 284–7) on Japanese metaphors and see also Nisbett (2003: 191–229).
7 For a contrary view, see Carlson's (1996: 51–3) discussion about the difficulty of separating the real from the imaginary worlds of human action.
8 On the differences between higher mammals and humans with regard to consciousness, see Edelman (2004: 97–112).
9 For an overview of the kinds of conversations going on among cognitive scientists and moral philosophers, see May, Friedman, and Clark (1996). Mark Johnson (1993) is also useful.

References

Bucci, W. (1997) *Psychoanalysis and Cognitive Science: A Multiple Code Theory*, New York: Guilford.

Carlson, M. (1996) *Performance: A Critical Introduction*, London: Routledge.

Crane, M.T. (2001) *Shakespeare's Brain: Reading with Cognitive Theory*, Princeton, NJ: Princeton University Press.

D'Andrade, R. (1995) *The Development of Cognitive Anthropology*, Cambridge: Cambridge University Press.

Damasio, A. (1999) *The Feeling of What Happens: Body and Emotion in the Making of Consciousness*, New York: Harcourt.

—— (2000) *Descartes' Error: Emotion, Reason, and the Human Brain*, New York: Quill.

—— (2003) *Looking for Spinoza: Joy, Sorrow, and the Feeling Brain*, New York: Harcourt.

Dennett, D. (1991) *Consciousness Explained*, Boston, MA: Little, Brown.

de Saussure, F. (1974) *Course in General Linguistics*, New York: Fontana/Collins.

Edelman, G.M. (2004) *Wider Than the Sky: The Phenomenal Gift of Consciousness*, New Haven, CT: Yale University Press.

Edelman, G.M. and Tononi, G. (2000) *A Universe of Consciousness: How Matter Becomes Imagination*, New York: Basic Books.

Fauconnier, G. and Turner, M. (2002) *The Way We Think: Conceptual Blending and the Mind's Hidden Complexities*, New York: Basic Books.

Flanagan, O. (1991) *Varieties of Moral Personality: Ethics and Psychological Realism*, Cambridge, MA: Harvard University. Press.

Garner, S.B. (1994) *Bodied Spaces: Phenomenology and Performance in Contemporary Drama*, Ithaca, NY: Cornell University Press.

Giora, R. (2003) *On Our Mind: Salience, Context, and Figurative Language*, Oxford: Oxford University Press.

Goffman, E. (1974) *Frame Analysis*, Garden City, NY: Doubleday.

Gordon, R.M. (1996a) "Simulation and the Explanation of Action," in Kogler, H.H. and Steuber, K.R. (eds) *Empathy and Agency: The Problem of Understanding in the Human Sciences*, Boulder, CO: Westview Press, 62–82.

—— (1996b) "Simulation, Sympathy, and the Impartial Spectator," in May, L., Friedman, M., and Clark, A. (eds) *Mind and Morals: Essays on Cognitive Science and Ethics*, Cambridge, MA: MIT Press, 165–80.

Hart, F.E. (1998) "Matter, system, and early modern studies: outlines for a materialist linguistics," *Configurations,* 6: 311–43.

Johnson, M. (1993) *Moral Imagination: The Implication of Cognitive Science for Ethics*, Chicago, IL: University of Chicago Press.

Lakoff, G. and Johnson, M. (1999) *Philosophy in the Flesh: The Embodied Mind and Its Challenge to Western Thought*, New York: Basic Books.

Lott, E. (1993) *Love and Theft: Blackface Minstrelsy and the American Working Class*, New York: Oxford University Press.

Mandler, J. (1992) "How to build a baby: II conceptual primitives," *Psychological Review*, 99: 587–604.

May, L., Friedman, M., and Clark, A. (1996) *Mind and Morals: Essays on Cognitive Science and Ethics*, Cambridge, MA: MIT Press.

McConachie, B. (2003) *American Theater in the Culture of the Cold War: Producing and Contesting Containment, 1947–1962*, Iowa City, IA: University of Iowa Press.

Nisbett, R.E. (2003) *The Geography of Thought: How Asians and Westerners Think Differently . . . and Why*, New York: Free Press.

Palmer, A. (2004) *Fictional Minds*, Lincoln, NE: University of Nebraska Press.

Pao, A.C. (2001) "Changing faces: recasting national identity in all-Asian–American dramas," *Theatre Journal*, 53: 389–409.

Rosch, E. and Lloyd, B.B. (1978) *Cognition and Categorization*, Hillsdale, NJ: Erlbaum.

Silverman, K. (1983) *The Subject of Semiotics*, New York: Oxford.

Shore, B. (1996) *Culture in the Mind: Cognition, Culture, and the Problem of Meaning*, New York: Oxford.

Taylor, J.R. (1995) *Linguistic Categorization: Prototypes in Linguistic Theory*, 2nd edn, Oxford: Clarendon.

Thagard, P. (2000) *Coherence in Thought and Action*, Cambridge, MA: MIT Press.

Vermeule, B. (in progress) *Making Sense of Fictional People*.

Vielmetter, G. (2000) "The Theory of Holistic Simulation: Beyond Interpretivism and Postempiricism," in Kogler, H.H. and Steuber, K.R. (eds) *Empathy and Agency: The Problem of Understanding in the Human Sciences*, Boulder, CO: Westview Press, 83–102.

Walton, K. (1990) *Mimesis as Make-Believe: On the Foundations of the Representational Arts*, Cambridge, MA: Harvard University Press.

Wilshire, B. (1990) "The concept of the paratheatrical," *TDR*, 34: 177–8.

Zunshine, L. (2004) "Richardson's 'Clarissa' and a Theory of Mind," in Richardson, A. and Spolsky, E. (eds) *The Work of Fiction: Cognition, Culture, and Complexity*, Aldershot/Burlington, VT: Ashgate Publishing.

—— (2006) *Why We Read Fiction: Theory of Mind and the Novel*, Columbus, OH: Ohio State University Press.

Section 1

Performance theory and cognition

1 Performance, phenomenology, and the cognitive turn

F. Elizabeth Hart

In an effort to counterbalance the abstracting effects of semiotics as an approach to performance – in an effort, that is, to reclaim the materiality of props, lighting, stage space, costumes, and of course the human body itself from a theory that would reduce such *things* to *signs* – theorists and practitioners of theatre have increasingly turned to phenomenology, hoping, if not actually to eliminate semiotics from the spectrum of approaches, then at least to find a perspective that may reconcile the varying materialities that comprise *both* things and signs. Mark Fortier has aptly articulated the growing frustration over the collapse of all things material in performance into language or – as many tend to reduce language – into semiotics: "To treat everything as language or as dominated by language seems a distortion of the nature of theatre as rooted in the physical and the sensual, as much as it is in words and ideas" (Fortier 1997: 3–4).

Two critics in particular, Bert O. States (1985, 1992) and Stanton Garner (1994), have offered especially compelling defenses of phenomenology as a tool for conceptualizing the full, lived experience of theatre, i.e., its usefulness as a descriptor of the perceptual dimension that constitutes theatre as much as, if not more than, the verbal.[1] The key study, in my view, is Garner's *Bodied Spaces* (1994), which, in its focus on the phenomenology of Maurice Merleau-Ponty, has contributed to the growing sense of the relevance of Merleau-Ponty's philosophy across a range of late twentieth- and early twenty-first-century discourses. Building on both the late writings of Edmund Husserl and those of Merleau-Ponty's contemporary and fellow existentialist Jean-Paul Sartre, Merleau-Ponty sought to resituate subjectivity not within Husserl's transcendental essences but within the physical body of the human perceiver, in short, "returning the body to the field of subjectivity" (Garner 1994: 27). In his monumental *Phenomenology of Perception* (1961), Merleau-Ponty established the body as the ground of all rationality, stressing, in a radical departure from Husserl, the body's dynamic interface with the world outside it. Perception arising from this interface establishes a pre-propositional or pre-reflective realm of consciousness, which in turn forms the basis of philosophical and scientific – i.e., abstract – thought. Of particular importance to Merleau-Ponty's view was his understanding of consciousness as *embodied*, as itself a response to the lived-in body within a lived-in world. Such consciousness, embedded and interactive within a network of temporally dynamic connections, is obviously a far cry from Husserl's sealed-off realm of idealized perception. "Whereas Husserl's phenomenology suspends the materiality of an 'outside' that includes the body for the sake of ideal self-presence," notes Garner, "Merleau-Ponty posited a consciousness caught up in the ambiguity of corporeality, directed toward a world of which it is inextricably and materially a part" (Garner 1994: 27).

Such a model of the phenomenal body and consciousness seems clearly useful for performance theorists as they strive to conceptualize the *thingness* of theatre and of performance in general. But ironically the very notion of embodiment – the hinge upon which Merleau-Ponty's revised understanding of subjectivity hangs – is also a key concept underlying Judith Butler's popular theory of (gender) performativity. I call this ironic because Butler's performativity, with its emphasis on the body's realization of a material identity through the discourses of culture, is arguably but a thinly veiled version of the very semiotics that phenomenology contradicts. To compound the irony, it is well known that among Butler's sources for her formation of performativity theory was Merleau-Ponty himself, albeit the later Merleau-Ponty of *The Visible and the Invisible* (1968). In fact, critics typically recognize performativity as a blend of phenomenology and J.L. Austin's speech-act theory, citing especially Butler's debt to Merleau-Ponty for the all-important idea of the "performative embodiment": the act by which the human body obediently expresses its assumption of the cultural restrictions that determine its materiality.[2] Butler's view, bolstered by the linguistic claims of Derrida, Foucault, Althusser, and – hovering behind each of these theorists – Saussure, posits a body that has no inherent agency, no basis for self-assertion prior to its interpellation into subjectivity. Indeed, sometimes her writings hesitatingly and obliquely suggest that the body may possess no (and perhaps she means *access* to its) biological materiality prior to its discursive, i.e., linguistic, constitution (e.g., Butler 1990: 136–41). Embodiment, in Butler's scenario, is thus something that happens *to* the body, is an imposition *upon* the body by culture; while the subject's agency, if it exists, can only manifest from variations within iterations and reiterations of this imposition.

One must recognize the efficacy of Butler's quasi-semiotics for gender, feminist, queer, and other identity-based critiques, both in literary/cultural studies and in theatre/performance studies. Her theories, because they have focused acute attention on the culturally dependent forms of the body's self-expression, have generated fresh and useful analyses of the mechanisms governing processes of cultural construction – all to the good. But what's troubling is the fact that, at their deepest levels, Butler's models of identity-formation are predicated on an outmoded and untenable science of language, the Saussurean semiotics that undergirds each of her poststructuralist influences (as noted above). In its determination to locate meaning within the gap between sign and signifier and in the arbitrary connection between phoneme and semantic unit, Saussurean semiotics aggressively *disembodies* both meaning and language, leaving philosophers like Derrida and Foucault apparently no choice but to conjure a hoped-for materiality out of a hopelessly abstracted system. It is therefore intensely ironic that Butler should derive a theory of embodiment from Saussure's legacy; and it is particularly striking how her theory opposes, as an etiology, Merleau-Ponty's theory of the embodied consciousness, the latter emerging from a – yes – biologically material body. Yet it seems to me that these opposing conceptions of what it means to be embodied have gone unnoticed within today's culture studies, an oversight that I find curious given the centrality of "embodiment" as a concept within both critical frameworks and especially given Butler's explicit deployment of Merleau-Ponty.

In this essay, my address to this contradiction will call for some shifting of the theoretical sands. I will argue that theatre and performance critics interested in reconciling phenomenological and semiotic approaches will never be able to achieve their goal so long as semiotics remains defined within a Saussurean framework or – perhaps more to the point – so long as the term "semiotics" continues to collapse all aspects of language into *sign*. (The alternative, taken as a disciplinary given by today's linguists, configures the sign in its phonetic and graphic forms to be one relatively minor aspect of language as a whole.) I assert that Butler and her fellow poststructuralists are actually quite right to say that language and discourse contribute to the formation and even the material realization of human subjects; however, I contend that the language and discourse at issue in these processes are somewhat different from the way poststructuralism has typically defined them, and that the difference is crucial for understanding, first, how such subject- or identity-formation actually takes place, and second, *to what extent* we should credit discursively formulated subjectivity and identity with having such embodiment capabilities. The key theoretical difference, as I will elaborate here, is the claim that language and discourse are *themselves* embodied: They are *cognitively* embodied, arising from the embodied human minds that anchor Merleau-Ponty's embodied consciousness and, *from* this embodied condition, acquiring the semantic and syntactic structures necessary to facilitate social construction, i.e., communication.[3] Embodiment by and through the mechanisms of language and discourse therefore constitutes but one aspect of a circulating *system* of both cognitive and cultural embodiment, as I hope to show.

Making such an argument requires an interdisciplinary leap outside the humanities into another domain in which embodiment now serves as a central concept: the domain of cognitive science. In recent years, cognitive studies have taken a noticeable turn toward the human body as the source of both information to and constraint upon the mind, the very entity that until recently was thought to be essentially transcendent in its relationship to the body. In disciplines embracing both the philosophy of mind and the sciences of the mind (including cognitive neuroscience, cognitive psychology, linguistics, artificial intelligence studies, and others), the conceptual barriers separating the mind from the brain and the brain from the body have to some extent given way to imagery of a fluid interaction between the three, belying easy generalizations about cognitive cause-and-effect. Nonetheless, it is becoming increasingly clear that Merleau-Ponty's embodied consciousness is a cannily accurate description of what the scientists now see as the material grounding of knowledge, of the mind-brain's dependence on the body's concrete situatedness within the physical and social worlds that encompass it.

In what follows, I will explore how this cognitive embodiment registers within one area that has been especially symptomatic of the cognitive turn, the field of cognitive linguistics. I hope to demonstrate how the insights of cognitive linguistics (and of related areas in cognitive science) may suggest a resolution to contradictory notions of embodiment within the humanities. What I intend to show with my analysis is that the Butlerian sense of embodiment, while it has been enabling for us as a critical tool, has also been misleading as an etiology of embodiment. The more likely scenario, taken from a cognitive-scientific orientation, is that embodiment is *primarily* a cognitive phenomenon, a phenomenon that creates the instruments of communication – language, discourse, sign, and gesture – through which a secondary order of constructivity becomes activated. While it is tempting to consider this secondary order of constructivity *as* "embodiment" (because its effects are more clearly evident to us), doing so turns out to be reductive since this secondary form of embodiment is simply not the same qualitatively as the primary order of embodiment through which the body's basic materiality finds its conceptual and expressive forms. Nevertheless, this secondary order of constructivity does participate indirectly – that is, recursively – in processes of cognitive embodiment since social context helps determine what forms of cognitive embodiment are most viable and thus which ones become stabilized within a given culture.

I will develop these claims and their relevance to theatre/performance through a focus on a limited but important aspect of any theatre or performance event: the embodied conceptualization of the *performance space*. Specifically, I will look at intersections between language/discourse and cognitively embodied space in two examples, the text of the Chorus to Shakespeare's *Henry V* and a recent London production of the play *After Mrs. Rochester*. With these analyses, I want to show that a reconciliation between *things* and *language* – including but, importantly, not exclusively linguistic signs – may indeed be possible but only within an analysis that uses cognitive embodiment as its starting point.

The role played by cognitive literary/cultural studies

In one sense, embodiment has defined performance since the origins of theatre in prehistoric ritual. Characters, whether of humans, animals, or gods, have always been represented in performance through the bodies of actors. This is true but for a few exceptions that include puppet theatre, which uses as proxy representations of bodies, and, as Marvin Carlson points out, performance art, which utilizes bodies but not always as representations of characters (Carlson 1996: 6). When talking about embodiment in the context of performance theory, however, it is easy to elide the element of intentionality in our eagerness to register the valences of physical features – facial expressions, gestures, gender, sexual attractiveness, etc. – assuming but not exploring the fact that behind every actor's use of his or her body is a body of *knowledge*, and that out of that knowledge emerges a focused intentionality that participates along with the body in creating a performance. It may sound simplistic to say so, but surely such intentionality emerges from – or at least is mediated by – the actor's *brain*. And while we may not be accustomed to thinking about the brain as a part of the body, we must recognize that indeed the brain is an organ like the heart or the kidneys, without which the body would cease to function unaided *as* a body. But even a critic like Butler, (who wants very much to understand the mechanics of embodiment, and whose investigations have taken her to psychoanalysis and to the poststructuralists who use psychoanalysis to understand subject-formation) does not acknowledge the direct role of the brain and thereby misses, as Mary Thomas Crane has remarked, "the material site where discourse enters the body, where entry into the symbolic occurs, and therefore where the subject is constructed" (Crane 2001: 7). What makes Butler's appropriation of Merleau-Ponty all the more interesting is the fact that at least Merleau-Ponty recognizes an embodied *consciousness*, assuming, as the word "consciousness" implies, a locus of psychic knowledge and awareness. And while his later works to which Butler appeals do expand on this epistemology by exploring the means – especially in language – through which the body interacts with and is acted upon by the world, there is no sense in which Merleau-Ponty himself ever abandons his original model of an embodied consciousness that participates in these exchanges.

In the decades since Merleau-Ponty's death, a new generation of cognitive scientists, most notably Gerald Edelman (1992), Antonio Damasio (1999, 1994), and Daniel Dennett (1991), has stepped forward to challenge the long-held axioms of Cartesian rationalism, not least of which Descartes' division between the mind and the body. The result has been an increasingly detailed map of the mechanisms by which the human cognitive apparatus is shaped by the body and thus the ways in which knowledge itself reflects mind-embodiment. And it is through this logic of mind-embodiment that cognitive researchers have pushed Merleau-Ponty's philosophy past the point of speculation and into the realm of scientific inquiry. The linguist George

Lakoff and the philosopher Mark Johnson, both innovators in the field of cognitive linguistics, write that "Cognitive science provides a new and important take on an age-old philosophical problem of what is real and how we can know it.... Our sense of what is real begins with and depends crucially upon our bodies, especially our sensorimotor apparatus, which enables us to perceive, move, and manipulate, and the detailed structures of our brains, which have been shaped by both evolution and experience" (Lakoff and Johnson 1999: 17).[4] Here, what amounts to a radical assertion that all knowledge is in fact mediated by the body would seem to be yet another expression of Husserlian phenomenology – except that today's cognitive science acknowledges that the body's boundaries with the world are porous and unstable and that embodiment is contingent upon both physical and cultural determinants. (Importantly, from a phenomenological standpoint, not only does the dichotomy between mind and body break down, but that between subjectivity and objectivity is also dissolved.)

My own orientation to these developments is through a new field within the humanities called "cognitive approaches to literature," whose practitioners have turned to the science of mind-embodiment in their efforts to formulate more human-friendly literary and cultural theories. To varying degrees, cognitive literary and cultural critics either reject poststructuralism wholesale; or they seek to revise poststructuralist insights by calling into question the Saussurean roots of deconstruction while simultaneously confirming the theorized effects of socially constructive discourse and ideology.[5] The latter group, in which I count myself, appeals both to the cognitive-scientific study of physiological mind-embodiment and to the understanding of cultural theorists of embodiment as a form of cultural inscription, coming closer, perhaps, than any other set of critics to implementing a true fusion of phenomenology and semiotics. By "semiotics," however, these critics mean language (and with it discourse) that emerges from embodied cognition and *not* the disembodied sign system of Saussure's linguistics or its consequent deconstructions. According to the cognitive literary/cultural view, language includes a semiotic dimension to the extent that it depends on arbitrary signs to communicate embodied meaning; but meaning itself, far from being arbitrary, is motivated by complex networks of cognitive connections. Yet having thus rejected Saussure's over-reduction of language to signs, cognitive literary/culture critics also offer limited endorsements of the Foucauldian or Butlerian assertion that language and discourse possess the power of social constructivity. This power might best be described as a kind of feedback system through which social context helps set the range of forms of cognitive embodiment that are most relevant to – and therefore most "natural" within – a given culture. In this way, cognitive literary/cultural theory actively merges the primary and secondary tiers of embodiment alluded to earlier in this essay.

This merger takes the form of a material continuum between the two forms of embodiment, one tapping into the primary cognitive materiality of mind and body, the other into the secondary materiality of language and discourse as the social manifestation of mind and body (c.f., the primary and secondary orders of constructivity, described earlier). Matter, in other words, flows in an interconnected stream between the embodied mind and its representations of embodied experience in language and discourse. Such a material continuum allows literary and cultural theorists to counterbalance the reductive tendencies of Saussurean semiotics, envisioning, as Crane puts it, "embodied and enacted materiality as co-existing on equal terms with discourse and representation, . . . go[ing] beyond phenomenology in offering an account of how embodied action shapes thought and language" (Crane 2001: 171).[6] Moreover, Crane writes, this material continuum bears similar implications for performance theory in the sense that, "If we are able to view discourse and embodiment, representation and experience, as mutually constitutive aspects of performance rather than assuming that discourse and representation subsume the other two, [then] a way is cleared for a broader view of the evolving concepts of theat[re] and performance" (Ibid.: 171).

Space as metaphor, metaphor as space

To illustrate the dynamics of this material continuum, I turn to the subject of the *performance space*, where intersections between language (including its semiotic dimension) and embodied cognition are both fundamental to the performance experience and an exploitably rich aspect of that experience. Performance space is obviously a central concern if what we are trying to gauge is the flow of materiality from the realm of the phenomenal (Crane's "embodiment and experience") to the linguistic/semiotic (Crane's "discourse and representation") or vice versa. The centrality of space to theatre is uncontroversial, a subject of studies undertaken decades ago by Antonin Artaud (1970), Anne Ubersfeld (1977, 1981), Steen Jansen (1982, 1984), and others; and more recently by Garner (1994), Una Chaudhuri (1995), and Gay McAuley (1999). Artaud argued for the need to separate the written text of performance from conceptualization of the performance space, maintaining that "the stage is a tangible, physical place that needs to be filled[,] and it ought to be allowed to speak its own concrete language" (quoted in McAuley 1999: 5). McAuley, too, stresses the difference that the physicality of stage space makes when evaluating the relative materialities of text and performance, going so far as to assert "the primacy of the theatrical over the written" (Ibid.: 5) and claiming for space the status of being "*the* medium of theatre" (Ibid.: 278, italics added). McAuley writes that the stage itself "distinguishes theatre from other dramatic media such as film, radio, and television":

> From the physical reality of the theatre building, its location in relation to other buildings and the social activities they accommodate, the organization of the audience and the practitioner spaces within this building, to the stage itself, the fictional worlds created on and around

it, and the modes of representation it facilitates, space is crucial to understanding the nature of the performance event and how meanings are constructed and communicated in the theatre.

(Ibid.: 278)

Space *is* crucial, even definitive, in the process of conveying meaning during performance. But how exactly does stage space *produce* meaning, and in what sense can we say that that meaning is "embodied"? Garner claims that the nature of stage space is one of "experiential duality," in which the differing experiences of spectators and actors require the same phenomenal space on which to be realized, the first through the objectifying powers of the perspectival gaze, the second subjectively through the actor's bodily inhabitation. On these terms, Garner writes, "theatrical space is phenomenal space, governed by the body and its spatial concerns, a non-Cartesian field of habitation which undermines the stance of objectivity and in which the categories of subject and object give way to a relationship of mutual implication" (Garner 1994: 3–4). I would observe further that stage space is "non-Cartesian" precisely in that it is a focus of privileged imagining, a socially sanctified site of legitimated *metaphor*, where metaphor is at its most concentrated and communal and – not unlike in religious ritual – where it comprises an epistemology of extraordinary cultural authority.

It is on the topic of metaphor that a cognitive approach may prove its relevance because it brings to bear on this discussion the tools of a science that – extraordinarily – takes seriously an epistemology based on metaphor. One of the characteristics of the cognitive-scientific turn toward mind-embodiment has been scientists' refusal to dismiss metaphor on the rationalist terms that demarcate "imagination" from "reason" or, in parallel terms, the "figurative" from the "literal," a demarcation that has traditionally resulted in the privileging of the latter terms over the former. Among these scientists, the cognitive linguists in particular have argued that we should revise our understanding of reason to include basic experiences of physical embodiment, experiences that serve us by constructing – via metaphor – the interconnected cognitive domains of thought and language. At the foundation of their claims is a philosophical orientation that they label "embodied realism" as distinct from "metaphysical realism," the latter associated with the Cartesian separation between subjects (human minds) and objects (things in the world). Descended from the realist philosophies of John Dewey and Hilary Putnam, the language theory of Ludwig Wittgenstein, and indeed the phenomenology of Merleau-Ponty, embodied realism combines into one set of concerns the questions inherent to ontology and epistemology by positing a fundamental fusion between human minds and the world. Both our experience of reality and our knowledge of that reality are contingent upon the brain and mind's shaping by the body, which is itself shaped by evolution and by the particularities of its experience. The relativity this gives rise to, however, is limited in degree since the body's particu-

lar experiences and the knowledge those experiences beget are both constrained by a positively experienced reality (positively in the sense that there
really *is* a reality out there), specifically, by the cultural, historical, and
environmental conditions in which the body is embedded.

Using this embodied realism as a philosophical foundation, cognitive linguistics represents an empirically driven, systematic analysis of what is, in
effect, Merleau-Ponty's embodied consciousness. Lakoff, Johnson, Raymond
Gibbs, Mark Turner, Gilles Fauconnier,[7] and many others now propose a
theory (or set of theories) of human knowledge-acquisition that we may
summarize as the following: kinesthetic and perceptual interactions between
the human body and its physical environments generate cognitive structures
that reflect the outlines of those environments and that serve in turn as the
templates for higher-level cognition. In particular, Lakoff and Johnson have
posited two forms of perceptual/conceptual constructs, the "basic-level category" and the "image schema," which provide the critical bridge between
the body's senses and the brain's neuronal structures. (Of these two kinds of
cognitive constructs, this essay will be more concerned with the image
schema, although I caution readers that no explanation of cognitive linguistics is complete without an account of basic-level categorization and other
tenets of prototype category theory.[8]) Image schemas are gestalt-like abstractions of sensorimotor experiences, stored in minimalist – and thus easily
retrievable – outlines in the memory. First developed in infancy, image
schemas can become permanent (i.e., neurologically stable) entities from
repeated use within a reality (which is always, to some extent, culturally specific) to which they consistently conform. Once developed and stabilized,
image schemas are used to structure higher levels of cognition via a process
of "metaphorical projection," which forms "primary metaphors" and
"complex metaphors" (examples below) that enable the brain to categorize
and assimilate both familiar and new experiences. Thus, image schemas
work with primary and complex metaphors to press embodied form onto
thought and language, importantly both enabling *and* constraining the
shapes of higher-level representations.

Of specific relevance to a discussion of stage space is the degree to which
image schemas are spatial in their content, so much so that Lakoff and
Johnson now typically refer to them as "spatial-relations concepts."[9] For
example, they argue that the human body's spatial positioning – its positions relative to physiological constants such as the body's upright stance,
front-back orientation, bilateral symmetry, or the effects on our bodies of
gravity – contributes to a significant proportion of the image schemas that
lend their shapes to complex (and complex systems of) thought. Our physical sense of having an interior as well as an exterior to our bodies leads us to
project in/out design onto countless intangible domains: we work *out* our
ideas; we take *in* advice; we drown *out* unwanted noise; we *in*vite orphaned
children *in*to our lives. The image schema for in/out bodily orientation
presupposes a discrete entity – a container – influenced by a force whose

trajectory either distances itself from the container (out) or intersects with the container (in). This combination of abstract boundaries and trajectories composes the image schema of CONTAINER (to which, as with all subsequent image schemas, I will refer with capital letters). Similar examples hold for other of our experiences of spatial orientation, e.g., left/right, front/back, toward/away-from, up/down, or near/far orientations, all of which provide us with the experiential foundation for more complex representations. Bilateral symmetry – having two arms, two hands, two eyes and ears, etc., each in seeming proportion with the other – supplies the cognitive template for the more complex uses of *balance* as a metaphor (noting, however, that BALANCE is also designated as an image schema by Lakoff and Johnson (1999: 35)) and thus for progressively more complex conceptual systems, e.g., *justice, argumentation, psychological health, modern marriage,* even *algebra,* all of which accrue semantic content metaphorically from the basic experience of proportionality.[10] (From this point on, I will cite metaphors in italics to distinguish them from image schemas.)

In addition to the body's physiology, its capacity for self-propulsion also serves as an important source of image schemas. Our sensorimotor experience of simply moving our bodies from one place to another gives us the image schema of SOURCE–PATH–GOAL, involving a starting point, a progression along a vector, and an endpoint (the latter perhaps an obstacle we first encountered as crawling infants). Although simple in its outlines, the PATH schema gives rise to some of our most complex abstractions, including the ideas of *life* (we typically conceive of life as movement along a path or more complexly as a journey), *death* (conceived of as the destination on that path or journey), and *causation* (things that happen to us along that path or journey seem linked sequentially owing to the linear trajectory of PATH). Concepts thus developed from the minimal outlines of physical locomotion provide us with a large but also largely unconscious inventory of primary metaphors and their verbal counterparts: e.g., *states are locations* ("I'm working *towards* buying a house"); *causation is forced movement* ("She was *compelled into* making this decision"); and *purposes are destinations* ("We *took the steps* necessary to revitalize our community"), to cite only a few.[11] These primary metaphors, alone or in combination, may go on to become the basis for more complex metaphors, verbal expressions, and whole systems of thought. For instance, the *purposes are destinations* primary metaphor, when combined with the *life is a journey* metaphor, renders the more complex but still largely unconscious metaphor *A purposeful life is a journey*, complete with various entailments including moral injunctions, which we internalize as axiomatically inherent to the metaphor. To list examples of such entailments (taken verbatim from Lakoff and Johnson's discussion):

- A purposeful life requires planning a means for achieving your purposes.
- Purposeful lives may have difficulties, and you should try to anticipate them.

- You should provide yourself with what you need to pursue a purposeful life.
- As a prudent person with life goals[,] you should have an overall life plan indicating what goals to set out to achieve next. You should always know what you have achieved so far and what you are going to do next.

(Ibid.: 62)

Such assumptions – apparently "natural" or "logical" truths – are then incorporated into whole systems of cultural practice, including the philosophical and theological systems that govern other systems, such as governmental, educational, and commercial institutions. Thus, our highest-level representations, those that constitute the complexities of whole societies, seem to owe a great deal of their form to cognitively embodied structures like image schemas and their translations via metaphor.

The implications for theatre and performance studies – as for literary studies – are no doubt many; and considering particularly theatre's dependence on space as one of its defining characteristics, the impact of a "spatial-relations" cognition theory on performance analysis could take up volumes of discussion. Recognizing the possibilities already, the theatre historian Bruce McConachie has been actively exploring the impact of the CONTAINER schema (projections arising from in/out orientation) on a range of issues related to the theatre, from the evolution of stage types to the social atmosphere of markedly period productions such as 1950s Cold War Broadway or community theatre in the post-Civil Rights American South. McConachie strongly endorses the contribution that cognitive theory has already made to the study of theatre and performance history: "Lakoff and Johnson open the way for historians to understand the brain as the material site where ecology and culture join to shape history and performance" (McConachie 2001: 571).

Of particular relevance to any analysis of stage space are McConachie's discussions of the image schemas underlying different stage types and "spatiality," or spectators' social experiences arising from these audience-stage arrangements. McConachie shows, for example, that traditional proscenium staging owes both its structure and its illusion of spectator objectivity to image schemas related to near/far and center/periphery, schemas based on human sight patterns that promote the idea of marginalization (Ibid.: 587–8). Alternatively, promenade staging depends more on the image schema of CONTAINMENT, in which actors and spectators occupy almost the same space, enabling a mutuality of actor-spectator gaze and thus promoting an overall sense of inclusiveness or community (McConachie 2002: 108). Not only the narrative but the ethical dimension of a theatrical experience will differ radically for both actors and spectators depending on the dynamics of the gaze alone, revealing the usefulness for performance theory of understanding exactly what embodied structures lie beneath a given choice of staging. There is, as well, an historical dimension:

Whichever embodied structures predominate at a given moment in theatre history will likely depend on what metaphors reign within the dominant discourses of that period, as McConachie demonstrates in his analysis of the role of promenade staging in the racially anxious but self-consciously progressive community theatre of Colquitt, Georgia, USA (Ibid.: 112–13).

My own approach to stage space recognizes, along with McConachie, the basic role of image schemas in conceptualizing stage type and spatiality. However, in an attempt to reveal the continuity between phenomenal and semiotic aspects of performance, I want to take McConachie's analysis a step further to consider how (at least in text-based performances) the textual/verbal dimension of performance – far from operating at an essentially different level from processes of nonverbal conceptualization – actually works in tandem with those nonverbal processes to generate spatially inflected meaning. Using the close-literary-reading techniques of cognitive poetics,[12] a subfield of cognitive literary/cultural studies that accepts the cognitive linguists' claims for a cognitively embodied substructure to language,[13] I hypothesize that there exists a material interplay between, on the one hand, cognitively embodied conceptualizations of stage space and, on the other, a performance's text- and speech-bound realizations of rhetoric and narrative. I hope to show that this parallel processing between space and text/speech renders a complex complementarity since *both*, as the linguists assert, find their origins in the same or similar cognitively embodied figures. I begin with a brief analysis of the CONTAINER schema as a component of the poetry of the opening of Shakespeare's *Henry V*; then I take a more in-depth look at the complex of image schemas and primary/complex metaphors embodying the narrative of a London production in the fall of 2003 of the play *After Mrs. Rochester*. My purpose, first, is to illustrate the continuity of embodied materiality between the phenomenal (i.e., physical) and the linguistic/discursive (including the semiotic) dimensions of performance, a continuity stemming from their shared investment in the materiality underlying Merleau-Ponty's embodied consciousness. Second, I want to show that this shared materiality enables embodiment to manifest in *both* ways, as they are exemplified, for instance, in the performance criticism of Garner and Butler. By this I mean that we find embodiment in its *primary* cognitive form emanating in a bottom-up direction from the body/mind toward culture (theorized by Garner); but we also find it in its *secondary* discursive form imposing itself in a top-down direction from culture toward the individual body/subject (theorized by Butler). And the result, I argue, is that some degree of agency must finally reside in both.

The cognitive poetics of stage space

One need only step to the center of the restored Shakespeare's Globe Theatre on London's Bankside to *feel* quite viscerally – given its steeply rising balcony seats encircling almost the entire open-air theatre, including alcoves behind and above the stage – why the Chorus of *Henry V* refers to the Globe as a "cockpit" (1.0.11) and then, two lines later, as "this wooden O" (1.0.13). For Shakespeare and his fellow actors, the "Globe" name offered endless opportunities for puns on the idea that the theatre was a microcosm of the world at large since it was rounded in shape not unlike the Earth and likewise offered up abundant life as its by-product. However, unlike the inhabitants of the planet, Shakespeare's theatre-goers stepped *into* the bowl-like roundness of the Globe's interior rather than loitering about on its surface as we do the planet, and this meant that the metaphor linking the activity of *playing* with the larger activity of *living* had to shift toward the image of the raised stage as the key site where this microcosm could come into focus: "All the world's a stage/And all the men and women merely players," as Jaques puts it (*As You Like It*, 2.7.139–40); or, as Macbeth famously laments: "Life's but a walking shadow, a poor player,/That struts and frets his hour upon the stage,/And then is heard no more" (*Macbeth*, 5.5.24–6).[14]

The opening Chorus from *Henry V* weaves both of these metaphors into one long artful appeal to its audience's "imaginary puissance" (1.0.25), asking viewers to conjure within this "wooden O" a much wider scene than the one presented: "O for a Muse of fire, that would ascend/The brightest heaven of invention!/A kingdom for a stage, princes to act,/And monarchs to behold the swelling scene!" (1.0.1–4). The Chorus admits the mere stage's inadequacies – "But pardon, gentles all,/The flat unraised spirits that hath dar'd/On this unworthy scaffold to bring forth/So great an object" (1.0.8–11) – yet he also encourages his listeners to build upon the sight of that stage, to embellish its bare outlines with lavish imagery in the same way that, numerically, "a crooked figure may/Attest in little place a million,/And [thus] let us, ciphers to this great accompt,/On your imaginary forces work" (1.0.15–18). As critics have long recognized, these opening lines of the Chorus represent an attempt on Shakespeare's part to overcome the limits of the neoclassical stage, to posit an epic form for the drama that will permit him to stage war on a geographical scale – crossing the English Channel from England to France and back again – never before performed. To do this, he must co-opt his audience's imagination, what he terms their "imaginary puissance," with carefully crafted rhetoric that will cue them together as one imagining community toward the same or similar large-scale and theatrically self-conscious fantasy.

Now, begging my reader's patience, I must pause to offer some additional terminology derived partly from cognitive poetics (the subfield of literary stylistics that builds upon the theories and methods of the cognitive linguists) and partly from my own deductions regarding the interplay between space and language in performance. Cognitive theorists have made a difficult but important distinction between *image schemas*, which are thought-based, extra-linguistic, minimalist abstractions, and *rich images*, which are the detailed, concrete, and often language-based manifestations of underlying image schemas or nonmetaphorical visual images.[15] Although image schemas and rich imagery are connected to each other, they are also quite different, and their difference is critical. The image schema is a conceptual abstraction that reflects sensorimotor and kinesthetic experience and is generally a deeply entrenched structure of an individual's long-term memory. The rich image, by contrast, is concrete, specific, fleeting, and ephemeral, and it only occurs to us by virtue of either the linguistic medium (as a function of text or speech) or direct (generally visual) perception. For example, the abstract notion of *compulsion* depends for its conceptual structure on generalized SOURCE–PATH–GOAL orientation; whereas, the rich image of a "speeding car," whether written or spoken as a phrase or spotted in an elementary school zone, lacks the generalized character of the image schema but nonetheless depends for its comprehensibility on our having had prior experience with the SOURCE–PATH–GOAL schema. If, let's say, sitting in my own car at a traffic light, I ruefully predict the impact of that car on a group of children occupying a distant crosswalk, then "speeding car" has proven itself to be a symptom of – indeed my best *evidence* for – the existence of SOURCE–PATH–GOAL within my cognitive makeup. In literary and dramatic texts, the deliberate clustering of rich images with other related rich images enables us to generate "readings" that intuit the underlying image-schematic patterns. (The aim of a cognitive poetics, of course, is to identify such patterns overtly.) Adding to this model for the sake of my analysis to follow, I propose a parallel scenario in which we find both connection and difference between *conceptual metaphors* and what we might call *rhetorical metaphors*: The first are the thought-bound projections of image-schematic patterns onto text or stage – independent of the linguistic – while the second are the linguistically expressed *results* of conceptual metaphoricity, signifying in tandem with accumulated rich imagery.

   To return to Shakespeare's *Henry V*, we find, not surprisingly, that the language Shakespeare uses to conduct his choral experiment in communal imagining draws on rich images of things-that-encircle in order to tap into the less specific but more cognitively fundamental image schema of CONTAINMENT. The words I have italicized in the following lines are examples of rich images that reinforce the CONTAINMENT schema: "Can this *cockpit hold*/The vasty *fields* of France? Or may we *cram*/*Within* this wooden *O* the very casques/That did affright the air at Agincourt?" (1.0.11–14); and just as pointedly: "Suppose *within* the *girdle* of these *walls*/Are now *confined* two mighty monarchies" (1.0.19–20). These two monarchies are soon "part[ed] asunder" by "a perilous narrow ocean" (1.0.22) (the English Channel), but this subsequent image of division and opposition is only imaginable within the "girdle" of mental geography that now encompasses them both. "Girdle" is a rich image understandable in terms of CONTAINER, while "girdle" as "wall" or "theatre wall" or even "fortressed town," once it has been contextualized within the Chorus's blank verse, becomes a rhetorical metaphor inferred from the interaction of the rich image "girdle" with the conceptual-metaphorical projection of CON-TAINMENT.

But notice here that the Chorus succeeds in shaping the audience's willing imagination not because of its rhetorical inventiveness *but quite the opposite*: because of its rhetorical appeal to what is most familiar, to what is, in effect, most basic to the embodied minds of its audience. The more visceral the appeal in this sense, the more it resonates throughout a given spectator's inventory of embodied knowledge – and the more *similarly* it resonates among multiple members of the audience, regardless of their many social differences, as would an experience as basic to all people's lives as being contained. I stress "similarly" here because no two audience members' embodied experiences will ever be exactly alike; nor will their projections of those experiences onto new domains of experience be absolute replications, even in circumstances such as watching the same performance in which individuals respond cognitively to the same stimulation. However, if the appeal is truly fundamental, truly an echo of basic-level image schemas, then such experiences and the cognitive responses they generate may in fact be sufficiently *alike* to promote an isomorphism or structural similarity between different individuals' imaginative constructs. And such approximate isomorphism may be all that is needed for Shakespeare to achieve the goal of unifying his audience's vision.

But even more to the point, what this example demonstrates is that the language of a performance is itself sufficiently isomorphic with the embodied structures within the minds of speakers and listeners to inspire a *coupling* with those structures and thus a prompting of them into a state of readiness for further use. Put another way, the cognitive linguists believe that we could not conceptualize the semantics of "girdle" without having a prior understanding of the enclosing behaviors of containers. But this power to embody must work both ways because – and as I simply assume in my discussion above of Shakespeare's "rhetorical appeal" – the utterance, via semiotic signs, of the word "girdle," followed by its amplification through rhetorical metaphor, serves to cue or highlight within an audience member's mind an image schema for CONTAINMENT, even if only for the flicker of time it takes for the brain's neurons to fire. Then, once foregrounded in this way, CONTAINMENT may remain prominent within the audience member's continuing processes of interpretation, injecting its image-schematic structure into multiple semantic and rhetorical frameworks and thereby creating structural coherence – though not necessarily equivalence – between many if not most audience members' perception of the performance. Thus, although meanings and the words they beget are themselves by-products of mind-embodiment, they can also share in the act of *embodying*, bodying-forth in an audience member's mind the very structures that had originally begotten *them*.

In this sense, then, language may be said to play a role in embodiment, exemplifying something akin to Butler's theory of performativity. It is crucial to note, however, that *this* embodiment represents the secondary rather than the primary or (what I earlier specified as the) cognitive form of embodiment, the latter of which manifests a greater degree of *materiality* despite the fact that both exist along the same material continuum. And although semiotic signs are engaged within this complex feedback process since meanings and words cannot be transmitted without recourse to the medium of signs, nonetheless, the semiotic aspect of language can hardly be said to dominate or control this process as it would, presumably, in Butler's poststructuralist model. Thus, the kind of "embodiment" that a critic like Butler wishes to draw our attention to, taking place through language and discourse and carrying with it the stamp of the social, can neither be wholly equated with Merleau-Ponty's embodied consciousness nor dismissed altogether within the processes of embodiment.

Let me turn now to my second illustration to explore once again the cognitive embodiment of the performance space. The coupling between linguistic (including semiotic) and phenomenal levels of performance occurs not only through rich text- and speech-based imagery, as I have tried to demonstrate, but through something else that is highly dependent on language for both its development and transmission: the cognitive dimensions of a performance's *narrative*. To a major extent, all narrative, whether literary or theatrical, depends on the embodiment of space to conceptualize *time*, that most basic component of any plot and hence of any story. Here I would like to show that the play *After Mrs. Rochester*, written by Polly Teale and performed under her direction for British audiences in 2003, serves as a particularly vivid example of the coupling between theatrical narrative (with its dependence on *time*) and embodied stage space.

After Mrs. Rochester tells the life story of the novelist Jean Rhys, whose 1966 *Wide Sargasso Sea* also tells a life story, that of the mad, sequestered wife of Charlotte Brontë's *Jane Eyre*. Like Bertha Mason, the mad Mrs. Rochester of Brontë's novel, Rhys was a Creole native of West India who, at some point in her youth, having read *Jane Eyre*, began to identify with the fictional Bertha. Teale recreates Rhys' childhood in Dominica, her discovery of Brontë, and her move to England where she worked as a chorus girl, artist's model, and possibly a prostitute between periods of being "kept" by a string of men. Rhys had always been a writer, but it was not until after an ill-fated love affair with the novelist Ford Maddox Ford that she began to publish her fiction. As she grew older, she became an alcoholic and violent (spending time in jail at one point for assaulting a neighbor). Her only child, a daughter, had to be raised by others. Rhys died in 1979 after three failed marriages and the onset of mental illness – but not before completing *Wide Sargasso Sea*, which won the Royal Society of Literature Award. Through her writing of the novel, Rhys seemed finally to have exorcized her obsession with Bertha, who had also known, as one London critic put it, "the warmth of the Caribbean sun, the chill of an English winter, and the exploitation of heartless men" (Johns 2003).

LIBRARY, UNIVERSITY OF CHESTER

As one might expect from biography, the play relates many of these details of Rhys' life, but it is the *way* that Teale captures Rhys' life story that is of interest. The entire play takes place within the confines of a single locked room, cluttered with papers and suitcases and overshadowed by an enormous wooden wardrobe. It is the room in Rhys' house in Devon to where, in 1957, she has sequestered herself in late middle age, hiding from the world in order to write and drink but hiding particularly from her grown daughter, who now seeks her out. Rhys, as portrayed by Diana Quick, sits disheveled on the floor near the wardrobe, pen and paper on her lap, while her daughter bangs on the door. Oddly, beside Rhys on the floor lies a woman in ragged Victorian lingerie, writhing, moaning, and occasionally spitting curses through streams of black hair that spill across her face. We notice – and at first think it strange – that there is no interaction between Rhys and the writhing woman (played by Sarah Ball), no acknowledgment on Rhys' part that she is even present. But soon we realize that the woman herself is a metaphor: she is, if we know Brontë's *Jane Eyre*, Mrs. Rochester; or she is, if we don't know Brontë's novel – and then eventually even if we *do* – the expression of Rhys' own madness, the madwoman locked in the attic of Rhys' psyche. The daughter temporarily gives up and goes away, leaving Rhys to concentrate on the task at hand: the composing of *Wide Sargasso Sea*.

As she writes, she verbalizes memories of her childhood, and so begins a series of voice-over and acted flashbacks to Rhys as a girl growing up white among the black natives of Dominica, brought up to be English yet stimulated by her friendships with native girls and by her exposure to native culture. We see this young Rhys, played not by Quick but by another actor, Madeleine Potter, being confronted by her parents about her native-leaning ways, coming upon *Jane Eyre* for the first time, and eventually reconciling herself to the fact that she will be sent to England for formal schooling. However – and this is the play's central device – during this flashback and others to come, the *older* Rhys and the writhing Mrs. Rochester also occupy the stage and continue to share it with the younger Rhys for the duration of the play. In other words, all three aspects of Rhys remain constantly present to the audience, each one expressing a particular period of Rhys' life but each one also performing her time period or mental state separately from the others. Though ever-present on stage, the three Rhys characters only rarely acknowledge each other, and when they do it is mainly for symbolic effect, such as when the older Rhys enfolds the younger in her arms to comfort her(self) after a trauma.

The surprising thing is not that the audience grasps Teale's device of offering parallel performances using isolated characters within a shared space; rather, it is how quickly and automatically they catch onto and accept it. What *should* surprise us (but doesn't) is the idea that all three actors can represent the same character at the same time; yet audience members have no difficulty distinguishing between the different phases of that one

character, even when all three actors are speaking or emoting simultaneously. This is because the cognitive apparatus required to make Teale's
device work is actually so basic, so fundamental to our embodied consciousness, that after only a few minutes into the play the audience forgets how
complicated the device truly is. It is fundamental because it calls upon our
embodied understanding of plot and of a plot's transmission via verbal
expression, both of which are dependent on our embodied concepts for *time*.
Time, as Lakoff and Johnson observe, has no material essence in and of itself
and so must be conceived of "relative to other concepts such as motion,
space, and events" (Lakoff and Johnson 1999: 137). Indeed, "Most of our
understanding of time is a metaphorical version of our understanding of
motion in space" (Ibid.: 139). And among the illustrations they offer are
metaphors taken from our most commonplace, everyday characterizations of
time and of our various spatial relationships to it. For instance, they point to
the *time orientation* metaphor, in which we (humans) are figured as an object
oriented in some specific relationship to time, which is figured as another
object removed at a distance from us (in front of us, alongside us, or in back
of us); or the *moving time* metaphor, in which we become a stationary object
relative to which time moves (coming toward us, passing us, moving behind
us); or finally the *moving observer* metaphor, in which we take on the role of
the moving agent relative to stationary time (we move toward the "future,"
pass through "now," and move "past" time) (Ibid.: 137–69).

All of these are complex metaphors that stem from primary metaphors
based on the SOURCE–PATH–GOAL schema. The metaphors differ from
each other mainly in terms of which of the two entities they endow with
agency (whether "we" or time) and thus over which one will exemplify the
necessary passage through a *space*. (In the case of the *time orientation*
metaphor, both "we" and time are stationary, but the mere existence of a
dividing space signifies a direct line or SOURCE–PATH–GOAL schema.)
The result of these metaphors embedded within conventional stories is a
sense of linear sequentiality that is the defining characteristic of plot and
arguably of narrative itself. In fact, the isomorphism between these *time*
metaphors and the principle metaphor we use to conceptualize *life – life is a
journey*, which is also based on the SOURCE–PATH–GOAL schema –
ensures that most narratives are sequential in their structure (and one can see
how this would be especially true of biographical narratives, such as Teale's
story of Rhys' life).

Teale's device in *After Mrs. Rochester* skillfully manipulates this conventional cognitive dependence on sequentiality. We are led by the older Rhys'
words to expect that the appearance of the young Rhys will bring a chronological sequencing of her life. And that, for the most part, is exactly what we
see performed and hear described: she appears as a youth, she grows older,
she grows older still, and then the play ends. But Teale's device also forces a
highlighting of other aspects of the same metaphors for *time* that underline
the sequencing of verbal narration, specifically the aspects of those

metaphors that emphasize the movement of agents through space. The space of the stage gives Teale the opportunity to dramatize several trajectories within the same life simultaneously because each actor representing this same character enacts different aspects or phases of that life by virtue of the simple fact that *each actor moves within her own discrete stage space*. Consequently, from one perspective, the audience expects and finds sequentiality; but from another, it experiences multiple sequences playing themselves out simultaneously. Both perspectives, taken together, illustrate how the narrative of *After Mrs. Rochester* – constituted within language and dependent on the medium of the linguistic sign – is nevertheless also inseparable from, indeed is continuous with, the phenomenal space in which it is enacted. Interestingly, while literary theorists tend to talk about narrative as if it is solely a product of textuality, it becomes obvious through an example like this that the *performance* of a narrative actively belies textuality in the Derridean sense, revealing the strength of any story's deep alliances to the phenomenal in which it is embedded. In particular, a cognitive analysis of a performed narrative better enables us to articulate the complex marriage between texts (language, discourse, sign) and the *thingness* of performance because human cognition is the material condition enabling *all* understanding, including all specialized epistemological scenarios such as the processes of socialization that underlie historicist explanations of these phenomena.

Conclusions

Again, language plays a role in embodiment to the extent that the textual/verbal combines with cognitively embodied space in *After Mrs. Rochester* to give its audience a multidimensional experience; and in this sense, performance enacts the complementary interaction between the phenomenal and the linguistic, including (but not reducing to) the semiotic sign. Material embodiment emerges from what Merleau-Ponty called the embodied consciousness, which I have elaborated here in the form of a cognitive-linguistic reading of embodied conceptualization and textuality /verbalization. Less material but nonetheless *still* material (since it springs from embodied consciousness) is language and, concomitant with language, the semiotic sign. This linguistic/semiotic dimension, by definition encapsulating the social, feeds recursively back into embodied consciousness, helping to set the conditions for future states of embodied consciousness and – even more to the point – performing a secondary order of embodiment whose nature is both cognitive and social. Together the two forms of embodiment – cognitive embodiment and linguistic or discursive embodiment – comprise the processes of identity-formation and subject-interpellation that poststructuralism (by itself) must labor to explain. Within this revisionary model, agency as a force for enacting and indeed *performing* social difference and change cannot be conceptualized as a function of *either* the cognitive *or* the social – one or the other – but rather as both together in complex alliance. This alliance mirrors the alliance with which we began between phenomenology and semiotics because, indeed, and thanks to Merleau-Ponty, the terms may now take on a parallel structure.

What I offer here is not a reconciliation between phenomenology and semiotics as performance theorists have understood either to this point. Rather, I shift the ground under both of these terms and the approaches to the theatre that they represent respectively; and I defend this shift as a necessary consequence of the relevance of cognitive science to many of the questions that both literary and theatre/performance theorists must ask. Cast onto the common ground of cognitive embodiment, both the *things* and the *signs* (or more inclusively, language) that make up the full theatrical experience emerge jointly from the materiality of the human body. And both take shape – complexly, and in the general context of human behaviors, uniquely – in the very fact of performance.

Notes

1 Two others worth mentioning are Read (1993) and Erickson (1995).
2 See Butler (1990, 1993). For critics' descriptions and analyses of Butler's theory, see Judovitz (2001: 8–9), Apter (1996: 15–34, esp. 15), and Crane (2000: 117, 150).
3 This statement is a compressed summary of ongoing research in cognitive semantics and cognitive grammar, subfields within the larger field of cognitive linguistics. Some noted practitioners include Sweester (1990), Langacker (1987, 1991), Fauconnier (1994, 1997), Goldberg (1994), Coulson (2001), Fauconnier and Turner (2002), and others in a field that has become increasingly international in scope in recent years.
4 Varela *et al.* (1991) offer another summary of Merleau-Ponty's relevance to today's cognitive science.
5 The first kind, often referred to as "cognitive-evolutionary critics" or "evolutionary literary theorists," seek to counter the effects of poststructuralism by appealing to the tenets of evolutionary psychology. The second kind, the "cognitive literary critics," find in cognitive science a basis for both supporting and refining the claims of poststructuralism. I offer an extended comparison and contrast between these two approaches in Hart (2001). See also Richardson (2004: 12–14).
6 Some examples of monographs or collections representing cognitive approaches to literature and culture studies include Spolsky (1993, 2001), Crane (2000), and Richardson and Spolsky (2004), to name only a few.
7 For a variety of accounts of metaphor as a means of knowledge-acquisition, see Lakoff and Johnson (1980, 1999), Gibbs (1994), Turner (1995), Gibbs and Steen (1999), Turner and Fauconnier (1996, 1999), and Fauconnier and Turner (2002), to mention only some.
8 See Lakoff and Johnson (1999: 17–20, 26–30) and Lakoff (1987: *passim.*). See Swettenham (this volume).
9 See Lakoff and Johnson (1999: 463). For empirical analyses of spatial-relations concepts, see Regier (1995, 1996).
10 My example of *balance* is a summary of Johnson's extended discussion (1987: 73–100).
11 These examples are taken from Lakoff and Johnson (1999: 204–5).

12 For diverse examples of cognitive poetics (theory and readings), see Tsur (1992), Crane (2000), M. Freeman (2002), and D.C. Freeman (2004). For an introduction to the field and essays exemplifying the range of applications, see the companion volumes of Stockwell (2002) and Gavins and Steen (2003).
13 As cited in note 3 above, some of the relevant works include Sweetser (1990), Langacker (1987, 1991), Fauconnier (1994, 1997), Goldberg (1994), Coulson (2001), and Fauconnnier and Turner (2002).
14 The latter quotation especially makes overt that the stage itself is "life," made possible by the journey-like strutting and fretting of the bad actor (traveling from one point on the stage to another), who eventually leaves the stage and is "heard no more" (i.e., he dies). In other words, the image schema of SOURCE–PATH–GOAL steps in where the CONTAINER schema becomes inadequate to represent life.
15 See Johnson (1987: 23–6) and Lakoff and Turner (1989: 99–100).

References

Apter, E. (1996) "Acting Out Orientalism: Sapphic Theatricality in Turn-of-the-Century Paris," in Diamond, E. (ed.) *Performance and Cultural Politics*, London and New York: Routledge.

Artaud, A. (1970) *The Theatre and Its Double*, trans. Corti, V., London: John Calder.

Butler, J. (1990) "Performance Acts and Gender Constitution: An Essay in Phenomenology and Feminist Theory," in Case, S.-E. (ed.) *Performing Feminisms: Feminist Critical Theory and Theatre*, Baltimore, MD and London: Johns Hopkins University Press.

—— (1993) *Bodies That Matter: On the Discursive Limits of 'Sex'*, New York: Routledge.

Carlson, M. (1996) *Performance: A Critical Introduction*, London and New York: Routledge.

Chaudhuri, U. (1995) *Staging Place: The Geography of Modern Drama*, Ann Arbor, MI: University of Michigan Press.

Coulson, S. (2001) *Semantic Leaps: Frame-Shifting and Conceptual Blending in Meaning Construction*, Cambridge and New York: Cambridge University Press.

Crane, M.T. (2000) *Shakespeare's Brain: Reading with Cognitive Theory*, Princeton, NJ: Princeton University Press.

—— (2001) "What was performance?" *Criticism*, 43(2): 169–87.

Damasio, A. (1994) *Descartes' Error: Emotion, Reason, and the Human Brain*, New York: Avon.

—— (1999) *The Feeling of What Happens: Body and Emotion in the Making of Consciousness*, New York: Harcourt Brace.

Dennett, D.C. (1991) *Consciousness Explained*, New York: Penguin Books.

Edelman, G. (1992) *Bright Air, Brilliant Fire: On the Matter of the Mind*, New York: Basic Books.

Erickson, J. (1995) *The Fate of the Object*, Ann Arbor, MI: University of Michigan Press.

Fauconnier, G. (1985; 2nd edn 1994) *Mental Spaces: Aspects of Meaning Construction in Natural Language*, Cambridge, MA: MIT Press; 2nd edn Cambridge University Press.

—— (1997) *Mappings in Thought and Language*, Cambridge and New York: Cambridge University Press.

Fauconnier, G. and Turner, M. (2002) *The Way We Think: Conceptual Blending and the Mind's Hidden Complexities*, New York: Basic Books.

Fortier, M. (1997) *Theory/Theatre: An Introduction*, London and New York: Routledge.

Freeman, D.C. (2004) "Othello and the 'Ocular Proof,'" in Bradshaw, G., Bishop, T., and Turner, M. (eds) *The Shakespearean International Yearbook 4: Shakespeare Studies Today*, Aldershot: Ashgate Publishing, 56–71.

Freeman, M. (2002) "The Body in the Word: A Cognitive Approach to the Shape of a Poetic Text," in Semino, E. and Culpeper, J. (eds) *Cognitive Stylistics: Language and Cognition in Text Analysis*, Amsterdam: John Benjamins, 23–47.

Garner, S. (1994) *Bodied Spaces: Phenomenology and Performance in Contemporary Drama*, Ithaca, NY: Cornell University Press.

Gavins, J. and Steen, G. (eds) (2003) *Cognitive Poetics in Practice*, London and New York: Routledge.

Gibbs, R.W. (1994) *The Poetics of Mind: Figurative Thought, Language, and Understanding*, New York: Cambridge University Press.

Gibbs, R.W. and Steen, G.J. (eds) (1999) *Metaphor in Cognitive Linguistics: Selected Papers from the Fifth International Cognitive Linguistics Conference*, Amsterdam and Philadelphia, PA: John Benjamins.

Goldberg, A. (1994) *Constructions: A Construction Grammar Approach to Argument Structure*, Chicago, IL: University of Chicago Press.

Hart, F.E. (2001) "The Epistemology of Cognitive Literary Studies," *Philosophy and Literature*, 25: 314–34.

Jansen, S. (1982) "L'Espace scenique dans le spectacle dramatique et dans le texte dramatique," *Revue Romane*, 17: 3–20.

—— (1984) "Le Role de l'Espace Scenique dans la Lecture du Texte Dramatique," in Schmid, H. and Van Kesteren, A. (eds) *Semiotics of Drama and Theatre*, Amsterdam: John Benjamins.

Johns, I. (2003) *The London Times*, 23 July.

Johnson, M. (1987) *The Body in the Mind: The Bodily Basis of Meaning, Imagination, and Reason*, Chicago, IL: University of Chicago Press.

Judovitz, D. (2001) *The Culture of the Body: Genealogies of Modernity*, Ann Arbor, MI: University of Michigan Press.

Lakoff, G. (1987) *Women, Fire, and Dangerous Things: What Categories Reveal About the Mind*, Chicago, IL: University of Chicago Press.

Lakoff, G. and Johnson, M. (1980) *Metaphors We Live By*, Chicago, IL: University of Chicago Press.

—— (1999) *Philosophy in the Flesh: The Embodied Mind and Its Challenge to Western Thought*, New York: Basic Books.

Lakoff, G. and Turner, M. (1989) *More Than Cool Reason: A Field Guide to Poetic Metaphor*, Chicago, IL: University of Chicago Press.

Langacker, R. (1987) *Foundations of Cognitive Grammar:* Vol. 1, *Theoretical Prerequisites*, Stanford, CA: Stanford University Press.

—— (1991) *Foundations of Cognitive Grammar:* Vol. 2, *Descriptive Application*, Stanford, CA: Stanford University Press.

McAuley, G. (1999) *Space in Performance: Making Meaning in the Theatre*, Ann Arbor, MI: University of Michigan Press.

McConachie, B. (2001) "Doing things with image schemas: the cognitive turn in theatre studies and the problem of experience for historians," *Theatre Journal*, 53: 569–94.

—— (2002) "Using cognitive science to understand spatiality and community in theater," *Contemporary Theatre Review*, 12(3): 97–114.

Merleau-Ponty, M. (1961) *Phenomenology of Perception*, trans. C. Smith, London: Routledge & Kegan Paul.

—— (1968) *The Visible and the Invisible: Followed by Working Notes*, trans. A. Lingis, Lefort, C. (ed.), Evanston: Northwestern University Press.

Read, A. (1993) *Theatre and Everyday Life*, London: Routledge.

Regier, T. (1995) "A model of the human capacity for categorizing spatial relations," *Cognitive Linguistics*, 6(1): 63–88.

—— (1996) *The Human Semantic Potential: Spatial Language and Constrained Connectionism*, Cambridge, MA: MIT Press.

Richardson, A. (2001) *British Romanticism and the Science of the Mind*, Cambridge: Cambridge University Press.

—— (2004) "Studies in literature and cognition: a field map," in Richardson, A. and Spolsky, E. (eds) *The Work of Fiction: Cognition, Culture, and Complexity*, Aldershot/Burlington, VT: Ashgate Publishing.

Richardson, A. and Spolsky, E. (eds) (2004) *The Work of Fiction: Cognition, Culture, and Complexity*, Aldershot/Burlington, VT: Ashgate Publishing.

Shakespeare, W. (1997 [1623]) *Henry V*, in Evans, G.B. and Tobin, J.J.M. (eds) *The Riverside Shakespeare*, 2nd edn, Boston, MA and New York: Houghton Mifflin Co.

—— (2004) "The Life of King Henry Fifth," in Bevington, D. (ed.) *The Complete Works of Shakespeare*, 5th edn, New York and London: Pearson Longman.

Spolsky, E. (1993) *Gaps in Nature: Literary Interpretation and the Modular Mind*, Albany, NY: State University of New York Press.

—— (2001) *Satisfying Skepticism: Embodied Knowledge in the Early Modern World*, Aldershot: Ashgate Publishing.

States, B.O. (1985) *Great Reckonings in Little Rooms: On the Phenomenology of Theatre*, Berkeley, CA: University of California Press.

—— (1992) "The Phenomenological Attitude," in Reinelt, J.G. and Roach, J.R. (eds) *Critical Theory and Performance*, Ann Arbor, MI: University of Michigan Press.

Stockwell, P. (ed.) (2002) *Cognitive Poetics: An Introduction*, London and New York: Routledge.

Sweetser, E. (1990) *From Etymology to Pragmatics: Metaphorical and Cultural Aspects of Semantic Structure*, Cambridge and New York: Cambridge University Press.

Tsur, R. (1992) *Toward a Theory of Cognitive Poetics*, Amsterdam: North-Holland.

Turner, M. (1995) *The Literary Mind*, New York: Oxford University Press.

Turner, M. and Fauconnier, G. (1996) "Conceptual integration and formal expression," *Metaphor and Symbolic Activity*, 10(3): 183–203.

—— (1999) "A mechanism for creativity," *Poetics Today*, 20(3): 397–418.

Ubersfeld, A. (1977) *Lire le Theatre*, Paris: Editions Sociales.

—— (1981) *L'Ecole du Spectateur*, Paris: Editions Sociales.

Varela, F.J., Thompson, E., and Rosch, E. (1991) *The Embodied Mind: Cognitive Science and the Human Experience*, Cambridge, MA: MIT Press.

2 Cognitive studies and epistemic competence in cultural history
Moving beyond Freud and Lacan

Bruce McConachie

Introduction

Slavoj Zizek begins his recent article "Lacan Between Cultural Studies and Cognitivism," published in the psychoanalytic journal *Umbr(a)*, with this call to arms: "We are witnessing today the struggle for intellectual hegemony – for who will occupy the universal place of the 'public intellectual' – between postmodern-deconstructionist cultural studies and the cognitivist popularizers of 'hard' sciences, that is the proponents of the so-called 'third culture'" (Zizek 2000: 9). Zizek attacks both camps in his essay, styling the cultural studies "deconstructionists" as relativists and the "cognitivist popularizers" as objectivists, so that he may present Lacanian psychoanalysis as a necessary third option. Along the way, Zizek dismisses those theorists of cultural studies who would lump Lacan and psychoanalysis with the other relativists. The problem with historicist relativism, for Zizek, is that it offers no epistemological escape from the "proto-Nietzschean notion that knowledge is not only embedded in, but also generated by a complex set of discursive strategies of power (re)production" (Ibid.: 14).

Like Zizek, Terry Eagleton scorns cultural relativists for their failure to recognize that nature puts limits on cultural construction. "There is a well-entrenched postmodern doctrine that the natural is no more than an insidious naturalization of culture," Eagleton remarks. He adds, "It is difficult to see how this applies to bleeding or to Mount Blanc" (Eagleton 2000: 93). In contrast to the culturalists, Eagleton urges that scholars seek to understand how the complimentary and conflict between nature and culture both inform and constrain what it means to be human: "If, as the culturalists maintain, we really were just cultural beings, or as the naturalists hold, just natural ones, then our lives would be a great deal less fraught. It is the fact that we are cusped between nature and culture – a cusping of considerable interest to psychoanalysis – which is the problem. It is not that culture is our nature, but that it is *of* our nature, which makes our life difficult" (italics in original) (Ibid.: 99). For Eagleton, a field like psychoanalysis reminds us that humans have a necessary stake in both nature and culture, but are inevitably fragmented within by the alliance between the somatic and the symbolic.

Eagleton's insights provide a sobering reality check against cultural relativism and a potent reminder as to why so many scholars of cultural studies have anchored their findings in the discourse of psychoanalysis. But is psychoanalysis, including its latter-day spin-off in Lacanian theory, the only or best way of understanding the dialectic joining the claims of culture and the necessities of nature? In accord with the materialism of Eagleton, Zizek privileges the epistemology of "modern science" as the best way to comprehend the mix of the symbolic and the somatic in human life and history (Zizek 2000: 14). But how scientific, really, is psychoanalysis?

In his *Umbr(a)* essay, Zizek's embrace of Lacan displays little regard for the epistemological subtleties of scientific discourse. His attempt to tar what he terms "cognitivism" with the brush of objectivism, for instance, is surprisingly misinformed. Cognitive literary theorist F. Elizabeth Hart has demonstrated that Zizek's essay simplifies and conflates the complex range of epistemologies currently at play in the field of cognitive studies. Where Zizek finds only "naïve scientism," Hart points to the "constrained constructivism," "internal realism," and "experientialism" of several cognitive scholars working in linguistics, psychology, and philosophy (Hart 2001: 321). Hart's discussion shows that most cognitive approaches deny the possibility of objective knowledge, but they hold that enough consistencies obtain in external reality to make human understanding reliable and relatively stable. Although Zizek's essay locates Lacan's position as a transcendent and scientific alternative to the rock of relativistic solipsism and the hard place of objectivist scientism, it may be that cognitive studies better equips historians to mediate between relativism and objectivism than psychoanalysis – and thus to gain insight into the dialectic of culture and nature at play in evolution and history.

Any comparison between the truth-values offered by psychoanalysis and cognitive studies necessarily involves a standard of epistemological judgment. I will rely on the normative standard established by David Henderson and Terence Horgan in their essay "Simulation and Epistemic Competence." Henderson and Horgan combine the insights of Quine's classic manifesto on epistemology with recent neuroscientific and psychological discoveries about the capabilities of human understanding. Following Quine, they acknowledge that the methods implementing our mental capacities must be "reliable" and that the truth claims generated by these processes should be "systematic." In addition to recommending these two criteria, the authors give extra credit for approaches to knowledge that are "robust." An epistemology is "robust" when its truth claims are "reliable" and "systematic" in several other environments beyond those occupied by the investigating scholar – "including those in which populations may be heterogeneous, for example" (Henderson and Horgan 2000: 120). To demonstrate that a modified notion of Henderson and Horgan's standard of epistemic competence is generally relevant to problems in historiography, I will draw on Mary Fulbrook's *Historical Theory*, a recent overview that evaluates several diverse approaches to the writing of history.[1] All of these theorists understand that no method can guarantee singular and unique Historical Truth; indeed, they agree that such a goal is epistemologically impossible. But this limitation does not prevent epistemological comparisons among different approaches to historical knowledge.

Deploying the Henderson and Horgan standard of epistemic competence, fitted to apply to history, I will show that cognitive studies offers a more empirically responsible path to knowledge in cultural history than psychoanalysis, including its Lacanian developments. A comparison for historiographical purposes of the relative merits of the psychoanalytic and the cognitive paradigms necessarily involves a case study. Luckily for me, a psychoanalytic historian has already arrived at an interpretation of a group of related historical events that has won wide applause among cultural scholars. Concerning their relative epistemic competence, then, I will compare Eric Lott's understanding of "wench" acts in his book on blackface minstrelsy, *Love and Theft*, to my own cognitive analysis of this entertainment. Wench acts featured a cross-dressed, blacked-up white male performing on the antebellum minstrel stage. Regarding Henderson and Horgan's standards of "reliability," "systematicity," and "robustness," as modified by Fulbrook's *Historical Theory*, cognitive studies proves epistemologically superior to psychoanalysis and ought to replace it for historical analysis.

I have divided this essay into four parts. Following this brief introduction, I will explicate Henderson and Horgan's standards for epistemic competence and adapt it to suit historical investigation. Next, I will examine the reliability of psychoanalysis and cognitive studies through close attention to the probable validity of their explanations of the wench act in nineteenth-century minstrelsy. Finally, I will compare both approaches in terms of their relative systematicity and robustness for historical understanding.

Standards for epistemic competence

In "Simulation and Epistemic Competence," Henderson and Horgan (2000) complement the conventional approach to knowledge, which consists of reasoning with language and other symbolic systems, with simulation, a mental competency that is pre-symbolic. The authors draw on a range of recent psychological findings and philosophical investigations that are challenging the near-exclusive focus on the human capacity to use symbols as the basis for truth in humanistic and social-scientific learning. As well as deploying theoretical knowledge, human beings, it seems, also utilize their capacity for empathy to understand, explain, and predict the practices, emotions, and beliefs of others. One important way of accomplishing these tasks, according to the conception of simulation advanced by Alvin Goldman and others, is to put ourselves in the shoes of another person, imagine the world as it would appear from her or his point of view, and "then deliberate, reason, and see what decision emerges" (Goldman 1995: 185). From the perspective of philosopher Robert Gordon, empathetic simulation can best be understood as "personal transformation" through a "recentering of my egocentric map" (Gordon 1995b: 56), in which the empathizer makes adjustments "for relevant differences" (Gordon 1995a: 63) with the other person. In attempting to understand the actions of a person in history, for example, a historian interested in applying Gordon's empathetic simulation would ask, "If I had been that person in that historical situation, what would I have done and why?" Significantly, Gordon's position is very close to the notion of empathy put forward by Konstantin Stanislavsky, the theorist of modern acting. According to Stanislavsky, actors intending to perform a fictitious role must imaginatively deploy simulation and put themselves in the "given circumstances" of the character they are playing on stage. Most actors and many cultural historians have understood empathy as a path to knowledge. They have not always trusted their "instincts," however.

And make no mistake – empathy begins as animal instinct. As philosopher Georg Vielmetter notes, the kinds of evidence humans get from empathetic understanding "is due to the biological constitution of higher mammals. So interpretation [through simulation] is basically a *natural process* controlled by our hard wiring" (italics in original) (Vielmetter 2000: 92). Vielmetter terms this kind of interpretation "transsubjective" because it is not a "one-person method"; it requires the imaginative projection of another person into the self and hence avoids the solipsism of introspection (Ibid.: 93). Although simulation alone can provide humans with social knowledge of the simple wants and opinions of others, most interpreters past the age of six qualify and amplify their empathetic knowledge of others with generalizations gleaned partly from rational symbolic processes. In their "Introduction" to *Empathy and Agency: The Problem of Understanding in the Human Sciences*, co-editors Hans Herbert Kogler and Karsten R. Steuber (2000) state that several simulation theorists allow for the possibility that we sometimes turn to theoretically generated ideas to understand others. But, Kogler and Steuber add, "for the simulation theorist such an appeal is a mere heuristic shortcut, since these generalizations are derived from prior simulations of other persons" (Ibid.: 9).

In matters of practical knowledge, simulation usually trumps reasoned theory because it calls into play our natural capacities and allows for human differences. Recently, Gordon compared the two approaches as the difference between "cold" and "hot" methodologies:

> Concerning the "theory of mind," or more broadly the methodology by which people anticipate and predict another's actions, there are basically two kinds of theory. One kind holds that we use what I call a cold methodology: a methodology that chiefly engages our intellectual processes, moving by inference from one set of beliefs to another, and makes no essential use of our capacities for emotion, motivation, and

practical reasoning. . . . The other kind imputes to us a hot methodology, which exploits one's own motivational and emotional resources and
one's own capacity for practical reasoning.

(Gordon 1996: 11)

Further, cold generalizations derived from our intellect are rarely precise
enough to allow for individual and situational differences. As Kogler and
Steuber explain, "Only because of our simulative abilities can we predict
that somebody who is worried because his child is very sick might forget to
take an umbrella, even if it is raining outside and he does not want to get
wet" (Kogler and Steuber 2000: 11). Human beings, they suggest, do not
store enough generalizations to account for and predict the particularities of
behavior. For example, "we do not have a general theory about what people
find funny," they state. "It is more plausible that we use our own judgment
and simulative capacities to predict how somebody will react to a joke"
(Ibid.: 11).

A connectionist model of the mind-brain, which most cognitive scientists
now favor over the older digital model, explains why simulation is more
foundational in generating reliable knowledge than abstract reasoning.
Unlike a computer, the neural network of the mind-brain in connectionism
lacks an executive component that activates and regulates subsidiary units.
Further, the connectionist model does not store and draw upon information
(or "memory") like a computer. Instead, when a "problem" is posed to the
connectionist neural network, various nodes in the mind-brain simultaneously send and receive signals until these nodes settle into a new configura-
tion; this new pattern is effectively the "answer." Learning, rather than
adding new "files" and "commands" to the system, alters the morphological
content of the mind-brain by shifting the "weights," as the connectionists
call them, among the nodes. This kind of system, according to Henderson
and Horgan, "will not, in general, generate predictions of people's specific
psychological state transitions" from a symbol-based theory because such
mental problems do not alter the allocated "weights" (Henderson and
Horgan 2000: 128). "The point," they conclude, "is just that the application
of theory alone, either explicit or implicit, cannot plausibly be the sole
component of our competence here. In general, the theoretical generalizations available to us will fail to be strongly predictive . . ." (Ibid.: 130). If
our minds worked like computers, theory-driven predictions about human
behavior derived from extensive memory banks and executive commands
would provide some reliability. In the connectionist mind-brain, however,
imaginative simulation is more reliable for generating plausible truth claims
than theory.

This is not to say that theory should be abandoned, of course. Henderson
and Horgan advocate a combination of "hot" and "cold" methods for the
production of reliable and systematic knowledge. Both simulation and
theory have their "blind spots," they note. Regarding theory, the connec-

tionist mind-brain cannot specify which theories might be relevant to which kinds of information. In particular, "where theory touches on cognitive processes that turn on an individual's sensitivity to her global belief set, theory is and will remain sketchy" (Ibid.: 133). Henderson and Horgan list two general "blind spots" that can afflict a person's reliance on simulation alone: inadequate information in setting up the simulation and cognitive inflexibility. For the first, simulators do not always know or do not take into account differences between themselves and the other person whose situation they are simulating. Second, the simulator may lack the imagination and cognitive knowledge to fully place him- or herself into the situation of the Other. A person who has not experienced extreme grief or great physical pain, for example, will have difficulty empathizing with someone who has undergone these experiences.

Given the "blind spots" inherent in each way of knowing, Henderson and Horgan conclude that applying both simulation and theory jointly, "in a sensitive and coordinated manner, should be reliable in yet a greater range of cases than applying either of them in a maximally exclusive fashion" (Ibid.: 136). To support their case for the cooperative application of both methods, Henderson and Horgan provide a telling example. Suppose, they say, that a white American male – they call him "Bob" – lives in the middle of Kansas among relatives and friends he has known most of his life. In such a narrow cognitive environment, simulation will provide Bob with a fairly reliable guide for predicting the behavior of others in his everyday life. Now suppose that Bob gets a job that requires him to move to Washington, DC, and to live and work with others from several different world cultures. The simulation that served him so well in Kansas now misleads him in significant ways; he has difficulty seeing the situation of others from their point of view because he lacks both the right information and the relevant cognitive experience. But Bob buys some books, gets on the Internet, and begins to pay closer attention to his co-workers and neighbors. In short, he puts together some general theories about various cultural Others and, by applying them, makes some progress in predicting their behavior. Eventually, he gets to the point where his theories are informing his ability to empathize with some of his new friends. This empathetic understanding is also refining his theories of cultural Others. After a difficult transition, Bob has learned to use theory and simulation together in what Henderson and Horgan would term a "robust" fashion (Ibid.: 137–9).

The synergy that emerges from the cooperative use of theory and simulation in a heterogeneous context creates the epistemic virtue of "robustness." Henderson and Horgan summarize their position:

> In worlds in which a folk face a cognitively homogeneous environment, simulation will be reliable. . . . In worlds in which they face a hetero-geneous social environment, the development and application of theory promises both to refine simulation, when it is feasible, and to cover for

the limitations of simulation, when refinement is not to be had. Theory, joined with simulation, seems the way to salvage reliability in the face of cognitive diversity (if it is to be salvaged).

(Ibid.: 139)

Henderson and Horgan advocate this synergy for scholarship, as well as for everyday life. Acknowledging that the combination of simulation and theory is only one component of epistemic competence in the social sciences, they nonetheless insist that it is an important one for both reliability and systematicity.[2]

How might Henderson and Horgan's standard of epistemic competence be applied to the writing of history? In *Historical Theory*, historiographer Mary Fulbrook develops normative guidelines for historical writing that are similar in epistemological ambition to those of the two cognitive epistemologists. On the one hand, her injunctions may be seen as extensions of Henderson and Horgan's standards into the field of history. On the other, Fulbrook recognizes significant differences between the truth claims of history and those of predictive social sciences that must be taken into account before any attempt can be made to apply Quinean standards of epistemic competence to historical discourse. For Fulbrook, the general aim of historical writing is the crafting of a reliable and persuasive interpretation and explanation of past events. Reliability, however, cannot usually be based upon experiments in which variables are controlled, tests may be repeated, and results are worked into systematic theories about human behavior. Nonetheless, the historian can ensure a high level of reliability through standards of evaluating and deploying evidence, comprehensiveness, informed simulation, and empirically responsible paradigms. While historical writing need not contribute to larger systems of explanation and prediction, the systems of interpretation embedded in a paradigm for constructing history should be open to revision, according to Fulbrook.

As a well-read historiographer, Fulbrook understands that multiple theoretical paradigms have divided the field of history into competing language communities. And she acknowledges that there is some "incommensurability," to use Kuhn's term, among these historical languages that will necessarily prevent any grand synthesis of historical knowledge. Even agreed upon "facts" and "evidence" will never be enough for consensus among historians because "there is not and arguably cannot be any such thing as a universal vocabulary for analyzing and redescribing the past" (Fulbrook 2002: 97). Further, according to Fulbrook, paradigm differences primarily have to do with "deep-rooted questions of philosophical anthropology" (Ibid.: 194). Some of these differences might be resolvable through empirical research, but many, such as the conflict between historians who emphasize the recurrence of long-term structures and others who point up individual differences and human innovation, are apparently matters of faith. At the end of the day, in history as in religion, she concludes that there is no arguing with faith.

Given these difficulties, Fulbrook's pragmatic suggestion is for the historian to be very careful about her or his choice of a symbol-based paradigm for interpretation. She notes that paradigms range over a spectrum of falsifiability – some are nearly hermetically closed in circles of self-confirmation while others are more open to fundamental change through empirical critique. Fulbrook advises scholars to join a "relatively broad community" where "openness of debate and rational agreement over interpretations of the past are possible, irrespective of differences in political and moral commitments in the present" (Ibid.: 96). To ensure this, she recommends that the "categories of analysis" deployed by this community of scholars should be at a "restricted level of empirical attribution" (Ibid.: 96). That is, Fulbrook advocates categories that describe historical specifics discernable in the evidence rather than whole historical processes or ontological generalizations; "working-class women" rather than "capitalism" or "sex-gender system," for example. She praises "empirically rooted" (Ibid.: 96) historians who arrive at generalizations and narratives through a synthesis of such specifics rather than those who deduce their stories from categories of historical or ontological wholes.

Fulbrook recognizes that the historian's choice of a paradigm community and its categories of analysis will partly determine what counts as "evidence," but this only makes the careful analysis and critique of paradigms more important. Further, this choice need not back the historian into selecting between postmodern despair and naïve empiricism. Although all historical narratives are necessarily partial, "not all candidates for 'partial narratives' are equally acceptable, illuminating or true" (Ibid.: 29). This is because "we can in principle develop and apply mutually agreed criteria for 'disconfirming' particular partial accounts (or parts thereof), using appropriately interpreted empirical evidence of a variety of sorts" (Ibid.: 29). The problematics of constructing a history of the Holocaust, for example, cannot be reduced to a matter of individual preferences among historians or to the dominant discourses of the day; the variety and immensity of the empirical evidence will make some partial histories more truthful than others. Consequently, asserts Fulbrook:

> We can in principle – at least within the very broad compass of 'western' notions of scholarship – develop and apply mutually agreed upon criteria for evaluating different accounts against each other, in terms of, for example:
>
> - range, comprehensiveness and interpretation of sources, netted within an appropriate conceptual framework which must itself be open in principle to critique and revision;
> - capacity to account for (i.e., satisfy curiosity about) a particular *explanandum* in the light of our existing contextual knowledge and particular interests;

- presentation and accessibility of historical accounts for a range of purposes to different audiences in the present.

(Ibid.: 29–30)

Among Fulbrook's criteria for evaluating different histories is evidence gleaned from historical simulation. Influenced by Max Weber's use of empathy to understand historical Others, Fulbrook lists simulation as one of several historical "tools" that depend upon "the creativity of the human imagination" (Ibid.: 187). Empathetic understanding can yield significant insight into "other cultures [and] other viewpoints" (Ibid.: 187), she states. Significantly, Fulbrook knows nothing about recent advances in simulation in the field of cognitive studies; she makes no distinction, for instance, between historical paradigms and simulation on the basis of symbolic or pre-symbolic methods. Fulbrook advocates empathy because she knows that its careful deployment has helped to produce reliable history from many historians in the past.

Together, Fulbrook's standards for good history and her cautious recognition of the inevitability of paradigmatic relativity place greater emphasis on "reliability" than on Henderson and Horgan's "systematicity." Although reliable history cannot rest on repeatability and predictability as in the sciences, informed simulation, standards of evaluating evidence, comprehensiveness, range, contextuality, and empirically responsible paradigms can guarantee a high degree of reliability. For Fulbrook, interpretations and explanations must be systematic in terms of the historical paradigm of investigation, but paradigms need not explain a comprehensive range of historical phenomena. Nonetheless, some interpretative paradigms are better than others on the basis of their categories of analysis and their fundamental openness to empirical challenge and revision. Historical knowledge based in Fulbrook's standards of reliability and systematicity would qualify as epistemologically "robust" in the definition put forward by Henderson and Horgan. This is because Fulbrook understands that engaging with the past is closely akin to interpreting and explaining a culture populated by heterogeneous Others.

Wench acts, as a case study

How do psychoanalysis and cognitive studies measure up in terms of the Henderson and Horgan standard of epistemic competence, as modified by Fulbrook's guidelines? More specifically, what can be said about both methods for producing valid truth claims in historical writing? Recognizing that no approach to historical knowledge can guarantee absolute truth, Henderson, Horgan, and Fulbrook have established a yardstick by which different methods may be judged for their relative epistemic competence – a yardstick that invites comparison between psychoanalysis and cognitive studies. Possible interpretations and explanations of wench acts in antebellum blackface minstrelsy provide a relevant case study to open up this epistemological comparison. How to understand the laughter evoked by blacked-up male actors cross-dressed as women in the 1840s and 1850s, in fact, has become a major historiographical problem for historians of minstrelsy. Race and gender intersected in wench acts, but what "race" and "gender" meant in these skits and how these constructions worked together for the audience is a matter of significant historiographical dispute. The choice of wench acts as a case study, then, promises historiographical as well as epistemological insight.

Wenches were already popular stage types in the US by 1843, the year minstrel entertainment crystallized into the general form that underwrote its immense success with urban, working-class audiences. One report notes that the first female impersonator in blackface appeared as early as 1835 (Mahar 1999: 316). Several historians of early minstrelsy trace the wench figure to the character of the Dame, a traditional role in American productions of English and French pantomime that was also performed by a cross-dressed male. Historian David Mayer notes that the usual Dame figure in British pantomime of the 1850s was a stereotypical aging female: "Ugliness allied to misplaced vanity, sexual voracity paired with squeamishness, assertiveness, slovenly housekeeping, appalling taste in clothes, excessive curiosity, and chronic and indiscrimate gossiping" (Mayer 2003: II, 995). Three of the first actors to gain success as minstrel wenches, George Christy, Barney Williams, and George Holland, had earlier won minor stardom as panto Dames and continued to perform Dame roles in panto pieces and Shakespearean burlesques during the antebellum years.

Within the pre-1860 minstrel show, the wench act was a specialty piece featuring at least three of the players and sometimes, apparently, the entire ensemble, which might number from five to a dozen performers. Typically, the number began with one or more musicians playing and singing a wench song – "Lucy Long," "Buffalo Gals," "Cynthia Sue," and "Lucy Neal" were popular wench tunes by the early 1850s. Several of the verses in these songs mocked sentimental and fashionable females and took particular aim at women's rights and abolitionism, a movement assumed to be dominated by women. After a brief musical introduction, the wench stepped onto the stage, usually a burley man in a silly wig and a mock-fashionable dress, sometimes displaying his big feet under white pantalettes. The audience applauded and laughed; it is clear that none of minstrelsy's savvy spectators mistook the white male wench as either black or female.

What happened next in typical antebellum wench acts is largely a matter of historical conjecture. Although some wench performers may have sung their song, most probably remained mute, the object of the song's satire, not the agent of its attack. Some female impersonators apparently adopted different poses in time to the music, presumably in mock display of their "female" charms. Most began dancing. Did they dance singly or with blacked-up male partners? Minstrel performers had been dancing shuffle steps and breakdowns by themselves since T.D. Rice began jumping "Jim Crow" in the 1820s and some wenches may have danced alone. On the other hand, an 1855 photograph shows a male minstrel bowing to a female imper-sonator, perhaps inviting him/her to dance. (The situation, however, is ambiguous; the black male seems to be carrying a piece of luggage and may be bowing to leave. Wenches performed in other skits besides comic songs and the scene in the photo may depict a moment of sentimental departure.)[3] A wench dancing with a male partner offered comic opportunities for foot stomps and butt kicks, opportunities not likely lost on wench performers. Vague contemporary comments about dancing wenches suggest an abun-dance of low physical comedy, which would accord with the origin of the wench figure in the panto Dame. A comic actor desiring laughs and familiar with Dame pratfalls might work the entire stage, creating ridiculous situ-ations and engaging in rough play with several other performers, dancing partners as well as seated musicians. There is no reliable evidence, however, that this occurred.

In *Love and Theft*, Eric Lott interprets the wench figure through the lens of psychoanalysis, drawing especially on Lacan's version of Freud's ideas. Following another Freudian, Robert Stoller, Lott asserts that minstrel wenches, like cross-dressed males in other forms of entertainment, helped the men in the audience to ward off castration anxiety. Further, powerful, masculinized women, says Lott, were a part of the general homosexual economy of minstrelsy. Lott cites examples from several songs and sketches that he believes demonstrate a pervasive white male desire for black men evident in many areas of antebellum minstrelsy. While he acknowledges the "riotous misogyny" of wench acts, he insists that the representation of males for other cross-dressed males within the fiction of blackface "brought homo-sexual desire to the stage" (Lott 1993: 164). "In the broadest sense," Lott concludes, "the blackface male's desire for his 'wench' acknowledges or rep-resents the relations of the white audience to blacks generally" (Ibid.: 166). Far from being incidental, Lott's conclusion about wench acts is key to a major line of argument in *Love and Theft*. The homoerotic desire among blacks and whites depicted in minstrelsy, Lott asserts, provided a significant basis for a cross-racial class alliance in antebellum New York City.

William J. Mahar, in *Behind the Burnt Cork Mask*, disputes Lott's find-ings. By examining the lyrics of "Lucy Long," the oldest and most popular of the wench songs, Mahar argues that wench acts were primarily about misogyny, not race. "It may be," he states, "that blackness and its racial implications were not the most important factors because audiences knew they were viewing a female impersonator. [In 'Lucy Long,'] it was the male wench's presentation of female promiscuity and the allure of [male] sexual freedom (at least in fantasy) that attracted [audience] interest" (Mahar 1999: 311). For Mahar, wench songs helped their mostly male spectators to fight the war between the sexes; they did not work on the audience to excite cross-racial homoeroticism. "Blackness is the cover under which the male

fantasy of exercising complete control over women is played out in the seemingly innocuous comic scene" (Ibid.: 312), Mahar concludes.

Mahar's take on wench acts qualifies Lott's psychoanalytic analysis, but it
does not overturn it. Lott, after all, does not deny that misogyny was a part of
the fun. Mahar's content analysis of "Lucy Long" is probably correct about
minstrel spectators' assuming that men had the right to treat women as
sexual objects, but Lott never supposes that the homoeroticism of minstrelsy
might somehow have altered the sexual orientations of most white men in the
audience to make them less interested in their wives and girlfriends. Further,
there are several grounds on which the historian might dispute Mahar's claim
that blackface was simply a convenient "cover" – that race, consequently, had
little to do with the dynamics of wench acts. With regard to the stage action
of a wench act, the historian might ask Mahar why he thinks the audience
paid much attention to the lyrics of "Lucy Long" at all. By 1850, most spectators had heard the song before, its music and lyrics were utterly conventional, and, in my experience, an audience will watch a comic dancer with
much more attention than they will listen to a familiar song.

Of course to bring my own experience as an actor, director, and spectator
into this discussion is to engage the simulation side of Henderson and
Horgan's epistemology. What I have just done is to put myself in the shoes
of an antebellum spectator at a minstrel show in order to imagine what
would interest me if I were seeking to enjoy a wench act. In this case, historical empathy places me/him in the midst of a raucous crowd of my/his white
male buddies, many of whom are drunk. Imaginative simulation also
requires me/him to enjoy the wench act on stage through racist and sexist
eyes. In this regard, practicing historical empathy is not for the squeamish;
Fulbrook, for example, notes the importance of identifying with concentration camp guards to fully understand the Holocaust.

The issue at hand, however, does not require quite this stretch of the
imagination. I do not have to push myself very far into the mind of my spectator to reach the easy conclusion that enjoying knockabout comedy was
more fun for the audience than listening to the exact words of the song.
Broad physical action has almost always trumped song lyrics on the stage,
regardless of the audience. Insofar as the wench may have danced to embody
the lyrics of "Lucy Long," however, Mahar may have a point. To imagine the
act in these terms involves a different and more difficult mode of historical
simulation – putting oneself inside the big shoes, long dress, black makeup,
and ridiculous wig of an antebellum actor playing the wench on the minstrel
stage. What did the actor do with such lyrics as, "Oh! Miss Lucy's teeth is
grinning/Just like an ear ob corn" and "If she makes a scolding wife,/As sure
as she was born,/I'll tote her down to Georgia,/And trade her off for corn"
(quoted in Mahar 1999: 308)? There would have been many ways for actor-
dancers, working within or against the rhythmic structure of the tune, to
get laughs out of these lines. The historian can be reasonably sure, however,
that evoking laughter was the performer's primary intention.

And this is where Lott's explanation falls apart. A simulation of the specific historical situation makes it very difficult to believe that actor-dancers playing minstrel wenches would try to induce erotic desire in their spectators. To avoid the "blind spot" of inadequate information in empathizing with minstrel actors and spectators and imagining their situation, the historian interested in Lott's explanation must look for evidence that speaks directly to the problematics of actor intention and audience response at that time and in that style of comedy. Olive Logan's description of the female impersonator on the minstrel stage, perhaps the best nineteenth-century description available, underlines the foolishness, not the desirability, of the wench figure in context: "Clad in some tawdry old gown of loud, crude colors, whose shortness and scantiness display long frilled 'panties' and No. 13 valise shoes ... the funny old gal is very often a gymnast of no mean amount of muscle, as her saltitory exercises in the break-down prove" (Lott 1993: 61). Logan's term "funny old gal" was the same one used to denote the Dame role in panto and burlesque, a figure that both beat up antagonists and usually got beaten up herself. This evidence points not to the comedy of drag in general, but to a specific kind of cross-dressed, knockabout humor that was common in the burlesques and pantomimes of the era. This style (both in drag and out) reigned supreme in the roughhouse clowning of George L. Fox, whose violent antics as Humpty Dumpty created hilarity among working-class audiences in mid-century New York City. The closest well-known parallels to antebellum wench impersonation in the twentieth century might be one of the Three Stooges parading as a woman, Billis singing "Honey Bun" in *South Pacific*, or Milton Berle in a dress.

Oddly, Lott cites Logan's description without understanding that ridiculous wenches probably evoked laughter, not homoerotic desire. It is very rare for spectators to laugh at sexually alluring figures. We might laugh *with* these people, but to laugh *at* them would be to turn them from objects of sexual interest into objects of ridicule. We do not need a fully developed theory of comedy to understand this; we know it from our experience. By simulating this aspect of antebellum audience response, the historian can bring her or his experience of sexual desire and laughter to bear in solving this problem of interpretation. Further, the knockabout, Three-Stooges style of minstrel wench comedy makes the combination of sexual turn-on and mocking laughter even more far-fetched. To go to simulation again, if I wanted to invite the laughter of ridicule as a minstrel wench, I/the performer might flirt with the audience, but in such a ridiculous manner that spectators would laugh at my/his attempt to arouse them. To suppose that many men in the antebellum minstrel audience were ever sexually excited by this "funny old gal" is incredible.

How might a historian attuned to the possibilities of cognitive studies proceed in interpreting and explaining wench acts? Clearly, simulating the historical situation of a performer or spectator involved in the act is a beginning, but Henderson, Horgan, and Fulbrook would expect the historian to enhance and qualify his or her application of empathy through more comprehensive evidence and better knowledge of the context, as well as through the deployment of relevant cognitive theories. While this essay is not the appropriate place to develop a complete history of the wench figure in antebellum minstrelsy, a start can be made toward that end by pursuing certain leads that appear promising.

Putting simulation together with a wider sampling of evidence, the historian can get more specific about the kind of rough comedy wench acts involved. Brawny men in dresses doing breakdowns and gymnastic stunts will not, by themselves, evoke much laughter. More likely, the fun occurred in the contrast between the pose of frail femininity adopted by the wench and the reality of male muscle underneath. Many later wench songs written after "Lucy Long" paint a sentimental portrait of a "yaller gal," often separated from her black lover and victimized by a white master. Apparently, performers of "yaller gals" borrowed much of their business from the "funny old gals" but also extended the possibilities of wench humor through this later type. In the version of "Lucy Neale" sung by the Virginia Minstrels in 1848, for example, a jealous white master sells the black singer of the song down the river to separate the lovers, and "Lucy" dies, presumably of a broken heart as well as from eating "too much corn and meal" (Bean 2001: 154–6). "Lucy Neale" invites the female impersonator playing Lucy to strike sentimental poses and dance with girlish coquetry. The comic contrast between this victimized (but still voracious) waif and the aggressive masculinity of the man under the dress must have been delicious.

This suggests that the male actor-dancers playing wenches often worked in two modes of performance, the representational and the virtuosic. That is, the performers used songs like "Lucy Neale" and mimed the motions of feminine allure to set up a believable "yaller gal" before they punctured this persona with the "saltitory" gymnastics and masculine horseplay mentioned by Logan and others. First they represented a winsome black female and then comically undercut her through male virtuosity. Other contextual evidence about minstrelsy supports the likelihood of this kind of comedy. Male wenches played in other skits that called for a believable representation of sentimental "yaller gals." Judging from the fact that many performers bragged about their truthful delineation of blacks, that blacks sometimes appeared on the minstrel stage, and that many spectators supposed that real black people did act like minstrel performers, it is clear that some measure of "realism" occurred in minstrelsy. But the performer's virtuosity in mime, dancing, pratfalls, and similar business must have been just as important as character believability in the success of wench acts. Many antebellum theatrical genres, including pantomime, burlesque, melodrama, and clowning, invited this kind of enjoyment. More specifically, panto Dames typically worked the same kind of contrast – an abrupt shift from squeamish old lady to clumsy and aggressive man – for laughs.

Philosophers of cognitive studies who work in the field of aesthetics have concluded that representational and virtuosic performances, the two modes that predominated in wench acts, correspond with actual, discrete modes of spectator response. Susan Feagin's *Reading With Feeling* uses several theories – most extensively Robert Gordon's insights into simulation and emotions – to survey the many ways that readers engage emotionally with fiction. Many of her conclusions may be translated from the situation of the reader and text to that of the spectator and actor; indeed, the spectator–actor situation is closer to the general reality of social interaction on which most psychological experiments relevant to Feagin's interests have been conducted. Feagin discusses seven types of engagement in all, which include sympathy, antipathy, empathy, and a category she lists as "response to an author's achievement or accomplishment" (Feagin 1996: 131).[4] The first three arise through engagement with the actual fictional narrative, while the last, which may be shortened to "virtuosity," is a meta-mode which situates the reader in a direct relationship with the author's performance. Spectators at a wench act, in other words, might sympathize with (or ridicule and dismiss, or put themselves in the place of) the "yaller gal" represented by the performer. Or they could directly applaud (or condemn) the performer's skill and accomplishment in puncturing the pretense of black femininity with male aggression.

A cognitive perspective on this kind of comedy also suggests the likely relationship between gender and race in wench acts. This relationship has been a contentious area of analysis for scholars. Mahar, for instance, concludes that wench acts primarily hinged on misogyny, while Lott, echoing most other scholars on minstrelsy, points to race as the main signifier and effective lure of minstrel wenches. In her dissertation on female impersonation in minstrelsy, Annemarie Bean theorizes that blackness and femininity worked together in wench acts but does not specify how their comedy might have facilitated this. Historians hampered by positivism, those Zizek terms "objectivists," will simply conclude that the "evidence" is insufficient to make any conclusions about the relationship between race and gender in wench acts. Zizek's "relativists" might call forth a variety of interpretative theories to understand race and gender in this historical situation, but how reliable could their explanations be? Historians attuned to possible cognitive interpretations, however, might advance an interpretation and formulate an explanation that at least draws on empirically tested theories to arrive at a probable conclusion.

From the point of view of George Lakoff and Mark Johnson's cognitive linguistics, the sudden shift from feminine "yaller gal" to masculine "funny old gal" suggests that both gendered and racial differences were a necessary part of the comedy. Of the two, gender probably played a more overt role. All of the performers on the minstrel stage embodied black characters; this made gender, not race, a primary signifier of difference on the representational level. On the level of virtuosity, however, the audience knew that white males performed all of the roles and directly applauded the performers, not their blacked-up characters, for their stunts and breakdowns. In cognitive linguistic terms, wench acts probably depended on what Lakoff and Johnson term a "Folk Theory of Essences" applied to the self. In this conception of the self, every person has an essence, a core nature, which makes him or her unique. Individuals may pretend to be another kind of person, perhaps even play at being a different gender, but their true inner self remains untouched (Lakoff and Johnson 1999: 282–4). The comedy of the wench act seems to have hinged on the abrupt revelation of a true white male self under the pretended self of a black female. Sometimes this occurred quite literally, as when big feet or strong knees erupted out from under the wench's dress. The cognitive, comic effect of this contrast was to reduce both femininity and blackness to a grotesque masquerade; in such circumstances, only masculinity and whiteness appeared to be natural and essential. The white males in the audience, then, probably enjoyed this comic unmasking in both racial and gendered terms.

Why did white, working-class males, the predominate audience for antebellum minstrelsy, find wench acts so funny? Probably because the new codes of Victorian respectability, which urged more affection and sentimental regard between men and women, were challenging older patriarchal principles of working-class life. As W.H. Lhamon noted, many minstrel acts attacked the new norms of domesticity, especially those that granted women greater authority in regulating the leisure hours and domestic behavior of the men in their lives (Lhamon 1998: 1–55). Historian Christine Stansell points to the difficulty many male workers experienced in supporting their families and the increasing economic opportunities for women in the cities. Challenged at the workplace and at home, men might take out their frustration on women in what Stansell calls the "great renegotiation of what, exactly, men and women owed each other" (Stansell 1987: 81). Wench acts were a part of this "renegotiation" in the 1840s and 1850s. On the representational level, it is likely that white male minstrels doubly degraded wenches as both powerless slaves and available prostitutes, the contemporary meaning of "wench." On the level of virtuosity, it seems that wench women lost any essential identity; they could be as grotesque, naïve, and voracious as their female impersonators decided. What better revenge against females usurping traditional male authority!

This tentative interpretation and explanation of wench acts based in an application of cognitive studies to history is more reliable than the psychoanalytical understanding offered by Lott. It better explains the comedy at the heart of the performance, it can account for more of the available evidence, and it is a better fit, contextually, with the experience of minstrel performers and working-class spectators in antebellum cities. With regard to the context, Lott finds little evidence of homoerotic desire among men across racial lines in antebellum cities. Granting that such evidence would be difficult to discover, the evidence for cross-racial class solidarity, which Lott presumes was partly the result of these homoerotic ties, is skimpy at best, and there is substantial evidence to counter it. On the whole, the psychoanalytic paradigm seems ill-suited to interpreting and explaining wench acts in a reliable way. An investigative paradigm based in cognitive studies, on the other hand, offers informed simulation and can accommodate the normative standards of empirical evidence proposed by Fulbrook. No more than any other method, a cognitive take on wench acts cannot deliver Historical Truth, but it is comparatively better than psychoanalysis.

Contrasting psychoanalysis and cognitive science

Is the relative unreliability of Lott's interpretation of wench acts based in the shortcomings of psychoanalysis, however, or is it simply the result of some anomalies that have little to do with the Freudian ideas that structure his paradigm? How closely tied is Lott's explanation to psychoanalytic dynamics? Fulbrook requires that historians critique their paradigms in terms of their openness to revision and their categories of analysis. In addition, Henderson and Horgan would demand that symbolic frameworks for truth claims be able to accommodate revision on the basis of pre-symbolic simulation. How do psychoanalysis and cognitive studies compare on the matter of systematicity when these standards are brought to bear?

Regarding the question of Lott's epistemological links to psychoanalysis, *Love and Theft* is deeply indebted to Freud and Lacan. The argument of half the book rests on varieties of Freudianism; antebellum blackface minstrelsy, according to Lott, entails both the "theft" of black cultural material and the "love" of black men by urban working-class white men. In the course of the "love" half of his narrative, Lott draws on Freud's interpretations of jokes, Melanie Klein's psychoanalytic understanding of infant sadism, Stallybrass and White's Freudian explanation of the imprint of desire on disgust, Freud's Oedipal complex, Mulvey's "male gaze," and even Slavoj Zizek on the constitution of desire. In short, Lott builds a substantial portion of his historical argument on the supposed validity of the paradigm of psychoanalysis and its Lacanian spin-off. This is not to say that all psychoanalytic analyses of wench acts would arrive at Lott's flawed conclusions. But it is clear that this paradigm has led him toward an unreliable interpretation.

To gain epistemic systematicity, Henderson, Horgan, and Fulbrook require that an explanatory paradigm remain open to empirical critique. Has new evidence led to the testing and revision of psychoanalysis since Freud founded the discipline? The simple answer is "no." In her *Psychoanalysis and Cognitive Science*, Wilma Bucci sets out to reconcile the theories of Freud and his disciples with those of second-generation cognitive scientists such as Edelman, Lakoff, Damasio, Rosch, Simon, and Kaplan. She recognizes that the basic project of both groups of researchers is the same: "to arrive at a general theory of the psychical apparatus" by using observable indicators to infer inner processes (Bucci 1997: 8). Although advocates of psychoanalysis continue to push its virtues in several academic fields, Bucci notes that "psychoanalysis as a theory of mind is at best a ghost of scientific psychology or any other scientific enterprise" (Ibid.: x). This is because psychoanalysis has primarily been taught in its own institutes and clinical programs. "[Freud's] metapsychology has not, in the century since its introduction, been subject to the empirical evaluation and theory development that is necessary for a scientific field" (Ibid.: 9). Specifically,

> the type of systematic inference that is applied in cognitive science and in all modern science requires explicit definitions that limit the meaning of the concepts, correspondence rules mapping hypothetical constructs and intervening variables onto observable events, and means of assessing reliability of observation. Each of the indicators that analysts rely on to make inferences about the conscious and unconscious states of other persons (as about one's own unconscious states) must itself be independently validated as having the implications that are assumed.
>
> (Ibid.: 10)

Bucci concludes that the concepts of Freudian psychoanalysis "do not and cannot begin to meet such constraints" (Ibid.: 10).[5] Just because such terms as "the unconscious" and "the Other" have entered common parlance does not make them valid; indeed, from a scientific point of view, the taken-for-granted aspect of psychoanalysis makes it more suspect.

Although Bucci credits Freud and his followers with some insights into psychological mechanisms that have withstood cognitive scientific analysis, she points out that his general theory of cognition and human development is much too simplistic and unverifiable to compete with the complexities of empirically based cognitive models. Zizek, however, seeks to turn this shortcoming of Lacan's version of psychoanalysis into a virtue. From Zizek's point of view, the realm of empirical evidence lies wholly within scientific positivism, which, following Kant, is limited to an objective understanding of the world that does not include human subjectivity. Zizek, in other words, simply refuses to recognize the validity of empirical evidence in gaining knowledge of human cognition. In "Lacan between cultural studies and cognitivism," Zizek purports to show that Lacan can provide a bridge "to overcome the abyss that separates the transcendental *a priori* horizon [of subjectivity] from the domain of positive scientific discoveries" (Zizek 2000: 27). This leads Zizek to plunge with Lacan into psychoanalytic notions of fantasy and to emerge with a category Zizek calls "the objectively subjective" (Ibid.: 29), a position beyond the claims of empirical evidence, that provides Zizek with a basis for truth and knowledge. In effect, Zizek posits Lacanian psychoanalysis as the best counter to the Kantian conundrum of the split between subjective and objective epistemologies.

But this is disingenuous philosophizing. As Zizek surely knows, there are other resolutions to Kant's problematic, and one of them is the "embodied realism" in Lakoff and Johnson's version of cognitive linguistics:

> Embodied realism can work for science in part because it rejects a strict subject–object dichotomy. Disembodied scientific realism creates an unbridgeable ontological chasm between "objects," which are "out there," and subjectivity, which is "in here." Once the separation is made, there are only two possible and equally erroneous conceptions of objectivity: Objectivity is either given by the "things themselves" (the objects) or by the intersubjective structures of consciousness shared by all people (the subjects). . . . What disembodied realism (what is sometimes called "metaphysical" or "external" realism) misses is that as embodied, imaginative creatures, *we never were separated or divorced from reality in the first place* (italics in original).
>
> (Lakoff and Johnson 1999: 93)[6]

Within embodied realism and all other forms of cognitive science, new empirical evidence can, in principle, always challenge established theoretical constructs. This does not mean that cognitive scientists are any more willing than other scientists to abandon conventional paradigms of knowledge; Kuhnian cautions are still in order here. (Nonetheless, the recent paradigm shift in cognitive studies from command-and-control computation to connectionist models of the mind-brain, on the basis of empirical evidence that could not be made to fit the older model, does suggest some flexibility.) On the whole, then, the paradigm of cognitive studies is more empirically responsible than versions of psychoanalysis. Regarding this measure of systematicity and reliability, cognitive studies provides a better paradigm for the writing of history.

A second measure of the usefulness of a particular paradigm for historians, very important for Fulbrook in particular, is the paradigm's categories of analysis. Given their proximity to historical evidence, paradigmatic analytical terms, according to Fulbrook, should avoid whole historical processes and broad ontological generalizations. Rather than describing wide varieties of evidence with one encompassing term, historians must use more discrete categories that allow them to micro-manage the particularities of the past. In truth, this measure of reliability is a problem for all psychologies, simply because the goal of every psychological system is to arrive at broad, synchronic generalizations about human cognition and behavior that hold true regardless of diachronic change. This difficulty plays out for historians committed to the truth of psychoanalysis when they find themselves interpreting a wide variety of phenomena as evidence of "the unconscious" or "the Oedipal complex" working in history.

Similarly, the Lacanian concepts of "the phallus," "the Other," and "the imaginary stage" can be used to explain an enormous range of historical activity, much of it apparently unrelated until examined under a Lacanian lens. These and similar categories allow Lott to presume that he can interpret the unconscious desires of white spectators in the 1850s through the same categories as a psychoanalyst might interpret a patient's problems in 1993, the publication date of *Love and Theft*. Indeed, so confident is Lott about the applicability of Freud and Lacan to all periods of history that he reads Norman Mailer's fantasies about the sexual potency of black males in the 1950s back into the desires of white spectators a hundred years before (Lott 1993: 54–5). Lacanian "desire" is ubiquitous in his book; it is difficult for the reader to know what, if anything, lies beyond its imperializing gaze.

Of course, historians must acknowledge some degree of commonality connecting them with past historical agents, or the writing of history becomes impossible. In my own analysis of wench acts, I drew upon such cognitive categories as "empathy," "sympathy," and the "folk theory of essences." This terminology, like other cognitive-scientific language, also presumes durability over time. But there are two major differences between these terms and those of psychoanalysis. First, all such cognitive language seeks to describe empirically verifiable phenomena and is, consequently, falsifiable. If cognitive scientists discover tomorrow that empathetic projection does not occur, I could not use the term "empathy," and "simulation" would lose validity as an historical method.

Second, although cognitive studies also purports to be transhistorical, its complex understanding of human cognition gives it a more extensive, historically flexible, and less reductive vocabulary than psychoanalysis for cultural analysis. In *Shakespeare's Brain: Reading with Cognitive Theory*, for example, the literary historian Mary Thomas Crane draws on cognitive psychologist Jean Mandler's theory of perceptual analysis to represent and explain particularities of Shakespeare's language that both individuate his thinking and connect the plays to his age (Crane 2001: 3–35). Mandler's psychology, which is supported by the convergent findings of Lakoff's linguistics and Gerald Edelman's neuroscience, gives Crane a vocabulary of "image schemas" and "spatial metaphors" that she can deploy with empirical confidence. Among the other terms deriving from this orientation are "subject," "self," and "agent," which are similar to but distinct from their Marxist or psychoanalytic counterparts. Further, while Mandler's "image schemas" and the metaphors that derive from them are rooted in the nature of the brain, they are responsive to historical shifts in the culture; the somatic-symbolic relationship in Mandler's psychology (unlike Freud's) is dynamic and ongoing. Following a series of comparisons among cognitive, Freudian, and Marxist psychologies, Crane concludes that "the concepts of a tripartite self (id, ego, superego) or of 'subject position' may themselves be too schematic to describe the multiplicity of competing processes going on within a given brain at any moment or to explain the effective integration of those processes" (Ibid.: 21).[7] In contrast to Crane's subtle handling of the intersection of the language of agency and Shakespeare's historical culture in *Hamlet*, Lott's deployment of psychoanalytic terms to understand working-class desire in 1850s minstrelsy is ham-fisted.

Finally, unlike cognitive studies, the implications of one version of the paradigm of psychoanalysis – the Lacanian – would prevent historical simulation. Where other paradigms of human action and belief are more or less indifferent to the possibility of engaging other modes of knowing outside of their preferred epistemology, the idea of human development at the heart of Lacan's psychoanalysis implicitly rules out any method not based in symbolic communication. For Lacan, the human subject is necessarily tied to language; the Freudian unconscious of the self is structured as a language, and adult humans relate to themselves and each other through symbolic communication. The only other register available to humans in everyday life is the imaginary, an inflexible state associated with infancy and various delusory conditions. Humans learn about the world and produce knowledge through the register of the symbolic; Lacanian psychoanalysis does not recognize a pre-symbolic capability of simulation as a mode of knowing.[8]

In practice, Lacanian therapists probably do use empathy to understand their patients; indeed, it would be surprising if they did not. But Lacanian theory cannot recognize such necessary communication as pre-symbolic. Consequently, if the application of Lacanian theory and other cognate theories is understood as the path to truth, the Lacanian historian could not use simulation as a method of interpretation. This is certainly true for Lott. Rather than engaging in an empathetic understanding of performers and spectators to interpret and explain their wench acts, Lott applies psychoanalytic, often Lacanian theories to arrive at an explanation. Lott's deployment of an exclusively "cold" methodology prevents him from engaging his "hot" imagination and emotion. For a theory that privileges sexual desire, Lacanian inhibition in this regard is sadly ironic. From Henderson and Horgan's point of view (and from Fulbrook's), the refusal of Lacanian theory to countenance simulation reduces its likelihood of producing reliable truth claims in historical studies.

Measuring Lacanian psychoanalysis and cognitive studies against Fulbrook's modification of Henderson and Horgan's standards of systematicity and reliability demonstrates the superiority of the cognitive to the psychoanalytic paradigm for historical writing. Although both paradigms promise a systematic investigation based in scientific protocols, psychoanalytic theorists, unlike the neurological, psychological, and linguistic scientists working in cognitive studies, do not admit the validity of empirical challenges to their founding ideas. This shortcoming in the Freudian paradigm is compounded by categories of analysis that are not only untestable but also too global for reliable historical judgments. Plus, Lacan's version of psychoanalysis inhibits the historian from the imaginative use of simulation. If *Love and Theft* may be taken as a representative example, psychoanalysis leads historians to conclusions that tend to be foreordained, more dependent on the paradigm than on empirically responsible methods for examining the relevant evidence.

Psychoanalysis, especially Lacan's synthesis of Freudian ideas and language development, has been widely influential over the past 25 years in cultural and theatrical studies; it has provided the theoretical basis for truth claims ranging from gaze theory to Judith Butler's notions of performativity. If the shortcomings of Lott's understandings of wench acts are any indication, it is time to reexamine conclusions based on the psychoanalytic paradigm. Cognitive studies, which seeks answers to many of the same cultural and historical questions posed by psychoanalysis, can provide an alternative. Overall, the reliability and systematicity of the psychoanalytic paradigm for historical understanding are much less robust than they are in the cognitive one.

Notes

1 On Quinean standards for epistemology, see Quine (1969). While Mary Fulbrook does not directly endorse these standards, she comes close to Quine's position by discarding relativism in favor of partial historical truths (Fulbrook 2002: 185–96).
2 Several of the contributors to *Empathy and Agency* recognize that the "simulation vs. theory" debate in contemporary cognitive studies bears some resemblance to the interpretation vs. explanation controversy in classical hermeneutics. For an overview of this debate and its relevance to contemporary hermeneutics, see Kogler and Steuber's "Introduction" (Kogler and Steuber 2000: 7–46). In "Simulation and Epistemic Competence," Henderson and Horgan hold that their "hybrid model," which combines simulation and theory, renders the terms of older debate *passé* (Henderson and Horgan 2000: 140).
3 See Mahar (1999: 313), for this illustration.
4 On a reader's emotional engagement with fiction, see also Scarry (1999).
5 In *A Clinical Introduction to Lacanian Psychoanalysis* (1997), Bruce Fink underscores the effectiveness of Lacanian therapy, but clinical success does not and cannot translate into empirical verifiability and epistemological reliability.
6 In his article Zizek (1998) discusses Daniel Dennett's theory of the self but does not engage the range of responses to Kantian epistemology posed by cognitive studies.
7 For another application of cognitive theories to historical understanding, see McConachie (2003).
8 On Lacanian psychoanalysis, see Lacan (1977), Mitchell and Rose (1982), and Zizek (1991). Also Fink (1995) and Copjec (1995). For Lacan, because the invasion of language structures a person's image of her/his body and language (following Saussure) entails the play of presence and absence, selves are doomed always to mis-recognize both Self and Other. Lacanian selves could never gain true knowledge of others through simulation; the attempt at projection necessarily breaks up on the rocks of self fragmentation. In contrast, the cognitive version of the self noted by Damasio (1999) emphasizes the perception of bodily integration and its perceived ability, consequently, to act in the world, including actions involving simulation.

References

Bean, A. (2001) "Female Impersonation in Nineteenth-Century American Blackface Minstrelsy," Ph.D. Diss., New York University.
Bucci, W. (1997) *Psychoanalysis and Cognitive Science: A Multiple Code Theory*, New York: Guilford Press.

Cockrell, D. (1997) *Demons of Disorder: Early Blackface Minstrels and Their World*, Cambridge: Cambridge University Press.

Copjec, J. (1995) *Read My Desire: Lacan Against the Historicists*, Cambridge, MA: MIT Press.

Crane, M.T. (2001) *Shakespeare's Brain: Reading with Cognitive Theory*, Princeton, NJ: Princeton University Press.

Damasio, A. (1999) *The Feeling of What Happens: Body and Emotion in the Making of Consciousness*, New York: Harcourt.

Eagleton, T. (2000) *The Idea of Culture*, Malden: Blackwell.

Feagin, S. (1996) *Reading with Feeling: The Aesthetics of Appreciation*, Ithaca, NY: Cornell University Press.

Fink, B. (1995) *The Lacanian Subject: Between Language and Jouissance*, Princeton, NJ: Princeton University Press.

—— (1997) *A Clinical Introduction to Lacanian Psychoanalysis*, Cambridge, MA: Harvard University Press.

Fulbrook, M. (2002) *Historical Theory*, London: Routledge.

Goldman, A. (1995) "Interpretation Psychologized," in Davis, M. and Stone, T. (eds) *Folk Psychology*, Oxford: Blackwell, 185–208.

Gordon, R.M. (1995a) "Folk Psychology as Simulation," in Davies, M. and Stone, T. (eds) *Folk Psychology*, Oxford: Blackwell, 60–73.

—— (1995b) "Simulation Without Introspection from You and Me," in Davies, M. and Stone, T. (eds) *Mental Simulation*, Oxford: Blackwell, 53–67.

—— (1996) " 'Radical' Simulationism," in Carruthers, P. and Smith, P. (eds) *Theories of Theories of Mind*, Cambridge: Cambridge University Press, 11–21.

Hart, F.E. (2001) "The epistemology of cognitive literary studies," *Philosophy and Literature*, 25 (2): 314–34.

Henderson, D. and Horgan, T. (2000) "Simulation and Epistemic Competence," in Kogler, H.H. and Stueber, K.R. (eds) *Empathy and Agency: The Problem of Understanding in the Human Sciences*, Boulder, CO: Westview Press, 119–43.

Kogler, H.H. and Steuber, K.R. (2000) "Introduction: Empathy, Simulation, and Interpretation in the Philosophy of Social Science," in Kogler, H.H. and Steuber, K.R. (eds) *Empathy and Agency: The Problem of Understanding in the Human Sciences*, Boulder, CO: Westview Press, 1–61.

Lacan, J. (1977) *Ecrits: A Selection*, New York: Norton.

Lakoff, G. and Johnson, M. (1999) *Philosophy in the Flesh: The Embodied Mind and Its Challenge to Western Thought*, New York: Basic Books.

Lhamon W.T., Jr (1998) *Raising Cain: Blackface Performance from Jim Crow to Hip Hop*, Cambridge, MA: Harvard University Press.

Lott, E. (1993) *Love and Theft: Blackface Minstrelsy and the American Working Class*, New York: Oxford University Press.

Mahar, W.J. (1999) *Behind the Burnt Cork Mask: Early Blackface Minstrelsy and Antebellum American Culture*, Chicago, IL: University of Illinois Press.

Mayer, D. (2003) "Pantomime, British," in Kennedy, D. (ed.) *Oxford Encyclopedia of Theatre and Performance*, 2 vols, Oxford: Oxford University Press: 995–7.

McConachie, B. (1992) *Melodramatic Formations: American Theatre and Society, 1820–1870*, Iowa City, IA: Iowa University Press.

—— (2003) *American Theater in the Culture of the Cold War: Producing and Contesting Containment, 1947–1962*, Iowa City, IA: Iowa University Press.

Mitchell, J. and Rose, J. (eds) (1982) *Jacques Lacan and the école Freudienne: Feminine Sexuality*, New York: Norton.

Quine, W.V.O. (1969) *Ontological Relativity and Other Essays*, New York: Columbia University Press.

Scarry, E. (1999) *Dreaming By the Book*, New York: Farrar, Strauss, and Giroux.

Senelick, L. (1988) *The Age and Stage of George L. Fox, 1825–1877*, Hanover, NH: University Press of New England.

Stansell, C. (1987) *City of Women: Sex and Class in New York, 1789–1860*, Urbana, IL: Illinois University Press.

Toll, R.C. (1974) *Blacking-Up: The Minstrel Show in Nineteenth-Century America*, New York: Oxford University Press.

Vielmetter, G. (2000) "The Theory of Holistic Simulation: Beyond Interpretivism and Postempiricism," in Kogler, H.H. and Steuber, K.R. (eds) *Empathy and Agency: The Problem of Understanding in the Human Sciences*, Boulder, CO: Westview Press, 83–102.

Winans, R.B. (1996) "Early Minstrel Show Music, 1843–1852," in Bean, A., Hatch, J.V., and McNamara, B. (eds) *Inside the Minstrel Mask: Readings in Nineteenth-Century Blackface Minstrelsy*, Hanover, NH: Wesleyan University Press.

Zizek, S. (1991) *Looking Awry: An Introduction to Jacques Lacan Through Popular Culture*, Cambridge, MA: MIT Press.

—— (1998) "The Cartesian Subject Versus the Cartesian Theater," in Zizek, S. (ed.) *Cogito and the Unconscious*, Durham, NC: Duke University Press, 247–74.

—— (2000) "Lacan between cultural studies and cognitivism," *Umbr(a): A Journal of the Unconscious*, 9: 33.

3   Performance strategies, image schemas, and communication frameworks

Tobin Nellhaus

Image schemas, according to contemporary cognitive science, are conceptual structures arising from sensorimotor and in some cases social experiences. They are not fully-fledged images or mental pictures, since they lack particularity and detail: they are abstract or recurrent patterns – tropes, if you will, of space, time, material and action. Examples include "container," "path," "force," "link," "cycle," "part-whole," "up-down," "center-periphery," "hot-cold," and so forth. As conceptual substructures, image schemas (and their elaboration into metaphoric imagery) organize and pervade every area of thought, from the nuts and bolts of categorization and grammar, through ordinary perception and idiomatic speech, to the heights of philosophy and ethics. For instance, even so basic a logical structure as the syllogism is founded on the "containment" schema: if all As are Bs (A is inside B) and C is an A (C is inside A), then C is a B (C is inside B) – a relation easily portrayed through the concentric circles of a Venn diagram. Cognitive science's most public face is probably the collaborative work of linguist George Lakoff and philosopher Mark Johnson in *Metaphors We Live By* (1980) and *Philosophy in the Flesh* (1999). The latter is especially significant for its deft analysis of the image schemas and metaphors underlying major philosophies in history.

Image schemas are fundamental to acting, performance space, dramatic narrative, and audience response. These elements form more-or-less integrated systems – performance strategies – each governed by a small set of image schemas and primary metaphors. That a handful of image schemas generate performance strategies is perhaps unsurprising, in the wake of the research already done on the role that image schemas play in performance.[1] Less well understood, however, is where these sets of schemas come from, why some culturally dominate while others are peripheral, why they change, and why their changes head in one direction rather than another. In short, basic questions remain on the social forces behind the cultural organization of image schemas and their heirarchization.

By itself, cognitive science cannot provide this analysis, because its methodological focus is upon the development and operation of image schemas in the individual mind. While the field occasionally acknowledges social aspects, it does not delve into them in any depth, nor can it. Thus cognitive science must be conjoined with an explanation for conceptual developments at the societal level. That explanation, I will argue, is provided by an understanding of communication practices, that is, the social use and development of speech, handwriting, printing, and electronics. Communication practices involve embodied experiences that generate a culture's dominant image schemas, which are embedded in performance strategies. Historiographically, this theory illuminates why and when theatrical practices undergo relatively sudden shifts in their dominant form (such as the type of performance space: locus and platea, U-shaped auditorium with perspective scenery, fan-shaped auditorium, and "missing fourth wall" sets, etc.), and the conceptual dynamics of the new form itself. Conversely, the theory I'm proposing also helps fill a gap in Lakoff and Johnson's arguments about the metaphoric basis for philosophy, by revealing that the choice of metaphors is not arbitrary but rather is historically conditioned at least in part by communication practices.[2]

From image schemas to performance strategies

Performance strategies embrace the entire arena of materials and techniques that playwrights, actors, directors, designers, managers, and other theatre personnel use or assume when constructing plays. They include performance space, performance time, dramatic action, scenery, sound, characterization, language, acting, genre concepts, expected audience behavioral norms, stage/audience dynamics, attitudes, pre- and post-performance discourse, and so forth. Although these elements can't all be controlled by the people involved, within a single production and often across many productions throughout a culture the elements tend to cohere into a regular system (akin to the regularities of a Foucauldian discursive formation).

Performance strategies emerge from agents' interactions with multiple social structures and forces, each other, and their own bodies in the context of performing before an audience. Agency is a core element of what theatre is "about." In theatrical performance, actors (real agents) create characters (virtual agents); the latter therefore are simultaneously products or causal *effects* of actual agency, *causes* of action in the dramas, and *indexes* of what it is to be an agent (Nellhaus 2000: 12–18). As agents, characters typically strive to solve problems, satisfy a need, ward off some danger, face a challenge, or in some other way remove impediments or fulfill desires. To do so, they adopt certain strategies, or at least ad hoc tactics. Performers, directors, and other theatre artists likewise seek to solve problems, though their problems are usually very different: how best to make sense of a script, how to make the transition from page to stage, how to communicate with their prospective audience, how to make optimal use of their financial, material, and organizational resources, and so forth. They too employ various strategies to achieve their ends. Not all of these strategies directly pertain to the performance itself, of course, but the ones that do usually focus on the performance's intelligibility and artistic success. Toward these ends, performance strategies involve selecting and organizing underlying image schemas deriving from sensorimotor and social experiences. And since some schemas derive from experiences with fundamental social relationships (or the institutions through which such relationships are maintained) or play an exceptional role in reproducing or transforming social relations, a few image schemas may obtain a foundational role in conditioning and enabling performance strategies.

For an example of how a small set of image schemas may structure performance strategies, I will consider the "sentimental" dramaturgy of the early eighteenth century. The present section will focus on describing the performance strategies and the ideas behind them; the subsequent section will consider their causal basis.[3] However, since I am claiming that the metaphoric underpinnings of these strategies constitute a relatively coherent network, I must briefly sketch the main elements of early eighteenth-century theatre and drama and then describe some of the key metaphors of the period.

The theatre buildings divided their audiences into a pit, a horseshoe of boxes, and galleries rising above them, with chandeliers lighting the entire interior; thus the auditorium created a sense of communal observation while demarcating social stratification. The back half of the stage contained wing flats and shutters for perspective scenery; the acting area included a forestage. During the English Renaissance, double-casting was commonplace; but when the theatres reopened in 1660, productions of new plays largely ended this practice, and actors played one and only one role in each play. Beginning in the early eighteenth century, theatre men like Richard Steele and Colley Cibber increasingly enjoined actors to speak the script, the whole script, and nothing but the script, and they lauded the actor Robert Wilks for striving to be letter perfect, setting an example for other players.[4] (Of course, Cibber himself had no qualms about radically reworking Shakespeare's plays.) The acting style itself was organized around gestures and "points," that is, gestural moments and tableaux encapsulating pinnacles of dramatic tension or expression, and a considerable amount of critical discourse at the time focused on emphasizing and elaborating on performers' gestural skills.

Starting in the 1690s, genres developed in which characters (increasingly from the merchant class) offered a new standard of behavior to the audience. Dramatists were becoming less interested in characters' wit and extrinsic behavior; now their attention was primarily on the characters' judgment, self-examination, inward struggles, and intrinsic merit. Pathetic incidents and meditative moments provided opportunities for exploring characters' inner qualities. Asides and soliloquies revealed less about plot and more about character; the characters were ultimately judged by their inner moral worth rather than their actions. Exemplary characters became a hallmark of sentimental drama (Peters 1990: 25–30; Loftis 1959: 196, 199).

Along with these pragmatics of theatrical performance were various conceptual systems through which audiences interpreted performance and its context. These systems operated not just within the theatre space, but rather were general attitudes and assumptions – cultural commonplaces, as it were, which were regularly articulated in guides to behavior and in mainstream periodicals such as *The Spectator* papers (edited and for the most part written by Richard Steele and Joseph Addison). Behavior manuals were, from today's perspective, remarkably specific and formalized: along with offering advice on how to respond to, say, haughtiness, they instructed their readers in the correct postures and gestures for taking one's leave, expressing anger, feeling perplexed, and so on. One of the striking aspects of these guides was the superiority they accorded to gesture over speech. Gesture was frequently considered purer, more lofty than the spoken word. Such views persistently appear in discussions of acting as well. For example, Steele – no fan of opera – praised the operatic castrato Nicolini for his gestural skills, and the actor Barton Booth evidently had similar talents. The underlying concept was that, whether on stage or in everyday life, gestures and facial expressions were necessary and immediate representations of a person's feelings, thoughts, and even intrinsic merit.[5]

Gesture drew its cultural significance in part from a metaphor: gesture was analogous to writing. Gesture, like writing, was opposed to the voice; it held positions in a spatial frame, like letters on a page; it revealed the inner self to the public eye just as writing did. Fluidity of writing and fluidity of movement were understood as essentially the same.[6] Just as words were the language of the mind, gestures were the language of the body. Gestural language was a confessional tongue in which one always admitted something – or had to be seen as admitting something. If words provided the text, gestures revealed the subtext (cf. Roach 1989: 111). The order of truth in verbal language was determined by logic and syntax, which were assumed to be universally valid and reflections of nature; the order of truth in gestural language was determined by nature, which assigned expressions to the passions, and these too were universal to all people. On the one hand, words and gestures (as mind and body) together composed a whole person and were the means through which people represented themselves; on the other hand, words and gestures conjoined as two ways of writing, of marking positions in the visual field.

Ultimately, these equations of writing and gesture derived from a yet deeper equivalency, for they shared in a metaphor that defined human beings: in the late seventeenth and early eighteenth centuries, and into even our own day, discourse drew a fundamental equation between people and texts. This equivalency appears throughout Locke's *Essay Concerning Human Understanding* (first published in 1690), particularly in his depiction of the mind at birth as "white Paper, void of all Characters, without any *Ideas*" (§2.1.2); it is on this blank sheet that sensation and reflection write their texts. The image recurs in many writings of this period. William Congreve used the metaphor in his plays. For example, in *Love For Love* (1695), Valentine tells Angelica, "You are all white, a sheet of lovely spotless Paper, when you first are Born; but you are to be scrawl'd and blotted by every Goose's Quill" (4.1.637–9). Likewise, in *The Double-Dealer* (1694), Lady Plyant complains, "Have I, I say, preserv'd myself, like a fair Sheet of Paper, for you to make a Blot upon?" (2.1.259–60). Following the metaphor's entailment that a lack of writing is mental emptiness, Steele wrote, "It is incredible to think how empty I have in this Time observ'd some Part of the Species to be, what mere Blanks they are when they first come abroad in the Morning, how utterly they are at a Stand till they are set going by some Paragraph in a News-Paper" (*The Spectator* 1965: 4); and Addison described "the Blanks of Society, as being altogether unfurnish'd with Ideas" (Ibid.: 10).[7] Given the equation between person and text, it is scarcely surprising that during this era biography and autobiography (the writing-out of one's life) achieved great popularity. Interestingly, according to the *Oxford English Dictionary*, it was during roughly this period – the early to mid seventeenth century – that the meaning of "character" began to shift from the established senses of a written mark or a description to a newer sense of the human personality.

The notion that printed texts furnish the mind with ideas is closely akin to another common trope of this period, that texts are a sort of mirror in which the reader reads him- or herself. One's response to a text, one's judgment of it, reset or recalled (one might say, reprinted) one's own character. Thus, by reading and reflecting on *The Spectator* (that watchful commentator on behavior), the reader saw a mirror of his or her own inner being. Indeed, the reader's judgment itself received a judgment, an enjoyable correction. This understanding of reading extended to perceptions of people's behavior: one looked at outward signs in order to penetrate into their inner meaning and respond with an emotional reflection. The reflex of seeing behavior, reading character, and responding with spontaneous feeling is, in a nutshell, the theory of sentiment – the principal innovation in drama of the time. Through that reflex the emotions of one person inspired sympathetic feelings in the observer. The reflex of sentiment became the reflection of the observer's inward self.

The dynamic of sentimental response also ensconced the reader in a particular social milieu. *The Tatler* and *The Spectator* took as one of their core themes the idea that family and friends formed circles of affection, in which the individual could retreat and disclose his or her inward self. The club or coffeehouse, which *The Tatler* often invoked through its department headings as sources of "news," and which *The Spectator* recalled in its imaginary Spectator Club, suggested a milieu of urbane sociality and membership – an intimate, benevolent community. Among family and friends, critical or satiric laughter could not be allowed, for it would create division and ill-feeling. The journals set politics outside their doors probably for the same reason. People were expected to enter the community with good-natured benevolence or, at worst, tolerant irony. In fact these papers asserted that it was one's duty to bring ease and pleasure to the rest of one's community.[8] Thus, the journals created an atmosphere inviting the reader to come and partake. Moreover, at least in principle, everyone could join its community. In the papers' ideology, true distinction lay in behavior, thoughts and sentiments, not in social class (*The Tatler* 1987: 69). However, there was more than ideology involved: as I will explain more fully in the next section, the papers adopted several practical strategies in order to connect readers to the publication and to each other, and the ideology emerged from these. In drama, the emphasis on forming an intimate community added pressure toward using sentimental incident and attenuating the battles of wit; theatrically, that desire encouraged the use of the U-shaped auditorium with a lit house in which the ladies and gentlemen in the pit and boxes would observe each other observing each other – not always nicely, to be sure (gentility was among Steele's goals for reforming the theatre), but intimately nevertheless.

Underlying an important array of early eighteenth-century performance strategies and their interpretive frameworks, then, is a handful of image schemas and metaphors drawn from reading and writing – not principally the printed content (though that certainly helped) but the process itself. The image of knowledge was, centrally, that its paradigmatic medium was writing (printed texts). Truth was texts, and texts were truth. Knowledge was nature imprinted on the mind. Minds were texts written on blank paper and available for reading, and reading imprinted on the reader's own text-like mind: to read is to be written upon. Selfhood thus resolved into that inner imprint, and understanding that text required reading the signs that the person necessarily produced in order to divine the inward character. Society became a gathering of readers, whose efforts to read each other drew them into a community of sentiment.

From communication structures to image schemas

Whereas the previous section considered the way image schemas establish performance strategies, this section addresses the underlying forces that cause these schemas to arise. That so many image schemas generating early eighteenth-century performance strategies pertain to writing is no coincidence. The schemas emerged from embodied experiences of communication – not simply the communication technology, but also the entire framework in which a society utilizes, develops, and values the various means of communication. If this assertion is true, then it should follow that during a given historical era, certain image schemas for performance are especially pervasive or serve as presuppositions for other developments. This is similar to the view that there are (or can be) dominant image schemas. The latter position has been argued by Bruce McConachie, who has shown that during the 1950s the schema of containment was prominent in American theatre and drama (McConachie 2001: 569–94; 2003: *passim.*). However, there are also image schemas of a more fundamental sort, which serve as assumptions on which others depend. So, to continue with 1950s American theatre, the special role of the containment image depended in part on underlying assumptions of individualism, "imaginary fourth-wall" staging, etc., all of which are founded on image schemas that dominate by being the conditions of possibility for other images. In other words, image schemas in cultural elaborations are hierarchized: Some are more basic, pervasive and enduring than others, which are more variable or "tactical."

The most fundamental image schemas concern the relationship between the agent who thinks and acts and the world around her – in other words, epistemological and ontological assumptions, such as Cartesianism, empiricism, rationalism, and so forth, particularly as they pertain to concepts of agency. The notion that sensations print concepts upon the mind is one such epistemological image schema. The idea that people are essentially isolated individuals whose social relationships are exterior accessories to their existence (everyone their own Robinson Crusoe) is an ontological image schema concerning the concept of agency. So too is the belief that our true selves are hidden deep within us and that selfhood consists solely of internal development. All three are of course images of containment but more specifically of being self-contained. In this regard, what is striking is not (or not simply) the use of the containment schema, but that what is contained is one's self. This is different from the notion of a body possessing a soul. Agency is understood not outwardly, in terms of its relation to the social and religious order of things, but inwardly, in terms of an individual development and waywardness that identifies the person as "unique."

Image schemas derive from embodied practices (both sensorimotor and social), but their nature is cognitive: they are matters of ideation, perception, and knowledge, which are rooted in the way that the mind engages with the world outside the mind, but they do not invent that world. And because image schemes, which are so fundamental to thought, are knowledge frames that emerge from embodied practices, the embodied practice most closely connected to the process of obtaining knowledge of the world will have an especially important, reflexive role in the further development of knowledge. Now, we develop a huge amount of practical knowledge and skill from direct experience, which is where Lakoff and Johnson place their emphasis; but clearly we do not obtain most of our knowledge *about* the world (discursive knowledge) that way. Few people travel around the world to learn if it is spherical, conduct the experiments necessary to discover that we need to breathe oxygen and not neon, or dig up bones to convince themselves of the theory of evolution. Instead, we listen to other people, read books, watch television, tune in to the radio; and conversely, to provide knowledge to others, we rely on speaking, writing, drawing, and the like. The embodied practice (or set of practices) most deeply connected to the process of obtaining discursive knowledge is communication.

The general theory, then, is that a society's use and deployment of the modes of communication available to it (which may include speech, hand-writing, printing, and electronics) have fundamental cognitive effects. The total system of modes of communication – what I call the communication framework – involves embodied practices of communicating and social rela-tionships toward and between the various modes of communication. As a complex and dynamic whole, the communication framework generates image schemas establishing epistemological and ontological assumptions. Those assumptions in turn are re-embodied in performance, both in the the-atrical practices and in the dramatic text; that is, these assumptions establish the foundations of the performance strategies of the period. I must empha-size that what is at issue is *not* simply the effects of a technology, but also how the technology is used and developed and the roles that it plays within a society. Major effects may arise when the social utilization of a communi-cation technology changes, even though the technology itself does not.

The communication framework of the early eighteenth century introduced a new type of print culture. During this period, the production, distribution, and consumption of printed matter was undergoing a crucial shift: during its first 250 years the printing press was used principally for books and broad-sheets, but at the turn of the eighteenth century, regular periodical publica-tion became economically and logistically sustainable for the first time. Journalistic print culture was born, eventually bringing major social transfor-mations in its wake – the result not of a technological revolution (the print-ing press remained exactly the same), but a revolution in the social use of a well-established technology. Book culture continued unscathed and even benefitted from the rise of the periodical press, but new image schemas and new inflections of old schemas entered cultural dynamics.

By no means am I suggesting that the spoken word lost all importance: on the contrary, oral skills were crucial in many contexts (such as the art of con-versation and maintaining the ties of friendship and family). However, print-ing was taking an increasingly dominant function in the everyday operations of life, administration, law, leisure, and so on. A key indicator of the shift can be found in jurisprudence: the validity of legal claims increasingly depended on documentary evidence; in contrast, during the Middle Ages oral testimony and memorial objects were preferred over always forge-able writings (Clanchy 1979: 23–4, 50–7, 203–7). Fundamentally, truth was now to be found in writing. This idea is considerably broader than the truth accorded to the Bible. During the Middle Ages, the truth of the Bible, Augustine, and Aris-totle derived from the authority of their authorship, which was bestowed on them by God or the accolades of generations; but in most other respects, culture had a decidedly oral character. However, by the early eighteenth century, the truth borne by writings had begun to reside in their very textu-ality. People relied on documents of all sorts to ascertain agreements, estab-lish precedents, determine sources, provide evidence, offer best examples, and serve similar veridical activities. The neo-classical emulation of classical writers' *styles* is another instance of the new weight given to textuality.

Language in general tended to be epitomized by its written form. This contributed to a new emphasis on vision as the source of knowledge. Not only did vision become more crucial to thought, but its qualities altered. Within oral and manuscript cultures, visual imagery necessarily took a mnemonic role, embodied in physical symbols, emblems, allegorical person-ifications, and the pictorial works of the Art of Memory. Acts of imagination secured memory. But in print cultures, this mnemonic role became unneces-sary. Visual phenomena had fewer accretions of allegorical or figural mater-ial; the result was a much more "literal" or naturalistic style of viewing. This is not to say that conventions were absent from the newer style of viewing, or that things seen were not systematically interpreted. "Literal viewing" was conventional, since it was predicated on specific social practices and rela-tionships. But the Enlightenment convention dispensed with communal mnemonic symbolism and introduced individual judgment as the crux of interpretation. Imagery was replaced by pictures. In a similar vein, Foucault distinguishes between the presentation of objects, such as animals as a pro-cessional spectacle during the Renaissance, and the eighteenth-century arrangement of those same things according to a grid or table.[9] In these terms, the table and museum both store information; whereas, the spectacle promotes imagination. In other words, the advent of literal viewing led to the depiction of appearance rather than (allegorical) meaning. This shift to literal viewing provides one reason why verisimilitude became a goal in the-atrical staging.

Another reason for verisimilitude, and in particular the use of perspective scenery, involves the application of the "line" (continuous movement along a path) as print culture's paradigmatic image schema for rational thought, i.e., linearity. Now, it is important to understand how print culture generates linear thinking – and how it doesn't. One can find several theories in the writings of Walter J. Ong, who maintains that "Print situates words in space more relentlessly than writing ever did. Writing moves words from the sound world to a world of visual space, but print locks words into posi-tion in this space. Control of position is everything in print" (Ong 1982: 121). He offers three explanations for why printing has a deeper spatial ori-entation than manuscript. First, the typographic composition process involves locking letters and words into positions in space. Second, printed texts appear to be far more even and regular than manuscripts do, thus offer-ing a notion of repeatable exactitude. Third, textual reference systems – indexes, catalogs, and the like – disengage words or texts from their context and situate them within a continuous, sequentialized space (page number, shelf location, etc.) (Ong 1982: 121–9).

Ong's first explanation is decidedly technologistic: somehow printing technology itself communicates meaning to people who never see it. His second idea is better since it involves a process of reading and interpretation, but it ignores the social determinants of the reading process. Both theories are contradicted by the examples of East Asia: well before Gutenberg, printing was developed in China and movable type in Korea, but neither country is associated with a development of linear culture similar to that of post-Gutenberg Europe. Ong's third reason, however, is highly suggestive and involves both the storage of writing and its utilization. The facts that printed works are easily retained and that they rapidly proliferated created new problems because, once stored, books must be retrieved and the language within them located. This was solved by using writing's symbol system to analyze and organize the literature: indexes use the alphabet and page numbers to locate terms within a text, emphasizing the spatial character of a written work, and library catalogs place that text within a physical architecture of categories. An ordered list of isolated terms directs the reader to a position within a textual space made of words or books.[10]

I can explain this more fully after introducing another crucial image schema. The very existence of ideas was conceptualized by an analogy with writing. When Locke explained how all ideas are constituted out of simple ones, he suggested that this notion could be readily grasped "if we consider how many Words may be made out of the various composition of 24 Letters; or if going one step farther, we will but reflect on the variety of combinations that may be made, with barely one of the above-mentioned *Ideas*, *viz*. Number, whose stock is inexhaustible, and truly infinite: And what a large and immense field, doth Extension alone afford the Mathematician?" (Locke 1690: §2.7.10). Simple ideas are the letters and numerals that combine into the "words," the complex ideas, and ultimately the propositions that comprise thought. Thus, for Locke, writing was a model for both how we come to know things and for the way ideas themselves exist.

This atomistic concept of ideas suggests the possibility of a vast table charting all the possible combinations of simple ideas. It also suggests that this table could be completely and consistently ordered, for both letters and numbers have places within a fixed, unequivocal sequence that can be used to establish progression and hierarchy. Before printing, the alphabet was only occasionally used for organizing words and ideas, and even in the early seventeenth century people had to be instructed in its use. But thereafter, alphabetization was more and more common, as was systematic pagination.[11] The dictionary (increasingly popular in the early eighteenth century) was organized on the basis of letters as atomistic units, placed in a sequence of unit-combinations, *A* preceding *B*, *Aa* preceding *Ab* but both classified under *A*, and so on. The alphabet could thus present the possibility of, and offer a model for, placing knowledge into a comprehensive system providing sequence and subdivision, order and taxonomy. And knowledge was not just "placed" into that system: the structure of knowledge itself was like writing's, consisting of atomistic signs that were combined and put into a sequence to form more complex ideas. Locke's analogy between ideas and numbers further intimates not only that ideas could be ordered and measured, but that their relationships could be calculated. In various ways, then, letters and numerals encouraged spatialization and provided means whereby space could be divided, ordered, and measured. Visualized, this orderly and measured conceptual space consists of a grid and elevations stretching into the distance. Its rationality was ratified by the systematic nature of alphabetic writing and the truth borne by textuality as such; in other words, internal consistency was the mark of veracity and logicality.

On this model, then, linear thinking (that is, the line or path as the paradigmatic image schema for reasoning itself) emerged not directly from physical or technological characteristics of the printed page – much less the printing press – but rather from social experiences of using writing in particular ways and from the social primacy given to print. But thus far I have considered print culture generally: there were, however, additional features specific to journalistic print culture when newspapers and magazines entered cultural life. As noted earlier, this development involved no technological changes, only changes in how the technology was used and how its products were distributed and circulated. The new features are among the ones described earlier as part of early eighteenth-century performance strategies: an emphasis on pathos and inward struggles, the revelatory gesture, the reflexive perception underlying the sentimental response, the intimate and benevolent community. How did journalistic print culture foster such conceptual frameworks?

The key pragmatic distinction between books and periodicals lies in their methods of distribution. Unlike books, periodicals are distributed rapidly across a geographical region (in this period, usually a city), and are also distributed across time (such as daily or weekly). For all practical purposes, books were bought and read one person at a time without any coordination; in contrast, the periodical press was the first mass medium, and it faced certain challenges in making that mass into a public. For their economic survival, the periodical had to find ways to maintain its identity and create a readership that was unified across space, joining readers under one common umbrella; and unified across time, preventing each evanescent issue from acting as a wholly discrete publication. The most common strategy was to give the periodical a subject matter or general theme of recurring interest (business reports, advances in the natural sciences, scandals, and high society), and within that scope include a potpourri or "mosaic" of items, as if to present a snapshot or cross-section of the ever-changing present – so to speak, a slice of life.

The Tatler and *The Spectator* lie at the intersection of the changes in print culture and the changes in theatre, and not just because both were edited and in good part written by Richard Steele, whose play *The Conscious Lovers* was the greatest box-office smash of the early eighteenth century. In order to compensate for the loss of direct interchange among their readers, the two papers introduced a twist in the strategy for securing readership that profoundly shaped journalistic print culture: *The Tatler* and *The Spectator* strove to create the sense of an intimate, benevolent community. As I noted above, the two journals emphasized the idea that family and friends formed circles of affection allowing personal self-disclosure. But the journals also strove to generate a sense of community between the readers and the journal by incorporating letters to the editor. More than a note from a reader, these letters of personal opinion or experience could expand on topics recently considered or send the editors into a new direction; they could reply to the essays or to other letters; the editors could incorporate the letters in various ways and even directly respond to them. Letters came from all sorts of people, and many were personally revealing or even confessional in nature. The letters made the public presentation of the private person fundamental to social interchange. They were, in a way, fragments of autobiography. Michael Ketcham observes that the sheer variety of viewpoints in these letters itself modeled a tolerant community (Ketcham 1985: 11, 125–32).

Thus through both discursive and pragmatic means, *The Tatler* and *The Spectator* fostered a sense that within their pages an intimate community came to life and offered its readers the opportunity to enter its social and emotional circles.[12] The periodicals were preoccupied with observing people's behaviors and manners, and through the mechanism of letters to the editor, readers and writers observed each other and were observed, both of them subject to social judgments and understandings. More than a judgment, the reader had an emotional response of his or her own, a reflection prompted by a perception. However, perception (as reading) was the key source of knowledge; perception (as writing) printed upon the mind; one's own mind had then to be read, generating an emotional response that was written upon the body and in gesture; and so the sequence continues. Thus, we arrive at the cycle of sentimental response, in which the emotions and behavior of one person produced sympathetic feelings in the observer, and the reflex of sentiment reflected the observer's inward self. By reading and reflecting on *The Spectator*, the reader looked into a mirror of his or her own inner being.[13]

Circulating throughout these varied discursive strategies, then, are a few basic tenets generated by print culture, especially during its journalistic phase: knowledge comes from "reading the signs," an image schema generalized to mean perception (especially vision); words are atomistic units that in the aggregate represent the mind but must form a linearly ordered and internally consistent sequence to do so; the logic (grammar) of such ordering is public and universal, even if minds are fundamentally private; and these private minds form a community by reading one another, in person or in text, a concept founded on the imaginary community formed by newspapers. Connecting all of these ideas is an underlying methodological individualism, paradigmatically based on the image of a solitary, silent reader.

Communication frameworks, image schemas, and theatre historiography

The communication framework (a society's overall system of using the various means of communication) involves embodied experiences that generate image schemas; the latter play a particularly central role in the development of theatrical performance strategies. The communication framework and its changes explain several matters in theatre history: the formation of the dominant performance strategies of a particular period; why some artistic options are explored but not others; how audiences made sense of performances and understood them as communicating something about the world; and why performance strategies remain relatively stable for a time and then undergo major, even drastic, shifts.

If performance strategies develop on the basis of the communication framework, then changes in communication methods must sooner or later cause changes in performance practices. *How* soon depends on a variety of issues, but the broad outline of theatre history does seem to correspond to the history of communication frameworks (better, certainly, than it matches other major social changes, like economic transformations). Greek tragedy shows traces of a societal "collision" between the traditional oral culture and a literate culture within Athens. Among the traces are a stylistic switch from stock phrases toward colloquial speech and with it the replacement of the epic dactyls by iambic verse; a change in the organization of narrative from episodic to linear (or "pyramidal") form; a progressive shift of emphasis from the chorus to the protagonist; and a slowly growing number of characters (Nellhaus 1989: 53–71).

Medieval theatre was also born from a manuscript culture but in a different societal context. The Church maintained a powerful connection between a particular text (the Bible) and the laity (largely, but decreasingly, illiterate) through its homiletic tradition. Oral culture was thus constantly embedded within manuscript culture and vice versa. The result was an orientation around symbolism and allegory, which were manifested in medieval theatre in allegorical characters, patterns of biblical figures and fulfillments, trade symbolism, and various elements of costuming and staging.

Print culture began in Europe in the mid-fifteenth century; by the end of the sixteenth, it had thoroughly permeated not just practical life but also discursive strategies and performance strategies in their wake: outdoor theatre moved inside, lost the *platea*, sprouted perspective scenery, and largely replaced characters that were biblical, allegorical, or civic (stereo)types with ones that were increasingly individual. Verisimilitude was being born. As I have shown, print culture altered somewhat with the rise of the periodical press in the late seventeenth century. Starting in the mid-nineteenth century, the Western world experienced successive waves of innovation in communication technologies: the telegraph, typewriter, radio, sound recording, motion picture, telephone, television, and computer network. These have injected all sorts of new dynamics into the communication framework, producing various ruptures in the dominant cultural paradigms. The upshot theatrically has been a broad eclecticism in performance strategies that has dominated (insofar as any eclecticism can dominate) the stage since the 1940s – though in general, some form of psychological realism has prevailed and prevails still.[14] There has scarcely been time for a new framework of communication to stabilize, much less establish a new set of fundamental image schemas for knowledge: at that level, Western societies are still essentially print cultures.

The process whereby one set of knowledge-paradigms supplants another is not simple. The new doesn't merely become more frequent as the old fades from memory. On the contrary, as the new model takes form, it precipitates a severe problem in how to determine the nature of knowledge. One might call this conflict a crisis of representation, provided "representation" is understood as concerning not a semiology of purely internal relations but rather the relationship between sign, mind, and world (within the context of intersubjective communication); and so it is a crisis in knowledge and in the image schemas that model that relationship. Thus, "representation" must be understood in the sense that invokes the otherness of being. Theatre performs this crisis of representation by becoming (so to speak) a problem to itself. This is one reason why, during major shifts in the communication framework, various forms of metatheatricality (especially plays within plays) tend to appear. But a crisis in representation is also a crisis in agency: if, as has been well demonstrated, agency is in significant part constituted discursively, a transformation in communication practices necessarily disrupts social understandings of agency and action. Because knowledge requires a knower, image schemas of knowledge are always closely connected to image schemas of a knowing or experiencing self who interacts with the world around it. Theatre itself is a model of agency – more precisely, social agency, i.e., the agent as enabled, constrained, and ensconced within social structures (Nellhaus 2000: 12–20).

Thus we return to the concept of performance strategies, which I described at the beginning of this article as a system or orientation through which agents adopt theatrical approaches to try to solve problems (at least discursively or symbolically). I hinted earlier at the significance to be given to models of agency (another way to conceptualize agential strategies) when I noted the individualism underpinning the discursive and performance strategies of the early eighteenth century. One aspect of that notion is an understanding of selfhood as being thoroughly interior. In the early eighteenth century, this involved an effort to confirm someone's (or one's own) inner moral worth, and the beginnings of psychological realism as dramatic emphasis shifted from plot to character. By the mid-1950s, the sense of personal depth had developed in the United States into "Method" acting, which emphasized the character's complex inner life and psychological intensity (sometimes meaning a "powderkeg" type of character or acting) (McConachie 2001: 592–3). The image schema of containment pervades both modes of characterization but with varying inflections as the precise concept of interior selfhood changes over the years. But other sorts of characterization also appeared, particularly during the first decades of the twentieth century, such as the expressionist character, which does not so much contain a self as have a self that's being contained – often by forces well beyond its control – rendering it individualistic in its weakness and isolation. In short, specific images can be layered onto a foundational schema as a sort of tactic within a general strategy. Such adjustments to characterization are also adjustments to a concept of agency that nevertheless endures for much longer swaths of history. In this case, agency has become a question of inwardness, personal or psychological conditions and processes, and, in a word, subjectivity.

Philosophy and the social organization of image schemas

The communication framework's generation of image schemas explains much about theatre history, but it also provides explanations for two other matters. In several chapters of *Philosophy in the Flesh*, Lakoff and Johnson analyze the metaphoric bases of various philosophies. However, although they discuss each philosophy in chronological order, they don't attempt any sort of historical explanation – the philosophies sometimes seem as though they are independent, historically contemporaneous positions from which one can pick and choose. But philosophies of science (or more broadly, ontology and epistemology) undergo sometimes massive transformations across history roughly in the same manner theatre does; and because the image schemas underlying performance strategies also underlie other discursive strategies, changes in communication practices explain several aspects of philosophical shifts, including their timing and general direction. I've already sketched one such analysis in my discussion of the atomistic and linear thinking that emerged in the early eighteenth century; I should add that as print culture has endured, so too have many of those conceptual features, primarily as varieties of empiricism and positivism (but also in their Romantic and poststructuralist opponents).

But we can extend the historical analysis backward, first by considering Lakoff and Johnson's analysis of the metaphors underlying Cartesian philosophy. They find that "the most fundamental metaphor Descartes uses is the commonplace Knowing is Seeing metaphor" (Lakoff and Johnson 1999: 393). The Knowing is Seeing metaphor itself is many centuries old, and can be found for instance in Plato (Ibid.: 85, 366–9). With Descartes, however, it assumes a new position, becoming the centerpiece of his philosophy, and its entailments are elaborated far more fully. Concomitantly, the (dare I say) focal question of philosophy becomes the nature of Knowledge. Before then, however, the key question concerned the nature of Being: nearly all of the major metaphors that Lakoff and Johnson find in classical Greek philosophers describe or define essence, but from Descartes on, the main role for the theory of essences is to define the essence of human beings as the capacity for reason. The importance and problematization of Being in pre-Cartesian philosophy squares with the strength of oral culture, which invested physical objects with meaning, veridical functions, and other cultural powers. In contrast, the

Knowing is Seeing metaphor in philosophy since Descartes takes its new centrality from the role of writing as the primary source of discursive knowledge
(knowledge about the world). Added support for this assessment comes from
what Lakoff and Johnson identify as the second most important metaphor in
Descartes: Thinking is Mathematical Calculation (Ibid.: 405–6). It too goes
as far back as the classical Greeks, but it assumed a new salience within print
culture: numeration, along with alphabetization, established the model of
knowing as the arrangement of ideas in an orderly, linear sequence. In short,
changes in communication frameworks not only introduce new metaphors
but also reorganize the roles played by older and, in some cases, quite basic
metaphors. The higher-level social structure for communication sets the conditions for the operation of older and lower-level cognitive structures through
which we interact with the world – it poses the questions which we strive to
answer by marshaling existing experience-based metaphors and developing
new ones. Models of agency are in part strategies for answering those questions. And performance strategies, especially approaches to acting and characterization, provide models of agency.

Finally, the theory I have outlined also fills a lacuna in Lakoff and
Johnson's analysis. One shortcoming of their theory is that the image
schemas and metaphors they analyze often appear as givens, and people's
choices among them within philosophy (and other fields of thought) are a
bit arbitrary. For example, the metaphor "theories are buildings" does
indeed underlie many phrases, such as "theory-construction," "supporting
evidence," and "building a conceptual framework" (Johnson 1987: 105). But
why buildings rather than cakes, sewing projects, or farming? Clearly there
are social determinants behind this and many other metaphors and image
schemas. While Lakoff and Johnson acknowledge such social determinants
and maintain that one key aspect of image schemas is their shared, public
character, they never delve into the nature of social and cultural determination and instead derive the shared and public character of image schemas
primarily from the human body (Ibid.: 175, 190). This gap invites essentialism or at the least a kind of decontextualization.

To avoid that danger, cognitive science must be incorporated into a more
socially oriented theory such as the one I have offered – not to explain all
metaphors (a social theory cannot explain metaphors that are strictly sensorimotor in origin), but to explain how some metaphors emerge and to explain
certain relations among metaphors. Such explanations are especially important for understanding metaphors about primarily mental activities and
high-level abstractions. Within the Lakoff and Johnson theory, there seems
little to govern which image schemas apply to such things and which ones
don't. But the sort of metaphors that describe the nature of thought, being,
and social agency are not arbitrary. Instead, the metaphors for those ideas are
in large part motivated (though not determined) by the communication
practices through which we obtain knowledge about the world around us
and about ourselves. That explanation begins to provide cognitive science

with the kind of social analysis it needs, because much as the mind develops through embodied interactions with the world, it also develops through interactions with people.

The shifts that theatre undergoes over history are not merely changes in style. Far from being arbitrary, these transformations are motivated – they embody in performance the image schemas that emerge from communication practices. Such image schemas are generative mechanisms whereby people develop more or less coherent performance strategies. Moreover, performance strategies are intimately linked both to philosophy and to concepts of agency. The latter lie at the heart of stage performance. Theatre is a model of social agency, including the agent's embeddedness between structures and discourses, and the latter are themselves conjoined in a particular social structure: the communication framework. In short, communication practices provide the foundations from which we develop our ways of performing, our understanding of our relations with the world, and our perception of what it is to be an agent within it.

Notes

1 McConachie's work (1993, 1994, 2001, 2003) is particularly extensive.
2 Philosophically, my argument is grounded in critical realism, which maintains that knowledge is socially produced yet we can in fact know the reality beyond our discourse, in part precisely because there is a difference between existence and our ideas about existence. Lakoff and Johnson's "embodied realism" takes very similar stands on the fundamental issues of epistemology and ontology. Critical realism, however, has a considerably stronger grasp of social dynamics and a more sophisticated ontological analysis. For further discussion see Nellhaus 1993; 2004; and forthcoming.
3 Strictly speaking, description and explanation are scarcely so discrete, but there does need to be a preliminary identification of the object of study.
4 Cibber 1968: 133, 270; *The Tatler* 1987: no. 89; *The Spectator* 1965: no. 502; Gildon 1710: 38.
5 *The Tatler* 1987: nos 66, 115, 182; *The Spectator* 1965: nos 38, 334, 518; Gildon 1710: 25, 41, 51; Victor 1733: 8–29, 32–3. See also Roach 1976: 189–205; and Downer 1966: 332–5.
6 See, for example, Gildon 1710: 87–8; and *The Spectator* 1965: no. 334.
7 Congreve 1967. See also Neill 1988: 10, 17 n. 22. Although the metaphor turns up in earlier texts, it appears to be more common after 1690; and the earlier metaphors often refer to the physical materials of books or the process of reading signs; whereas, the later ones generally focus on their textual nature and the inscribability of the mind and character.
8 On the intimate community in *The Spectator*, see Ketcham 1985: 3, 5, 17–18, 51, 63–64, 77, 161.
9 Foucault 1970: 131. On visualization in orally oriented cultures, see also Havelock 1963: 187–9.
10 Kernan attributes a similar importance to the library as a spatial "paradigm of knowledge": see Kernan 1987: 246–58.
11 See Eisenstein (1979: 89–107), whose discussion also considers the developments in indexing. Cohen (1977: 146 n. 29) similarly notes that "The alphabet itself was recognized as a conceptual tool in the seventeenth century."

12 Where the possibility of forming an intimate community was unavailable, another strategy emerged, initially in the Americas. From its beginnings as a simple venue for market information and official notices, the newspaper developed into an assemblage of articles and reports representing a "day in the life" of a particular region or country (and its relationship with other places), unified only by the coincidence of events on a particular date – a link that lies in the imagination – and the collective ceremony of a community reading it each day. Thus, the newspaper helped nurture "imagined communities" possessing a consciousness of nationhood. See Anderson 1991: 32–6, 61–5.

13 On the theory of sentiments, see Ketcham 1985: 13, 32, 41–3, 49–50, 53, 63. Ballad opera might be interpreted as the converse of sentimental drama: rather than draw together an audience through an emotional union with the characters in their pathos, they unite the audience by satirizing social elements that undermine its cohesion.

14 In an analysis that gracefully interweaves cultural study, cognitive science, and mode of communication theory, McConachie argues that radio had a major impact on the image schemas undergirding American drama in the 1940s and 1950s, and that television had likewise affected the plays of the subsequent decades (see McConachie 2003: 28–38, 48–50, 85–6, 283–5). McConachie does not thoroughly analyze modes of communication as systems of social practices and relationships, and at times his argument even flirts with technological determinism, but his point may be correct for all that.

References

Anderson, B. (1991) *Imagined Communities: Reflections on the Origin and Spread of Nationalism*, London: Verso.

Cibber, C. (1968) *An Apology for the Life of Colley Cibber*, ed. B.R.S. Fone, Ann Arbor, MI: University of Michigan Press.

Clanchy, M.T. (1979) *From Memory to Written Record, England 1066–1307*, London: Edward Arnold.

Cohen, M. (1977) *Sensible Words: Linguistic Practice in England, 1640–1785*, Baltimore, MD: Johns Hopkins University Press.

Congreve, W. (1967) *The Complete Plays of William Congreve*, ed. H. Davis, Chicago, IL: University of Chicago Press.

Downer, A.S. (1966) "Nature to Advantage Dressed: Eighteenth-Century Acting," in Loftis, J. (ed.) *Restoration Drama: Modern Essays in Criticism*, New York: Oxford University Press.

Eisenstein, E. (1979) *The Printing Press as an Agent of Change*, Cambridge: Cambridge University Press.

Foucault, M. (1970) *The Order of Things: An Archaeology of the Human Sciences*, New York: Vintage.

Gildon, C. (1710) *The Life of Thomas Betterton, the Late Eminent Tragedian*, London: Robert Gosling.

Havelock, E.A. (1963) *Preface to Plato*, Cambridge, MA: Harvard University Press, Belknap Press.

Johnson, M. (1987) *The Body in the Mind: The Bodily Basis of Meaning, Imagination, and Reason*, Chicago, IL: University of Chicago Press.

Kernan, A. (1987) *Printing Technology, Letters and Samuel Johnson*, Princeton, NJ: Princeton University Press.

Ketcham, M.G. (1985) *Transparent Designs: Reading, Performance, and Form in the "Spectator" Papers*, Athens, GA: University of Georgia Press.

Lakoff, G. and Johnson, M. (1980) *Metaphors We Live By*, Chicago, IL: University of Chicago Press.

—— (1999) *Philosophy in the Flesh: The Embodied Mind and Its Challenge to Western Thought*, New York: Basic Books.

Locke, J. (1690; reprinted 1975) *An Essay Concerning Human Understanding*, ed. P.H. Nidditch, Oxford: Oxford University Press, Clarendon.

Loftis, J.C. (1959) *Steele at Drury Lane*, Berkeley, CA: University of California Press.

McConachie, B. (1993) "Metaphors we act by: kinesthetics, cognitive psychology, and historical structures," *Journal of Dramatic Theory and Criticism*, 8(2): 23–45.

—— (1994) "Approaching performance history through cognitive psychology," *Assaph*, 10: 113–22.

—— (2001) "Doing things with image schemas: the cognitive turn in theatre studies and the problem of experience for historians," *Theatre Journal*, 53: 569–94.

—— (2003) *American Theater in the Culture of the Cold War: Producing and Contesting Containment, 1947–1962*, Iowa City, IA: University of Iowa Press.

Neill, M. (1988) "Horned beasts and china oranges: reading the signs in *The Country Wife*," *Eighteenth Century Life*, 12: 3–17.

Nellhaus, T. (1989) "Literacy, tyranny, and the invention of Greek tragedy," *Journal of Dramatic Theory and Criticism*, 3(2): 53–71.

—— (1993) "Science, history, theatre: theorizing in two alternatives to positivism," *Theatre Journal*, 45: 505–27.

—— (2000) "Social ontology and (meta)theatricality: reflexions on performance and communication in history," *Journal of Dramatic Theory and Criticism*, 14(2): 12–18.

—— (2004) "From embodiment to agency: cognitive science, critical realism, the framework of communication," *Journal of Critical Realism*, 3(1): 103–32.

—— (forthcoming) "Critical Realism and Performance Strategies," in Krasner, D. and Saltz, D. (eds) *Staging Philosophy: New Approaches to Theater and Performance*, Ann Arbor, MI: University of Michigan Press.

Ong, W.J. (1982) *Orality and Literacy*, London: Methuen.

Peters, J.S. (1990) *Congreve, the Drama, and the Printed Word*, Stanford, CA: Stanford University Press.

Roach, J. (1976) "Cavaliere Nicolini: London's first opera star," *Educational Theatre Journal*, 28: 189–205.

—— (1989) "Power's Body: The Inscription of Morality as Style," in Postlewait, T. and McConachie, B. (eds) *Interpreting the Theatrical Past: Essays in the Historiography of Performance*, Iowa City, IA: University of Iowa Press.

The Spectator (1965) ed. D.F. Bond, Oxford: Oxford University Press, Clarendon Press.

The Tatler (1987) ed. D.F. Bond, Oxford: Oxford University Press, Clarendon Press.

Victor, B. (1733) *Memoirs of the Life of Barton Booth, Esq.; With his Character*, London: John Watts.

Section 2

Drama and cognition

4 Essentialism and comedy

A cognitive reading of the motif of mislaid identity in Dryden's *Amphitryon* (1690)

Lisa Zunshine

This essay uses as its starting point a striking correspondence between two literary works coming from very dissimilar cultural backgrounds and written for completely different audiences. The first is a short children's poem by a twentieth-century Polish poet Yulian Tuvim (1894–1953) and the second is a late-seventeenth-century comedy *Amphitryon; or the Two Sosias*, John Dryden's adaptation (1690) of the ancient Greek legend of the conception of Hercules, made previously famous by such luminaries of the stage as Plautus and Molière. Incommensurable as these texts appear to be, both contain the same curious incident – indeed, Tuvim's poem contains nothing else – in which a character is persuaded that if somebody looks exactly like him, or even just wears his clothing, it must be him. Both persuasion scenes are quite amusing, and it is only afterwards, when one tries to figure out what is really going on in these quirky variations on the "twin" theme, that they may appear a bit unnerving. In what follows, I speculate on the possible cognitive-psychological underpinnings of both such amusement and such uneasiness. My ultimate goal is to consider this ambivalent emotional reaction when prompted by the *actual theatrical performance* as opposed to the same reaction arising in response to *reading* about the adventures of twins. If the workings of certain deep-seated cognitive proclivities inform our thinking about personal identity, how does the *physical presence* of the strikingly similar bodies on stage engage and experiment with such proclivities?

I begin by outlining the plots of Tuvim's poem and Dryden's play (the latter as compared to Plautus's and Molière's earlier versions) and attempting to reconstruct their respective audiences' immediate responses to the naïveté of the protagonists. In this part I also introduce the question that has pursued me since I first considered those responses: What shared assumptions about personal identity make those peculiar persuasion scenes both comprehensible and funny for audiences that have practically nothing in common? The second part lays out the theoretical background that should allow me to attempt to answer that question in the third part. Here I discuss several recent studies by cognitive-evolutionary scientists, including Scott Atran, Lawrence Hirschfeld, and Susan Gelman, that explore cognitive biases underlying our tendency to essentialize natural kinds – that is, the tendency to perceive natural kinds as having some invisible but enduring "essences" – the same biases that are arguably recruited in our reasoning about personal identities. Although one cannot do justice to these extensive works in one section of an essay, I do try to cover as much ground as possible and show how powerfully such research resonates with many issues at the foreground of contemporary cultural studies. The reason I go to some length in doing so is that I hope to persuade my readers that a cognitive interpretation of *Amphitryon*, inspired by the work of Atran and his colleagues, represents just one example of the remarkable interdisciplinary potential of this approach.

The literary texts that I use in this part to illustrate the points made by cognitive scientists include books by such authors as J.K. Rowling, Marge Piercy, and Michail Bulgakov, not immediately connected to either Dryden or Tuvim. The connection should become clearer as I move to the third part, in which I return to *Amphitryon* and show how this play's suggestive experimentation with the issue of personal identity builds on the same implicit essentialist assumptions that we use to make sense of a variety of magical or near-magical transformations of people and objects that take place in *Harry Potter*; *He, She and It*; and *The Dog's Heart*. In the fourth, closing part, I discuss the difference between the novelistic treatment of the topic of mislaid identity and its specifically theatrical incarnation. Drawing on literary-historical research into stage representations of twins, I particularly consider the ways in which the embodied nature of theatrical performance – the physical presence of actors – provides the crucial perceptual input for our essentialism-informed construction of the ever-elusive personal identity.

The first impressions: reading Tuvim, watching *Amphitryon*

I do not recall exactly how old I was when I first read Tuvim's poem, translated from Polish to Russian, and immediately learned it by heart, something that came easily to me in my Russian-speaking days. I know that I could not have been older than seven, for I had not started school yet (in Soviet Russia, children didn't begin formal schooling until they were seven), and I still remember with what amused superiority I considered the poem's protagonist, a young boy named Yurgán, who wakes up one morning and realizes that he cannot "find Yurgán." Note that Tuvim does not say that "Yurgán cannot find himself," or something along these lines, because that would complicate his little narrative with the more "adult" overtones of existential angst and difficulties of self-realization, and Tuvim does not seem to be interested in that. His Yurgán quite literally cannot find the physical entity known as Yurgán. He searches the bed, he looks around the house – nothing. He runs into the street where he meets a neighbor, to whom he complains that he "cannot find Yurgán." The neighbor replies, "Look here, you odd fellow, you are wearing Yurgán's jacket! See that torn pocket? You yourself are Yurgán!" (translation mine). The poem ends here with the boy happy about finally locating Yurgán. Thus the apparently absurd initial problem is resolved through winding up absurdity to a higher pitch: whoever wears Yurgán's jacket must be Yurgán.

The little poem has remained dormant in my Russian-speaking subconscious until, a couple of years ago, I came across Plautus's 200 BC tragicomedy *Amphitruo* featuring a comic character named Sosia, who also comes to believe that he has "mislaid" himself. If Yurgán checks for his missing self in bed and around the house, Sosia suspects that he left himself "by the harbor" – giving us a grownup version of Yurgán, whose world has significantly expanded, offering more places in which to "mislay" himself, but whose reasoning powers seem to have remained peculiarly narrow and thus vulnerable to outlandish suggestions.

Here is how Plautus's Sosia is led to suspect that he has forgotten himself somewhere else. The Theban general, Amphitryon, has been away from his wife, Alcmena, fighting the army of Teleboeans. The night he is supposed to return home, victorious, Jupiter assumes his shape and seduces Alcmena, impregnating her with Hercules. While Jupiter is busy with Alcmena, he employs another god, Mercury, to keep away Amphitryon's slave – Sosia – who is coming to inform Alcmena about the approach of her husband. Mercury replicates Jupiter's feat of impersonation; he takes on the form of Sosia and tells the real Sosia that *he* is an impostor who has no business hanging around Amphitryon's household. Confounded, the real Sosia begins to mull over the arguments of his assertive double:

> Sosia. Certainly when I consider
> This guy's looks and my own as well –
> For many's the time I've looked at myself
> In the mirror – we are exactly alike.
> He is wearing a cap and a cloak
> Exactly like the ones I wear;
> Legs and feet and height and haircut,
> Eyes, nose, lips – they're all alike;
> Cheeks and chin and beard and neck –
> Remarkable similarity!
>   (Passage and Mautinbaud 1974: 59–60)

Mercury substantiates his claims to Sosia's identity with heavy beatings, and Sosia is finally persuaded:

> Sosia. All right, all right, I'll go! Immortal
> Gods, I beg you, tell me this:
> How did I get mislaid? What happened?

> How did I lose my former shape?
> Did I forget myself and leave
> Myself down by the harbor there?
> This fellow certainly has my shape –
> Or at least the shape I used to have.
>
> (Ibid.: 60)

Plautus's play has gone through numerous adaptations in the last 22 centuries, including the anonymous English translation of the early 1600s *The Birthe of Hercules*; Jean Rotrou's (1638), Molière's (1668), Dryden's (1690), Johann Daniel Falk's (1804) and Henrich von Kleist's (1806) respective *Amphitryons*, Jean Giraudoux's *Amphitryon 38* (1929), Georg Kaiser's *Amphitryon Doubled* (1944), and others. Sometimes only parts from the original play have been used, as it was with Shakespeare's *The Comedy of Errors*, which is based primarily on Plautus's *Menaechmi* but borrows the scene in which Amphitryon is denied entrance to his own house to portray Antipholus of Ephesus raging by the barred door of the house he shares with his wife Adriana. On the whole, both the original legend, which had already been popular by 500 BC, and Plautus's rendition of it spawned an "astonishingly long line of … dramatic development" (Passage and Mautinbaud 1974: Preface, n.p.).

Dryden's play, considered by Earl Miner "one of the unrecognized masterpieces of English comedy" (quoted in Milhous and Hume 1985: 201), is based on Rotrou's and Molière's *Amphitryons*, but it departs from them significantly, expanding, in particular, the theme of the comic predicaments of Sosia (hence the new subtitle, the "Two Sosias"). We learn from Judith Milhous and Robert D. Hume's reconstruction of selected late seventeenth-century theatrical productions that in the first cast of Dryden's comedy the role of Sosia was played by James Nokes. Here is Colley Cibber's description of Nokes's typical demeanor in a comic role:

> The lauder the Laugh the graver was his Look upon it; and sure, the ridiculous Solemnity of his Features were [sic] enough to set a whole Bench of Bishops into a Titter. … In the ludicrous Distresses which, by the Laws of Comedy, Folly is often involv'd in, he sunk into such a mixture of piteous Pusillanimity and a Consternation so ruefully ridiculous and inconsolable, that when he had shook you to a Fatigue of Laughter it became a moot point whether you ought not to have pity'd him. When he debated any matter by himself, he would shut up his Mouth with a dumb studious Powt, and roll his full Eye into such a vacant Amazement, such a palpable Ignorance of what to think of it, that his silent Perplexity (which would sometimes hold him several Minutes) gave your Imagination as full a Content as the most absurd thing he could say upon it.
>
> (Ibid.: 217–18)

We can only imagine then with what delicious "mixture of piteous Pusilla-nimity and Consternation" Nokes's Sosia "debated . . . by himself" who he is or is not, all the while surveying surreptitiously the belligerent claimant to his identity:

> Sosia. He is damnable like me, that's certain. Imprimis: there's the patch upon my nose, with a pox to him. Item: a very foolish face with a long chin at end on't. Item: one pair of shambling legs with two splay feet belonging to them. And, *summa totalis*: from head to foot, all my bodily apparel.
>
> (Dryden 2001: 2.305–10)

Faced with such compelling evidence, Dryden's Sosia has no choice but to admit sorrowfully that this stranger *is* himself – "there is no denying it." "But what am I, then?" asks the befuddled character as he feels his identity slipping away from him: "For my mind gives me I am somebody still, if I knew but who I were" (Ibid.: 2.311–13).

In all these cases, the humor of the situation stems from the naïveté of the protagonists who are willing to accept that their identities are defined by external characteristics, such as a jacket with a torn pocket, the shape of "legs and feet," "height and haircut," or a "patch upon [the] nose" covering a venereal sore. We find the attitude of Tuvim's Yurgán as well as of Plautus's and Dryden's respective Sosias funny (the latter additionally set off by Nokes's brilliant acting) because it is clear to us that they really *should know better*. But – and here I pose a seemingly simple question, on whose deceptive simplicity my whole argument will turn – on what grounds should they know better? What is it that I knew as a preschooler, and the readers of Plautus were aware of two thousand years ago, and the Restoration audiences immediately recognized as belonging to the jurisprudence of "the Laws of Comedy," but that Yurgán and Sosia so spectacularly fail to grasp?

To answer this question I need a conceptual framework that can do two things simultaneously. On the one hand, it should allow me to cut across disparate historical milieus – for how much really does a child from twenti-eth-century provincial Russia have in common with an adult theatregoer in late-seventeenth-century London? On the other hand, it should be sensitive to culture-specific differences, for at no point can it reduce the cultural meaning of one representation to another. With such requirements in mind, I cannot think of a better framework than the one offered by the recent cog-nitive-evolutionary research on essentialism, although I invite my readers to disagree with me and come up with an alternative, if only because "my" explanation involves the liability of a many-page theoretical buildup from a discipline relatively unfamiliar to literary critics.

Essentialism and cognitive-evolutionary psychology[1]

I first came across the research on possible cognitive underpinnings of essentialism in Scott Atran's 1990 book *Cognitive Foundations of Natural History: Toward an Anthropology of Science.* Building on years of cross-cultural research by his colleagues and his wide-ranging study of folk biologies, Atran discusses the important difference in our conceptualization of natural kinds and of artifacts. Already, between the ages of three and four, children think of natural kinds (plants, animals, and people) in terms of their underlying, largely immutable and invisible "essences" (Atran 1990: 83) and of artifacts in terms of their "function."[2] The tendency to essentialize natural kinds does not disappear as children grow up, but rather expands and diversifies its application. In fact, it is this tendency that has allowed people all over the world to develop and maintain for thousands of years complicated systems of folk taxonomies, paradoxically both making possible the advent of contemporary scientific taxonomy and also holding science back by exaggerating, in Ernst Mayr's words, the "constancy of taxa and the sharpness of the gaps separating them" (Ibid.: 84).

The experiments that investigate children's capacity for essentializing are often structured as a series of transformations inflicted on an animal or artifact. Since the time of publication of Atran's book, such experiments have been replicated thousands of times in a broad variety of cultures, and they have become increasingly probing and complex. In a traditional experimental set-up, a child is presented with a toy animal or a picture of an animal wearing a very convincing "costume" of a different species or with some body parts missing or altered. When asked to comment on the species of the hybrid animal, for example, on a skunk wearing a zebra "outfit," even three-year-old children judge a skunk to be a skunk. The skunk seems to retain that underlying "skunkness" that makes him different from other animals. A tiger without legs is still a tiger, not a new species of animal. In other words, as the cognitive psychologist Paul Bloom observes, "In a child's mind, to be a specific animal is more than to have a certain appearance, it is to have a certain internal structure. It is only when the transformations are described as changing the *innards* of the animals – presumably their essences – that children, like adults, take them as changing the type of animal itself" (Bloom 2004: 47).

Children respond quite differently when it comes to evaluating the presumed "essence" of artifacts. A log, for example, is not judged as having any specific quality of "logness" about it; in fact, it seems to change its "identity" quite often: *depending on its current function*, it can be perceived as firewood, a bench, or a battering ram.[3] Another artifact, a cup with a sawed-off bottom, becomes a bracelet or a cookie-cutter – there is nothing that is perceived as intrinsically "cupful" about it. The experiments have demonstrated again and again that "transformations that radically change the appearance of an object result in judgments of category change for artifacts but stability for animals, implying that animals – but not artifacts – retain some essential qualities that persist despite external appearance changes" (Gelman 2003: 246). And indeed, one can think of a variety of everyday situations in which we relatively easily transcend our idea of what a certain artifact "really" is by changing its function. Even as I am typing this and drinking tea, I am using an old computer diskette as a coaster, and as far as I am concerned, it "is" a coaster now.

What I am presenting here is by necessity a sketchy and simplified account of a series of complex and lengthy arguments. To do justice to them, to think of their further application, or to quarrel with them, my readers will have to go "to the source." There is one point, however, that I need to make clear here because of its prominence in every cognitive-evolutionary study of essentialism: cognitive scientists stress that the tendency to perceive living/natural kinds in terms of their essences is "not a metaphysical claim about the structure of the world but rather a psychological claim about people's implicit assumptions" (Ibid.: 8). In other words, our tendency to essentialize by no means testifies to the actual existence of any underlying essences; instead, its cross-cultural prevalence reflects the particularities of the cognitive make-up of our species. The exact evolutionary history of a cognitive trait, or a cluster of cognitive traits, that underlies essentialism remains debated by psychologists and anthropologists. Approached as a psychological rather than a metaphysical phenomenon, essentialism emerges as "sketchy and implicit – a belief that category has a core, without knowing what that core is" – a "placeholder" notion (Ibid.: 9). People may "implicitly assume, for example, that there is some quality that bears have in common that confers category identity and causes their identifiable surface features, and they may use this belief to guide inductive inferences and produce explanations – without being able to identify any feature or trait as the bear essence. This belief can be considered an unarticulated heuristic rather than a detailed, well-worked-out theory" (Ibid.: 22).

Studies in cognitive neuroscience suggestively dovetail the research of Atran and his colleagues in cognitive-evolutionary psychology and anthropology. Hanna Damasio has pointed out recently that a patient with "a lesion in the left temporal lobe, but located posteriorly in the temporo-occipital junction away from the temporal pole, as well as from Wernicke's and Broca's area, will show a deficit in the retrieval of words denoting manipulable objects, [whereas] the retrieval of words for persons or animals is entirely normal" (Damasio 2001: 11). Another example comes from the work of Oliver Sacks, who describes a patient tentatively diagnosed with the neurological disorder known as Posterior Cortical Atrophy, who cannot, in particular, recognize the words that she reads (although her vision as such is perfect). At the time when the patient, Anna H., was first introduced to Sacks, she was not able to decipher the words shown to her, such as "cat." She "could, nevertheless, correctly sort them into salient categories, such as 'living' or 'non-living,' even though she had no conscious idea of their meaning" (Sacks 2002: 64). Such instances of selective neurological damage suggest that the differences in our conceptualization of living kinds and artifacts are supported by cognitive architectures that are *at least on some level* functionally distinct from each other.

If Atran's primary goal was to explore the role of essentialism in construction of folk-biological categories from antiquity to the present, Lawrence A. Hirschfeld's 1996 *Race in the Making: Cognition, Culture, and the Child's Construction of Human Kinds* focuses squarely on one of the most pernicious consequences of essentialism, racism. Arguing that we "are simply not likely to rid ourselves of racialist thinking by denying that [such thinking] is deeply grounded in our conceptual endowment" (Hirschfeld 1996: xiii), Hirschfeld shows how, given specific cultural-historical circumstances, our cognitive propensity for essentializing natural kinds can translate into racialism. Although, as Hirschfeld points out, "the races as socially defined . . . do not (even loosely) . . . pick up genuine reproductive populations" (Ibid.: 4) – essentialism "exploits certain real-world regularities" (Gelman 2003: 298), such as skin color (or, for that matter, gender or sexual orientation) to construe social identities as "natural." Hirschfeld's book is a must-read for any literary critic who wants to get a powerful interdisciplinary boost for her argument about a cultural construction of race because it provides a series of crucial insights into the ways we construct our everyday world and then rationalize our constructions as "natural."[4] The remarkable potential of a conceptual framework that considers the ways in which cultural constructions of social categories exploit our cognitive predispositions is already apparent in such thought-provoking works as, for example, the 2001 article "Can Race be Erased? Coalitional Computation and Social Categorization," by Robert Kurzban, *et al.* (2001).

One of the most recent studies of the cognitive underpinnings of essentialism is Susan A. Gelman's 2003 *The Essential Child: Origins of Essentialism in Everyday Thought*, which both builds on and extends Atran's and Hirschfeld's respective arguments. For example, Gelman differs from Atran in her reconstruction of the possible evolutionary history of essentialism, although their respective explanations are by no means mutually exclusive. Atran suggests that a "cross-cultural predisposition (and possibly innate predisposition) to think [about the organic world in terms of underlying essences] is perhaps partly accounted for in evolutionary terms by the empirical adequacy that presumption of essence afforded to human beings in dealing with a local biota [flora and fauna]" (Altran 1990: 63). Such a presumption "underpins the taxonomic stability of organic phenomenal types despite variation among individual exemplars" (Ibid.: 6). In other words, our Pleistocene ancestors could make certain inferences about every new (previously unencountered) organic specimen if they could recognize it as belonging to a certain category. For example, it would make sense to be wary of any tiger – not just the one who ate your cousin yesterday – because it is in the "nature" of tigers to prey on humans. Moreover, a tiger with three legs would still be perceived as a tiger, not a new three-legged species of animal with unknown properties, because it is in the "nature" of tigers to have four legs and the exception-on-hand testifies only to the peculiar personal history of this particular exemplar. Atran's view is thus that for millions of years such "essentialism" might have served as a cognitive "shortcut" instrumental in helping our ancestors to orient themselves amid the bewildering variety of natural kinds, including poisonous plants and predators. The ascription of imagined essences was useful for categorization and thus contributed to the survival of the human species. As such, it was selected for in thousands of consecutive generations and became a part of our cognitive makeup.

Unlike Atran, Gelman thinks that our tendency to essentialize is predicated not on one single cognitive adaptation, such as the adaptation for categorizing flora and fauna, but on many different cognitive abilities. As she puts it, "the cognitive capacities that give rise to essentialism are a varied assortment of abilities that emerged for other purposes but inevitably converge in essentialism" (Gelman 2003: 323). Gelman lists a series of independent cognitive capacities, such as the "basic capacity to distinguish appearance from reality," the capacity for "causal determinism" and for "tracking identity over time," that "individually and jointly" may lead to essentialism (Ibid.: 313). Viewed as an outcome of several fundamental cognitive processes, "essentialism is something we do neither because it is 'good' for survival, nor because it is 'bad' for people who are manipulated by essentialist rhetoric. Essentialism is something that we as humans cannot help but do" (Ibid.: 323). Note that both Atran and Gelman (as well as Hirschfeld and other cognitive-evolutionary psychologists) agree on the larger point of seeing essentialism as a "side effect" (Ibid.: 15) of other evolved cognitive adaptations. Their disagreement mainly lies in locating the "proper domain" for essentialist thinking. Atran sees it in folk-biological taxonomies; whereas, Gelman finds it in a cluster of cognitive biases not necessarily related to folk biology.

But let us say we accept the view that "*all and only* living kinds are conceived as physical sorts whose intrinsic 'natures' are presumed, even if unknown" (Atran 1990: 6; italics added), which means that the set of inference procedures used to deal with living things is very different from that for dealing with artifacts. How do we account, then, for the fact that in our everyday lives, we (both children and adults) regularly engage in a broad range of domain-crossing attributions, imputing essences to artifacts (for example, to works of art) and viewing various natural kinds in terms of their functions?[5] Such mental operations are clearly crucial for nuancing and reconfiguring our relationship with our world. Our language itself is quite sensitive to our domain-crossing tendencies, supplying us with such terms as objectification, commodification, anthropomorphization, and fetishization, as well as the recent addition inspired by Gilles Fauconnier and Mark Turner's (2002) important research on "conceptual blending."

Gelman agrees that essentialized artifacts "will support some novel inferences" – which is the primary conceptual "benefit," so to speak, of any essentializing – but she points out that these inferences are "quite limited compared to those of natural kind categories." For example, "artifacts can participate in rich causal theories, including those in archæology and cultural studies . . ., but such theories concern interactions between the object and the larger world, not properties intrinsic to the artifacts themselves" (Gelman 2003: 49).[6] Consider an ancient Roman coin unearthed at an archeological site. We perceive this coin as very special, its long history lending it that ineffable something that the most meticulously wrought modern copy would not possess. And yet what imbues it with this degree of essence is not something intrinsic to the coin itself, but rather its history of having participated in the complex social and cultural networks of a long-lost civilization.

To further illustrate the point that although we constantly and casually cross conceptual domains of artifacts and living/natural kinds the inferences that we can draw from a "domain-crossing" artifact are quite limited, we can turn to the veritable storehouse of such conceptual hybrids, J.K. Rowling's Harry Potter series. At one point in *Harry Potter and the Chamber of Secrets*, a boy named Draco Malfoy flatters one of his teachers, Professor Snape, leaving the latter rather pleased.[7] Even if you have never read any Harry Potter books, you can immediately infer, based on my intentionally stripped-down-of-any-details account of this episode, that the man named Snape needs to breathe, eat, sleep, and defecate; that he can talk on various topics, and that he has a broad range of states of mind; that he may have a special relationship with a group of people that constitutes his family; that he can learn to knit, to play drums, and sauté vegetables; and that he can do all these things not just on Tuesdays, or on special magical days, but every day. This list may strike you as silly, but the fact that we never even bother to consciously articulate to ourselves these and thousands of other automatically assumed possible qualities of "Snape" only shows how integral – to the point of not even being consciously perceptible anymore – this inferential process is to our making sense of the world. In other words, when we hear that a *human being* is flattered, we use our essentializing capacity to assume, if unconsciously, thousands of things about this person because they are in the "nature" of human beings.[8]

Now think of the doors at Hogwarts, the school of witchcraft and wizardry attended by Harry Potter and his friends. Like a majority of other artifacts in this school, these doors are magical: they "wouldn't open unless you asked politely, or tickled them in exactly the right place" (Rowling 1999: 132). They seem thus as appreciative of a certain form of flattery and attention as Professor Snape. We clearly have no problems with imagining this strange object that is simultaneously a door and a creature capable of a very human emotion. Yet compare the range of inferences we can draw from Snape's susceptibility to flattery to that we might draw from the similar susceptibility of the doors at Hogwarts. Can we assume that these doors need to breathe and eat? And if they are capable of appreciating attention while hanging on the door hinges at Hogwarts, will they have the same capability at a different, non-magical location? Can they learn any of the things that human beings can? Do they feel any particular emotions toward their family? And what is the doors' family, anyway – people who use them regularly? People who make them? Other doors? The adjacent walls? Furniture made of the same tree? The reason that we have a difficult time answering these questions is that we know that it is in the "nature" of doors to provide or debar access to a different space, and that's it. Doors are defined by their function, and the only reason that we may be able to attribute certain thoughts, emotions, and desires to this particular set of doors is that we transfer onto them some of the inferences that we would automatically make about a flattered human. In other words, a few essentialism-enabled assumptions about human beings do rub off on the flattered doors, but only a few and even those under some duress.[9]

It is equally significant that no matter how many times we read about a door that appreciates politeness in a novel, or no matter how many times we hear, for example, of a crying statue in real life, we will never assume that doors ordinarily can be influenced by flattery or that statues regularly cry. Quite a number of cultural representations thrive – that is, attract our attention and interest – precisely because they suggestively *violate* some sort of important conceptual "boundary" between an artifact and a natural kind, by perhaps forcing upon us the inferences that we generally are not prepared to associate with even a somewhat anthropomorphized artifact. Gelman uses as an example of such "boundary-crossing" artifacts the "hybrid toys created by the evil boy in the movie *Toy Story*" (Gelman 2003: 69); and I have discussed, in an essay published several years ago, the enduring fascination that we feel toward such ontological hybrids as Frankenstein's monster, who look and act like human beings and yet have been literally "made," artifact-like, by their creators.[10] We are similarly titillated by cyborgs, such as Yod from Marge Piercy's *He, She, and It*, or Andrew from Isaac Asimov's *Bicentennial Man*, because they are brought into the world with a defined "function" – as artifacts usually are – and then rebel against or outgrow that function by acquiring a complex world of human feelings and emotions. What is particularly remarkable about these representations is that they seem to retain their "out-of-the-ordinary" feel no matter how many times we have been exposed to similar conceptual curiosities and no matter how well we have been "prepared" for them by our everyday habit of, for example, casual anthropomorphizing.[11]

A broad array of cultural representations could thus be fruitfully considered as both exploiting and resisting our essentializing proclivities. Remarkably, even the enduring cultural anxiety about the theory of evolution could itself be grounded in our tendency to essentialize natural kinds, for biology is typically "misinterpreted . . . within an essentialist framework" (Ibid.: 285). Despite essentialist "assumptions about category immutability, categories do in fact transform from one to another, most notably in evolution. Yet children – and in some cases even adults – have trouble appreciating evolutionary accounts of species origins" (Ibid.: 66):

> What appears to be difficult is not the complexity of [the concepts of evolutionary theory], nor the scientific methods underlying the evidence, nor even the technical underpinnings of the work. Rather, even nontechnical concepts such as the following seem almost insurmountable: within-species variability, the lack of any single feature (either morphological or genetic) that is shared by all members of a species, and the lack of biological reality to 'racial' groupings of people. These conceptual difficulties call into question whether true conceptual reorganization takes place, or whether instead we are looking at the coexistence of multiple frameworks. . . . Adults remain susceptible to less obvious but still potent essentialist assumptions. In other words, essentialism is not strictly a childhood construction. It is a framework for organizing our knowledge of the world, a framework that persists throughout life.
>
> (Ibid.: 295)

Gelman's reasoning here raises a series of genuinely difficult issues. First of all, it is easy to misinterpret what she is saying and read into it the assertion that because essentialism "persists through life," its specific harmful consequences, such as, for instance, racism, must also persist through life. Gelman, of course, points out repeatedly throughout her book that "instantiations of essentialism" are "culture specific. . . . Essentialism is a species-general, universal, inevitable mode of thought, . . . but the form that it takes varies specifically according to the culture at hand, with the basic notion of essentialism becoming elaborated in each culture's complex theories of nature and society" (Ibid.: 283). The very fact that essentialism informs very different cultural formations in every society already indicates that whereas our tendency to essentialize may be "inevitable," there is nothing inevitable or unchangeable about each specific instantiation of essentialism. On the contrary, it seems that by understanding how susceptible we are to essentialist reasoning, we can successfully "deconstruct" and demystify each instance of such reasoning and see it for what it is – a specific cultural construction parasitizing on a more general cognitive predisposition.

To add further nuance to the thorny issue of the "inevitability" of essentialism, we may remember that cognitive-evolutionary psychologists have argued for some time now that we tend to essentialize abstract concepts themselves.[12] In other words, the very way in which we make sense of such terms as "inevitable" or "inherent" may hinder us from grasping their significance within the evolutionary framework.[13] For example, there is a huge difference between saying that we may have numerous evolved cognitive predispositions that are indeed "inherent" and automatically assuming, as we often do, that the instantiation of these dispositions somehow defines, delimits, and predicts the actual-world outcomes. The latter is completely false, and most cognitive-evolutionary psychologists are very sensitive to this issue (even though this aspect of their research rarely makes it into the lurid and heavily essentialist newspaper accounts of what is or what is not "in our genes"). The philosopher Elizabeth Grosz captures this difference aptly when she calls "Darwin's gift to the humanities" the emerging new understanding that within the evolutionary framework, "being is transformed into becoming, essence is transformed into existence, the past and the present are superceded by the future" (Grosz 2002: n.p.). She further notes that the "sciences which study evolution – evolutionary biology for example – become irremediably linked to the unpredictable, the non-deterministic, the movement of virtuality rather than the predictable regularity that other sciences tended to seek" (Ibid.). It may have taken these sciences "more than two thousand years . . . to escape the paralyzing grip of essentialism" (Mayr, quoted in Gelman 2003: 296), and the escape is far from complete, but it is possible.

The ever-receding "essence" of Sosia

I will be arguing shortly that the reason readers and viewers of Tuvim and Dryden can immediately appreciate the incongruity of their protagonists' over-reliance on appearances is that both writers have exploited, subconsciously and yet with complete assurance, our "inherent" tendency to think of natural kinds in terms of their invisible and yet enduring essences. First, however, I need to clarify how we move from essentializing natural kinds to essentializing individuals, for these two conceptual operations are not completely identical, and the authors in question certainly rely on the latter. Commenting on the difference between the two, Gelman observes that kind essentialism "takes one crucial step beyond individual essentialism. With kind essentialism the person assumes that the world is carved into preexisting natural categories"; whereas, "individual essentialism seems not to require any such commitment to kind realism" (Gelman 2003: 152).

Thus, you may "believe that your beloved pet Fido" has something special about him, "some 'Fido-ness' that he retains over time, that would show up even if he were to morph into a frog or a human, and that he carries with him after death, e.g., into heaven, or on reincarnation." Importantly, however, this "essence of Fido would be specific to Fido" and *not* something "shared with all other dogs."[14] In other words, the features that (we think) comprise the "essence" of each individual specimen are not identical to the features that (we think) comprise the "essence" of the natural kind to which this individual belongs. As "Lisa Zunshine" I (am perceived to) have that ineffable special something that makes me *me*; as a human being I (am perceived to) have a *different* set of special qualities that align me with other specimens of my kind. So, whereas, on the one hand, "essentializing of individual people recruits much the same cognitive mechanisms as essentializing of natural kinds" (Gelman 2003: 152), on the other hand, given a specific context, we can easily differentiate between the two.

Works of literature regularly draw on this ability, as does, for example, Michail Bulgakov's biting 1925 anti-Soviet satire *The Dog's Heart* (*Sobachye Serdze*). The novel centers on a scientific experiment during which a dog named Sharik is surgically transformed into a human being by receiving implants of a pituitary gland and the testicles of a dead criminal. As a man, the former dog exhibits the criminal inclinations of the deceased owner of the gland and testicles, whose *individual* "essence" has thus survived both physical death and reincarnation into a body of a different species. At the same time, in a darkly hilarious nod to *kind* essentialism, the budding Soviet proletarian "Mr. Sharikov" also possesses qualities presumably typical for *any* dog, such as inveterate hatred of cats. We are thus able to make sense of the nuances of "Mr. Sharikov's" hybrid personality because we are intuitively aware of the distinction between individual and kind essentialism.

In the cases of Plautus and Dryden, the exploitation of their audience's individual essentialism is particularly striking because they truly try to get at those "hidden, nonobvious properties that impart identity" (Gelman 2003: 151), only to demonstrate, ultimately, the futility of any attempt to define such properties. They systematically explore attributes other than one's appearance, such as character traits, family history, personal memories, actions, and social standing, which in principle could – but, importantly, *seem not to* – capture the essence of the individual. Tuvim does it as well, but in a more modest fashion, keeping in mind perhaps the young age of his intended readers. Yurgán's neighbor uses the torn pocket on his jacket to clinch the argument about the boy's identity ("See that torn pocket? You yourself are Yurgán!"). The appeal to the torn pocket may transcend the purely external – and hence relatively easily dismissible – considerations of identity because the rent garment can indicate something about the "inner nature" of Yurgán: perhaps he is sloppy, or rowdy, or absent-minded. Still, the poem's attempt to ground personality in the ownership of a jacket – even if the jacket has come to express some of its bearer's character – registers in our minds as a delightful play, a wink to the reader, who, young as she is, is already expected to know better.

In Plautus's play, Mercury not merely mimics Sosia's outward appearance but also appropriates his actions and memories. When Sosia attempts to hold on to his identity by asking,

> Am I not Sosia, Amphitryon's
> Servant . . .
> Didn't our ship arrive this very
> Night from the harbor of Persicus
> With me aboard it? Didn't my master
> Just now send me to the house?
> Am I not standing in front of the house
> Right now with a lantern in my hand?
>   (Passage and Mautinbaud 1974: 58)

Mercury eagerly responds by elaborating Sosia's story and providing details of Amphitryon's sail from Persicus and his earlier battle with the Teleboean king. He even describes a war trophy that Amphitryon keeps "in a little chest" and intends to give to his wife as a present. Sosia is duly impressed by the stranger's knowledge: "Well, he's beaten me. I've got/To find myself another name" (Ibid.: 58). In the last desperate bid for his slipping self, Sosia tests Mercury by asking what was it that he, Sosia, did while Amphitryon was fighting the enemy on the battlefield and Sosia was left "all alone in the tent, something that [the pretender, as Sosia hopes] will never know or be able to tell . . . not to save his life." Mercury immediately replies that he drank a "whole jugful of wine" – the correct answer and the one that compels our poor hero to cry out, "Then who am I, if I'm not Sosia,/Will you kindly tell me that?" (Ibid.: 59)

Dryden draws out the discussion of what Sosia did "all alone" (Dryden 2001: 2.295) in the tent, mentioning the "lusty gammon of . . . bacon" (2.296–7) that Sosia apparently devoured while hiding from the battle, and thus bringing into a sharper relief the plight of the character who can no longer rely on his personal memories to protect his identity. In doing so, he follows and amplifies Molière's version of the Roman original. He also develops further Molière's suggestion that one's origins and family history appear to be as ineffective gatekeepers of one's self as are private memories. Molière's Mercury overwhelms the dumbfounded Sosia with the knowledge of the intricacies of his family history, as he pontificates:

> . . . Sosia is my name, with utter certitude,
> The son of Davos, skilled in shepherd arts,
> The brother of young Harpax, deceased in foreign parts,
> The spouse of Cleanthis, the prude
> Whose whims will make me lose my mind.
> (Passage and Mautinbaud 1974: 147)

Dryden's Mercury also recites Sosia's lineage and compounds it with yet another particular that calls on Sosia's intensely personal – and embarrassing – recollection. Speaking of Sosia's wife, he observes that she, with "a devilish shrew of her tongue and a vixen of her hands . . ., keeps [him] to hard duty abed, and beats [him] every morning when [he has] risen from her side without having first . . ." – here Sosia interrupts him by saying that he understands him "by many a sorrowful token" and adds in a melancholy aside, "This must be I" (Dryden 2001: 2.248–54). He seems by now to be deprived of whatever personal identity could be conferred by genealogy, memory, and sexual history.

The social self is the one to which Sosia continues to cling fast. In Plautus's play, Amphitryon remains Sosia's last hope for refuting Mercury's claims to his identity, although this hope is complicated by Sosia's dreams of freedom from servitude. Having exhausted the "tests" that should reveal Mercury's imposture, Sosia decides to go find Amphitryon:

> . . . Well, I'd better go to the harbor
> And tell my master all about this.
> Unless he doesn't recognize
> Me either – I hope to God he won't!
> Then I can shave my head today
> And then put on a free man's hat.
> (Passage and Mautinbaud
1974: 60–1)

It appears that Sosia's conception of his identity is strongly aligned with his position as Amphitryon's slave. If it so happens that his master does not claim him as his servant, he is truly not Sosia anymore, a proposition that could be easily loaded with ideological overtones depending on the historical context of the play. For example, in the case of Dryden's *Amphitryon*, Sosia's temporary suspension of his identity – *until he hears from his master* (Dryden 2001: 2.329–35) – could easily function as an ironic comment on the post-revolutionary, Whiggish mentality of some of the members of his audience.[15] What is important for my present argument is that, however ideologically suggestive we may find the idea of defining the person's self by his social position, this definition is never *quite* satisfactory either. It could be argued that there is a significant variance in the degree to which different cultures countenance the equation of one's identity with one's social standing. I suspect, however, that even in those cultures in which such an equation is the strongest, borne out by a long tradition and a powerful doctrinal imposition, it is still ridden with cognitive tension that may eventually translate into political actions.

And, indeed, when Dryden's Sosia does meet his master, who immediately and familiarly threatens him with beatings – a welcome that according to Sosia's own earlier stipulation should leave no doubt in his mind that he *is* Sosia – it fails to convince him. Sosia readily admits that he is "but a slave and [Amphitryon is his] master" (3.8), but his freshly reconfirmed social status does nothing to restore his belief that he is indeed the only true Sosia. The memory of past physical abuse at Mercury's hands, coupled with the evidence of his senses, overrides the testimony provided by the actions of his master. Here is Sosia explaining to the incredulous and angry Amphitryon how he came to think that the other Sosia *is* him and perhaps even better than him:

> Sosia. I could never have believed it myself, if I had not been well-beaten into it. But a cudgel, you know, is a convincing argument in a brawny fist. What shall I say, but that I was compelled at last to acknowledge myself? I found that he was very I, without fraud, cozen,

or deceit. Besides, I viewed myself as in the mirror from head to foot. He was handsome, of a noble presence, a charming air, loose and free in all his motions – and saw he was so much I, that I should have reason to be better satisfied with my own person, if his hands had not been a little of the heaviest.

(Ibid.: 3.126–38)

Sosia's reasoning is funny, not least because of his grudging admiration for the other Sosia and his sly intimation that his "absent" (Ibid.: 3.152) self is apparently a gentleman, what with "a noble presence" and freedom "in all his motions." It almost seems that Sosia does not mind "sharing" his identity as long as his double's apparently elevated social status reflects well on him. This scene, thus, works on many different levels, and the "cognitive" reading that I am offering here does not claim to account for its complicated overall effect on a specific audience. Still, I suspect that *at least one reason* that viewers have been enjoying for the last 22 centuries Sosia's ludicrous exchanges with the false Sosia and with his master is that these exchanges tease and "work out" our evolved cognitive tendency to essentialize individuals. Plautus, Molière, and Dryden obligingly offer up for our consideration various personal qualities that seem to be able to capture a person's "essence" and then invite the audience to laugh at the naïveté of any character who buys such a reductionist reading of his identity. The laughter, however, barely covers, and is made more poignant by, a certain amount of anxiety, and here is why: on the one hand, viewers are reminded, as they witness Sosia's misadventures, that one's appearance *certainly* does not define one's identity; one's name *certainly* does not define one's identity; one's social standing does not *quite* define identity; one's memories do not *quite* define identity; one's origins do not *quite* define identity; one's actions do not *quite* define identity – although in different cultural-historical settings, each of these "non-definitions" would be weighed differently in relation to the others.

On the other hand, precisely because the "essence" that we attribute to individuals cannot be captured – for thinking that there is an essence is a function of our cognitive makeup rather than a reflection of the actual state of affairs – some nervousness would always accompany any failed endeavor to capture the "core" of the person. Certain "what ifs" would perpetually hover over such endeavors: *What if* the person's appearance really expresses something crucial about her core being, and we simply haven't yet found the correct way to map one onto another? (The persistence of various sumptuary laws, such as the English Sumptuary Statutes, enforced from the fourteenth to the seventeenth centuries, reflects, *at least in part*, this nagging suspicion.) *What if* one's memory is all that truly differentiates one person from another? (Movies such as *Total Recall* play with this idea.) *What if* one's origins determine who one is forever? (To make such an argument today one would use, or rather misuse, research on DNA and genes.) *What if* one's actions "define" the person's identity? *What if* one's social class truly determines it? Because we (cannot help but) assume that some essence *is* there, failing to capture it again and again does not invalidate in principle our implicit belief in it, but it does foster the continuous uncertainty about what does or does not truly express the "core" of a person, an uncertainty that takes myriad culturally specific forms. The staged exploration of that uncertainty could be comic – as in the case of Sosia – but it could also be tragic. *Amphitryon*, after all, is named after the character whose identity is "borrowed" by the philandering god, a borrowing that prompts a series of personal and social crises (some of them nearly fatal), the intensity of which varies from one translation to another.[16]

Speculating on twins and the theatre within a cognitive framework

With an eye on future research, I will now expand my argument and discuss some tentative ways in which a cognitive analysis of the motif of mislaid identity can be correlated with what we know about the broader tradition to which this motif properly belongs – the theatre's long-standing interest in the adventures of identical twins. I will suggest that just like the motif of the mislaid identity, the twin theme engages in a particularly focused way a cluster of cognitive adaptations associated with our essentializing tendencies. I will conclude by inquiring into the possible difference between the cognitive "work-out" provided for these adaptations by representations of twins *in performance* and comparable work demanded by the numerous novelistic treatments of the same topic.

"When a myth resorts to twins," writes René Girard in his essay on Plautus's and Molière's *Amphitryons* and Shakespeare's *The Comedy of Errors*, "it must be trying to make a point and this point cannot be the difference between the twins, otherwise why resort to twins? The point is obviously the absence of difference" (Girard 1981: 85). But the "absence of difference" can only be the point if it is immediately recognized by all concerned parties as blatantly contradicting certain assumptions about the world. And, indeed, argues Girard,

> In ... all comedies of twins, the characters deal with each other on the assumption that all of them are unique and immediately identifiable as such. If they did not cling to this assumption in the face of contrary evidence they would not become so confused. It takes more than the presence of undistinguishable twins, I repeat, to generate the comic effects; it takes this persistent refusal to acknowledge the possibility of beings, human or divine, less different from each other than we would like them to be.
>
> (Ibid.: 69)

Let me restate in stronger terms the point that Girard only hints at in the last line of the quotation above: The reason members of the audience can immediately appreciate the stubbornness with which the befuddled stage twins "cling to [the] assumption" of their uniqueness is that they – "we" – share in that however battered assumption. Note that I am not implying that this assumption is somehow fundamentally wrong and that there is no such thing as a unique personal identity. I am saying rather that our reasoning about this unique personal identity and our attempts to "define" it are profoundly informed, and perhaps "fatally flawed," by our proclivity for essentializing.

And so Sosia's ridiculous exchange with Mercury replicates and parodies the audience's implicit search for the evidence of some "core" difference between the two men. Having registered what he perceives as Mercury's striking resemblance to himself, Sosia reaches, one after another, for the conceptual knobs onto any of which we, too – had we been in his situation – would have pegged the evidence of our personal uniqueness (name, parentage, personal history, memories, social standing), and each one of them fails him. We laugh when Sosia gives up after trying those knobs because we feel that, unlike this poor chump, we do have extra knowledge that allows us to tell the real man from the impostor. *Read: we do have extra knowledge that continues to provide the welcome input for our essentialist biases, even when Sosia himself runs out of such material.* This is because, first, in our privileged position of spectators, we know that the other Sosia is "really" Mercury because we have seen the first act of the play in which Jupiter asked Mercury to impersonate Sosia.[17] Second, we are abetted in our superior knowledge of the "real" difference between the two Sosias by the material realities of a theatrical production.

The latter point is important and bears historical elaboration. A curious observation emerges out of the history of production of plays featuring twins, such as *The Comedy of Errors*. On the one hand, as John M. Mercer notes, "despite the blatantly nonrealistic plots of [such] plays, audiences and reviewers of *The Comedy of Errors* ... at least since the Restoration, have demanded a high degree of realism in the stage portrayal of the twins. In response, adapters, directors, and actors have done their best to satisfy this demand" (Mercer 1993: 97). On the other hand, on the occasions when directors and actors have truly succeeded in making the twins look identical, their audiences' response was mixed. In a 1990 production at Stratford, England, when the same actor played both Dromios, artfully working around the moments when the twins have to appear on stage together, one reviewer wrote that the spectators "could not enjoy the play's 'errors' of mistaken identity. He argued that it was not funny when the other characters mistook the twins – because he did the same" (Ibid.: 108). By contrast, another reviewer praised the 1883 production at the Strand in London precisely because Dromio's identity was "never for a moment in doubt, differing as [the two Dromios did] in voice, manner, and appearance" (Ibid.: 109).

The actions and costumes of the brothers, points out Mercer, "made them enough alike to be funny" and "no more than this [was] required. Drama by definition must create some illusion of reality, and [this play obligates] productions to establish *some* identity between the actors who play the twins" (Ibid.: 110).

The 1983 BBC's *The Comedy of Errors*, directed by James Cellan Jones, features one actor, Roger Daltrey, playing the two Dromios, and one actor, Michael Kitchen, playing the two Antipholi, with the use of the split screen in the last scene, when both sets of twins finally meet face to face. Because in this case the "twins" are indistinguishable, there is a real danger of making the action incomprehensible for the audience. To help us tell the brothers apart, Antipholus of Syracuse is portrayed as funnier, more emotionally flexible, and much kinder to "his" Dromio than is Antipholus of Ephesus, who is relatively rigid in his emotional reactions and habitually abusive toward his servant. Not surprisingly, Dromio of Syracuse comes across as a more cheerful and self-assured person than his much-beaten twin. Subtle differences in wardrobe (at one point, one Antipholus's collar is turned up while another's is turned down) and stature (one Dromio seems to slouch more than the other) help us to keep the brothers apart. Still, all these subtle details notwithstanding, at least one critic has insisted that the movie is "made less interesting [because] the actors don't play each twin as having a different personality, so it's difficult to tell who is who."[18]

Can certain properties of our cognitive propensity for attributing essences to individuals account *at least in part* for the audience's preference for twins who can be told apart without too strenuous an effort? When faced with the implied "absence of difference" between the two people, we immediately start looking for any evidence of dissimilarity between them (by contrast, when we see two identical chairs or cups or umbrellas, we do not have the same impulse to tell them apart and construe each as somehow special – unless, that is, they participate in some social interaction that involves *people*). Why do we do it? – a seemingly simple question that opens up a complex issue of our social cognition as entangled with our essentialist biases.

For, on the one hand, as *The Comedy of Errors* reminds us, there is a very good practical reason for wanting to be able to tell apart the two people who look alike. One of them may owe you money, or he could be your lawfully wedded husband; whereas, the other could be a stranger of no importance (yet!) or credit, who is looking to skip the town after getting enough gold from the duped citizens. Profoundly social beings as we are, we keep constant track of the (evolving) position of people around us in relation to various social networks that comprise the fabric of our lives. The two people who look the same present a challenge to this social awareness, for they cannot possibly have the same communal weight, history, and responsibility, and so not being able to tell one from the other can have a significant and possibly negative impact on our own social position. For instance, Angelo, the goldsmith from *The Comedy of Errors*, stands to lose his credit with respectable merchants after mistakenly giving the golden chain to the wrong Antipholus; and Dr. Pinch, a schoolmaster, is punished for blundering into the Antipholi affair by getting his beard "singed off with brands of fire" and his hair nicked so that he is made to look "like a fool" (5.2.171, 175). The danger of losing one's reputation can acquire sexual overtones: Adriana from *The Comedy of Errors* only has dinner with the man who looks like her husband, but Alcmena from *Amphitryon* actually conceives a child with the pretender!

Still, we cannot say that our historically enduring fascination with the theatrical twin motif can be accounted for by our real-life fear of being duped by twins. It is unlikely that at any point in human history – especially given the formerly high mortality of twins, both natural and induced by infanticide – the problem of telling them apart was so pressing as to leave a long-lasting mark on our psychological makeup. In other words, it is possible that plays such as *Amphitryon* and *The Comedy of Errors* skillfully manipulate our emotions and draw us in by appealing to a complex mix of our social and perceptual biases. These plays speak to our very real need to keep close tabs on who is who and who is where in our multi-level system of social hierarchies. But in addition to that, the plays also use this social aspect as a "flag of convenience"[19] in their endeavor to tease and exploit our essentialist proclivities. The plays featuring twins give us a "cognitively enjoyable" opportunity to exercise our essentialist biases at the same time that they tacitly assure us of the social value of such an exercise. They offer us a safe setting in which we can hunt for visual dissimilarities between the twins and construe those uncovered dissimilarities as a "proof" of our intuition about an "underlying, largely immutable, and invisible" (Atran 1990: 83) essence of each individual; but they also leave us with a pleasant vague feeling that we have learned some sort of a potentially useful lesson about keeping track of who is who in the social game. Theatrical representations of twins thus may derive much of their emotional appeal from engaging our essentialist biases – playing with them, teasing them, and validating them – but they delight by pretending to instruct.

I propose, only half-jokingly, that Dryden's new subtitle for *Amphitryon*, his "*The Two Sosias*," as well as the late-eighteenth-century "improvements" on the title of *The Comedy of Errors* – such as William Woods's *The Twins, or Which is Which?* (1780) and Monk Lewis's *The Twins; or Is It He or His Brother?* (1799)[20] – implicitly promised their audiences a cognitive "workout" for their essentializing capacities. It stands to reason, then, that the truly identical stage twins – when they are portrayed by the same actor who makes no effort to emphasize *some* dissimilarity between the two protagonists – give no input, so to speak, to such capacities. Unless some members of the audience take the incidental differences in the actor's portrayal of the twins and construe them (again, enabled by their own essentialist biases) into evidence of the systematic difference between the "brothers," they may not particularly enjoy the twin motif of the play.

Crucially, then, the theatre's engagement with our essentialist biases is *always embodied*. At any given historical juncture, any audience watching a specific performance of *Amphitryon* or *The Comedy of Errors* receives extra input for its essentializing deductions from the physical presence of the actors. When the late-seventeenth-century theatregoers saw that "mixture of piteous Pusillanimity and a Consternation" animating the face of James Nokes's Sosia as he surveyed his "charming" rival to his identity, they enjoyed that particular display of emotions for many different reasons. *At least one reason*, however, for this spectacle being such a treat was that Nokes's facial expressions and demeanor were strikingly different from that of the actor playing Mercury. The viewers could fairly feast on the multiple implications that this embodied difference provided for their endeavor of establishing the real Sosia as "essentially" and incontrovertibly distinct from the pretended Sosia. What heightened the dramatic irony of the situation was that the real Sosia himself remained left out of this perceptual loop, unable to reclaim his "core" uniqueness based on the fact that his emotions and demeanor were so distinct from those of his haughty double.

The perceptual availability of the richly embodied "evidence" of the "essential" difference between the presumed twins is what distinguishes theatrical explorations of the twin motif from its novelistic explorations, or, for that matter from the published versions of the plays. Consider the recent novel by the Mexican writer Ignacio Padilla originally called *Amphitryon* and published in English as *Shadow Without a Name* (2002). A brilliant heir to the doppelganger extravaganzas of Nabokov and Borges, Padilla leads the increasingly dizzy reader through a bloody military carnival where a person can change deeply and perhaps irrevocably after adapting somebody else's name, face, or professional status. We find this story about a "prisoner of a past and of a face not his own" (Ibid.: 191) both exciting and unnerving because, among many other things, it teases our essentialist predilections and lovingly cultivates the anxiety underlying our endeavors to locate and define the "core" of a given person. But even as Padilla's novel builds on some of the same essentialist biases as does Dryden's play, the physical presence of the actors in Dryden's *Amphitryon* adds a level of engagement with such biases that is in principle unavailable to the readers of the novel. For instance, a theatrical director wishing to adapt Padilla's book for the stage would have to decide how similar "in voice, manner, and appearance" she should make Franz T. Kretzschmar and Adolph Eichmann (the presumed doubles of the book), a very important question and one irrelevant for the novelist.

Different genres and different media thus appear to engage the same cognitive propensities in markedly different ways, satisfying and creating highly nuanced cognitive needs. Of course, even with the remarkable progress of the evolutionary cognitive science of the past 20 years, we are still a long way off from figuring out why certain theatrical or literary representations affect us the way they do. In the words of evolutionary anthropologist Dan Sperber, "our understanding of cognitive architecture is [still] way too poor, and the best we can do is try and speculate intelligently (which is great fun anyhow)" (Sperber 2001: 49). I wrote this essay both sobered by Sperber's warning and inspired by his parenthetical remark. Every single one of my speculations resulting from applying the cognitive-evolutionary studies of essentialism to the theatrical motif of mislaid identity and to the broader motif of twins could be wrong, but the questions that prompted those speculations are emphatically worth asking.

Notes

I am grateful to F. Elizabeth Hart and Christopher Hair for their thoughtful feedback on the previous versions of this essay.

1 Parts of this discussion dealing with Atran's argument have originally appeared in my essay "Rhetoric, Cognition, and Ideology in Anna Laetitia Barbauld's 1781 *Hymns in Prose for Children*" (Zunshine 2001).
2 For an important related discussion of Aristotelian essentialism, see Atran (1990: 83–122).
3 Note that a log is a potentially ambiguous example. In its "former existence" (as an oak, for instance) it would be classified as an organic object and thus conceptualized in terms of its underlying essence, rather than its function.
4 Other important questions explored at length in Gelman's study that I will not discuss here because it is simply impossible to do them justice in the present limited space are: To what extent does language promotes essentialism? Do children learn essentialist thinking from their parents? What happens if we complicate the experiments involving the appearance-changing animals, for example, by showing that we have "replaced" their innards completely? How do we explain the persistence of the popular and scientific misconception that young children show a "bias toward phenomenism (reporting just appearance, for both appearance and reality)" and on the whole perceive the world "solely in terms of surface appearances" (Gelman 2003: 74)? How and when does childhood essentialism become "integrated with scientific and cultural knowledge" (Ibid.: 287)? What is the difference between essentializing and categorizing?
5 See Bloom (2004: 54–7), and Jesse M. Bering, "The Folk Psychology of Souls," forthcoming.
6 In making this point, Gelman engages with and qualifies the influential earlier work on categorization of Eleanor Rosch. For discussion, see Gelman (2003: 49).
7 You can find the full account of the interaction between Draco and Snape in J.K. Rowling's *Harry Potter and the Chamber of Secrets* (Rowling 1999: 267). I have purposely withheld the details of the situation so as to make it as parallel to the following "doors" example as possible.
8 Elsewhere I discuss possible cognitive underpinnings of our ability to treat a fictional character (such as Snape) as a real-life person (Zunshine 2003). For the purposes of the present argument, I do not consider this issue at all, for, after all, the doors that I discuss in the next paragraph are not "real" doors either.
9 Compare it to Gelman's observation that three- and four-year-old children treat the "domain of people as special." She has found "that children treated adjectives for people as more powerful than adjectives for nonpeople" (Gelman 2003: 51).
10 See Zunshine (2001: 133).
11 It could be argued that in "other" cultures (always a hopeful location), people

are much more ready to take literally their animism, that is, "the transfer of notions of underlying causality from recognized (folk)biological to recognized nonbiological kinds" (Atran 1990: 217). This, however, is not the case, as has been demonstrated by Margaret Mead in 1932, Frank Keil in 1979, and Gelman in 1983. For a discussion of their respective findings, see Atran (1990: 216–17).

12 See, for example, Gelman and Wellman (1991: 213), and McIntosh (1997).

13 Compare it to Abbott's suggestive argument in "Unnaratable Knowledge" (2003).

14 Susan Gelman, e-mail communication (17 September 2003).

15 See, for example, Bywaters (1991: 62).

16 The German author Heinrich von Kleist enlarged this potential tragic aspect of *Amphitryon* in his 1807 translation, in which he has the sadistic Jupiter exploiting Aclmena's terrified suspicion that she has spent the night with a person other than her husband.

17 Imagine, however, that bending the laws of the genre, an evil philosopher appears on stage and asks us how Sosia is *really* different from Mercury. Won't we find ourselves reciting the same failed mantra that Sosia tried? Won't we be saying that Mercury is different from Sosia because he looks different and because his parentage, personal memories, and actions are all different from Sosia's? Essentialism is a clay crutch that dissipates into dust when we attempt to lean on it.

18 This anonymous comment comes from the Internet Movie Database: http://us.imdb.com/title/tt0085351/as of 12 January 2004. The comment itself is dated 15 May 2001.

19 I am using this expression in the sense borrowed from David Mamet's observation about his play *Oleanna*, in which, as he puts it, the issue of sexual harassment was "to a large extent, a flag of convenience for a play that's structured as a tragedy. Just like the issues of race relations and xenophobia are flags of convenience for *Othello*. It doesn't have anything to do with race" (Mamet 2003: 1473).

20 For a discussion of these titles, see Mercer (1993: 98).

References

Abbott, P. (2003) "Unnarratable Knowledge: The Difficulty of Understanding Evolution by Natural Selection," in Herman, D. (ed.) *Narrative Theory and the Cognitive Sciences*, Stanford, CA, Center for the Study of Language and Information, 143–62.

Atran, S. (1990) *Cognitive Foundations of Natural History: Toward an Anthropology of Science*, Cambridge: Cambridge University Press.

Bering, J.M. (forthcoming) "The Folk Psychology of Souls."

Bloom, P. (2004) *Descartes's Baby: How the Science of Child Development Explains What Makes Us Human*, New York: Basic Books.

Bywaters, D. (1991) *Dryden in Revolutionary England*, Berkeley, CA: University of California Press.

Damasio, H. (2001) "Words and Concepts in the Brain," in Branquinho, J. (ed.) *The Foundations of Cognitive Science*, Oxford: Clarendon Press, 109–20.

Dryden, J. [1690] *Amphitryon; or, the Two Sosias* (2001) Markley, R. and Dalporto, J. (eds) in Canfield, J.D. (gen. ed.) *Broadview Anthology of Restoration and Eighteenth-Century Drama*, New York: Broadview Press.

Fauconnier, G. and Turner, M. (2002) *The Way We Think: Conceptual Blending and the Mind's Hidden Complexities*, New York: Basic Books.

Gelman, S.A. (2003) *The Essential Child*, New York: Oxford University Press.

Gelman, S.A. and Wellman, H.M. (1991) "Insides and essences: early understandings of the non-obvious," *Cognition*, 38(3): 213–44.

Girard, R. (1981) "Comedies of Errors: Plautus – Shakespeare – Molière," in Konigsberg, I. (ed.) *American Criticism in the Poststructuralist Age*, Ann Arbor, MI: University of Michigan, 66–86.

Grosz, E. (2002) "Darwin and ontology," paper presented at the annual convention of the Modern Language Association, New York.

Hirschfeld, L.A. (1996) *Race in the Making: Cognition, Culture, and the Child's Construction of Human Kinds (Learning, Development, and Conceptual Change)*, Cambridge, MA: MIT Press.

Kurzban, R., Tooby, J., and Cosmides, L. (2001) "Can race be erased? Coalitional computation and social categorization," *Proceedings of the National Academy of Sciences*, 98(26): 15387–92.

Mamet, D. (2003) "Interview by Geoffrey Norman and John Rezek for *Playboy*, 1995," in Klaus, C.H., Gilbert, M., and Fields, B.S., Jr (eds) *Stages of Drama: Classical to Contemporary Theater*, Boston, MA: Bedford/St. Martin's, 1472–4.

Milhous, J. and Hume, R.D. (1985) *Producible Interpretation: Eight English Plays, 1675–1707*, Carbondale and Edwardsville, IL: Southern Illinois University Press.

McIntosh, J. (1997) "Cognition and power," Steen, F. (ed.) *Cogweb: Cognitive and Cultural Studies*, http://cogweb.ucla.edu/Culture/McIntosh.html.

Mercer, J.M. (1993) "Making the twins realistic in *The Comedy of Errors* and *Twelfth Night*," *Exploration in Renaissance Culture*, XIX: 97–113.

Padilla, I. (2002) *Shadow Without a Name*, trans. Bush, P. and McLean, A., New York: Farrar, Straus and Giroux.

Passage, C.E. and Mantinband, J.H. (1974) *Amphitryon: Three Plays in New Verse Translations. Plautus: Amphitruo, translated by J.H. Mantinband; Moliere: Amphitryon, translated by Charles E. Passage; Kleist: Amphitryon, translated by Charles E. Passage; Together with a Comprehensive Account of the Evolution of the Legend and its Subsequent History on the Stage*, Chapel Hill, NC: The University of North Carolina Press.

Rowling, J.K. (1999) *Harry Potter and the Chamber of Secrets*, New York: Arthur A. Levine Books/Scholastic Press.

Sacks, O. (2002) "The case of Anna H," *The New Yorker*, 7 October, 62–73.

Shakespeare, W. [1594] (1980) *The Comedy of Errors*, in Hardison, G.B. (ed.) *Shakespeare: The Complete Works*, Fort Worth: Harcourt Brace.

Sperber, D. (2001) "In Defense of Massive Modularity," in Dupoux, E. (ed.) *Language, Brain, and Cognitive Development: Essays in Honor of Jacques Mehler*, Cambridge, MA: MIT Press, 47–58.

Zunshine, L. (2003) "Theory of mind and experimental representations of fictional consciousness," *Narrative*, 11(3): 270–91.

—— (2001) "Rhetoric, cognition, and ideology in Anna Laetitia Barbauld's 1781 *Hymns in Prose for Children*," *Poetics Today*, 23(1): 231–59.

5 "It is required/You do awake your faith"

Learning to trust the body through performing *The Winter's Tale*

Naomi Rokotnitz

Alack, for lesser knowledge! How accursed/In being so blest!
(Leontes, *The Winter's Tale* 2.1.38–9)

The drama of the human condition comes solely from consciousness ... because it concerns knowledge obtained in a bargain that none of us struck: the cost of a better existence is the loss of innocence about that very existence.... But drama is not necessarily tragedy.
(Damasio 1999: 316)

Skepticism is part and parcel of "a bargain none of us struck." There is no denying that human knowledge is limited and that there seem to be multiple and sometimes conflicting truths.[1] Historically, this skeptical realization has led many thinkers to profound existential crises.[2] Deprived of guarantees to truth, people's willingness to trust, to invest their confidence in a particular fact, idea or person, becomes problematic; the universe becomes overwhelming. Nevertheless, we continue to aspire to understand one another, to trust and to reach truth(s). Skepticism, thus, plays a necessary and important role in our search for knowledge, but it need not either overshadow our endeavors or enforce a resignation to relativism.

In the first half of *The Winter's Tale*, Shakespeare demonstrates the potentially paralyzing effects of radical skepticism. In the second half of the play, he suggests how this paralysis may be combated, even countered, by attunement to the instinctive human propensity to trust. Trust, as will be argued in the following pages, arises from *embodied* experience and, crucially, from our ability to use that knowledge *empathetically* in order to understand others. This ability, we discover, is not automatic but requires gradual refinement through practice. Moreover, trust is founded upon a necessary union between biology and culture, body and mind.

The malady of reason[3]

In the prose-romance from which Shakespeare borrowed the plot for *The Winter's Tale*, King Leontes' suspicion that his wife is unfaithful is raised by somewhat misleading appearances.[4] In *The Winter's Tale*, however, Leontes' suspicion is presented not only as wholly unprompted but – as other characters in the play immediately concur – the product of "diseased opinion" (1.2.297). Leontes' diseased opinion rapidly develops into a jealous rage of such intensity that he seems mad. His madness is clearly not a justifiable response to any observation of his wife's behavior (as Leontes himself first thinks); nor is it an explosion of (sexual) jealousy or wrath (as his subjects first think). I follow the philosopher Stanley Cavell in identifying Leontes' madness as the result of unsupplemented logical reasoning – an "infection of [the] *brains*" (1.2.144; italics added).[5] It is logic that leads Leontes to jealousy and thence to the discovery of skepticism; and it is radical skepticism that leads him to despair.

Skepticism existed in the early modern period on both sides of the religious chasm, yet however skeptical of human knowledge, neither Luther nor Montaigne nor even Descartes doubted that, although humans may be blind to it, *absolute truth* exists in the form of an omnipotent God. This faith has traditionally grounded the standard interpretation of *The Winter's Tale* as an allegorical representation of human folly and a propagation of belief in divine mercy achieved through Perdita-Nature and Hermione-Grace, the curative forces that ultimately right human wrongs.[6] And yet, Shakespeare's was a time of profound religious controversy and renewed study of ancient skeptical texts. Many of Shakespeare's contemporaries were realizing that even if God is truth, this truth is not readily available to mere mortals.

The Winter's Tale demonstrates again and again just how difficult it is for humans to obtain secure knowledge. This is because, first, language, the tool of reason with which we tell of our knowing, is shown to be susceptible to misinterpretation and reinterpretation. Although the words of the oracle seem clear and explicit ("Hermione is chaste, Polixenes blameless, Camillo a true subject, Leontes a jealous tyrant" 3.2.130) they are insufficient to persuade King Leontes of the truth. Instead, it is Paulina, whose name suggests identification with St. Paul and his doctrine of justification by *faith*, who ensures that the oracle's prophecy comes about. Crucially, whether by hiding the queen, pretending she is dead, castigating Leontes, ensuring he does not remarry, or finally by orchestrating the (seemingly) miraculous resurrection of Hermione, Paulina uses secrets and lies – withholding information and disseminating misinformation – in order to reveal this truth.[7] Even more importantly, she uses words to disguise, rather than to explain, where her real efforts are concentrated: in the material world of *actions*.[8]

Thus we see that although language can articulate knowledge, it is nonetheless not the only means of obtaining knowledge and can also be deliberately manipulated to conceal knowledge. The Protestant epistemological claim for "sola scriptura" – meaning that the words of the Scriptures are enough to contain and explain all truths – is thus undermined. I do not believe that Shakespeare was seeking to delegitimize Protestant claims in order to revert back to Catholic superstition.[9] Instead, it seems to me that his play reveals the extent to which, in order to get at any kind of truth, reason and language must be supplemented. This supplementation draws upon experience of embodied knowledge.

However, firsthand experience of an event, such as seeing it – although it does not necessitate belief in another person's experience – still fails to guarantee infallible apprehension. Any police investigator will avow that any two witnesses can potentially see the same event and yet form different impressions of that event. Leontes' efforts to find unequivocal visible evidence that his son is his (the nose, the shape of the head) are to no avail because his confidence in appearances has been fundamentally shaken. Once his reason is tainted by suspicion, it colors all he sees.

Leontes gradually understands that not only is reason limited, but two of its informing sources, the modalities of hearing and seeing, are dangerously unreliable.[10] The third gentleman's bewilderment in Act 5 is expressed in the confusing possibility that "that which you hear you'll swear you see, there is such unity in the proofs" (5.2.32–3). Moreover, characters respond to their sensory input with surprising inconsistency. Although hearing the proclamation of the oracle was not sufficient to persuade Leontes of his erroneous accusations, merely hearing report of the deaths of his son and his wife is sufficient to persuade him, and he immediately admits his error.[11]

When the full force of the realization that meaning is uncertain dawns upon the consciousness of King Leontes, disillusionment, anxiety and inordinate self-pity develop into anger, which he translates into abuse of others. Leontes' madness is the expression of a crisis of faith: He is propelled into a dark abyss from which it appears that the entire world is unstable. He loses contact with reality because he no longer trusts that he can tell what is real and what is imagined.

The theory of "biological materialism" offered by the literary critic Ellen Spolsky provides a particularly useful rubric for my reading of *The Winter's Tale*. Spolsky argues that, as the human brain receives information from a number of different sensory inputs obtained by separate modules, it is inevitable that these modules will produce different and sometimes incommensurable readings of the environment (Spolsky 1993: 5). Knowledge attained through one modality is often in conflict with knowledge attained through other modalities. Spolsky shows that systematically denying the evidence provided by the body in favor of knowledge reached through reasoning alone may lead to a warped assessment of both self and world; it can also lead to ever more radical skepticism.

If this is so, then Leontes' crisis of faith is inevitable – there is no means of attaining a single, correct, comprehensive impression of reality. Spolsky argues, however, that this failure in fact works to our advantage: memories, analogies and inferences fill some of the gaps between dissonant kinds of knowledge categories, enabling problem-solving, adaptability, creativity and progress. Thus, our process of decision-making is most likely to be satisfying if it includes consideration of as many kinds of knowledge as possible. We then recognize that in deciding to follow one modality or another, we are not determining what is true but only what is appropriate or useful at a particular point in time.

This view is shared by David Henderson and Terence Horgan, who assert that "truth-conductivity (reliability) is not the sole decisive epistemic virtue" (Henderson and Horgan 2000: 120). What we require are "processes that are reliable and system-conducive" for whatever complex or heterogeneous an environment we may find ourselves in. For a capacity (cognitive or other) to be useful to us in terms of "epistemic competence" or "robustness," it has to be "a component of a set of capacities that is conducive to the truth and systematicity of our belief systems" (Ibid.: 121).

What then is at stake here? In order to combat radical skepticism and reground trust, body and mind must be understood as one. Our approach to reality – to truth – is best understood in terms of a general strategy or system that we deem reliable even if it cannot be watertight. Art, I suggest, is an effective means of encouraging acknowledgement of the necessary interdependence of body and mind and, even more importantly, of providing us with opportunities to *practice* and *refine* the complex and subtle ways through which we may better understand one another and reach for truth(s) in our lives. Truth often fits the needs of survival (e.g., live wires are dangerous). At other times, however, truth and survival only relate to each other indirectly. And indirections, I argue, are precisely the joints at which biology meets art.

Learning to trust

Leontes is not unique in feeling helpless when faced with the realization of the certainty of uncertainty. In fact, his response appears to be generic. Cavell claims that not only is tragedy "obedient to a skeptical structure" but that skepticism already bears "its own marks of a tragic structure" (Cavell 1987: 5). This view is supported by the movement of the tragic first half of the play, in which Leontes exaggerates the imagined betrayal of his trust to a level that requires his conceptual extinction of the whole world. His delight that he is blessed in his "just censure" and "true opinion" becomes in the very next line a dire realization that he is "accursed/In being so blest!" (2.1.37–9). His knowledge seems to him "venom" (2.1.41).

There seems to be a subtle but deliberate blurring of Leontes' consciousness of the magnitude of the implications of his doubt. When Leontes cries, "All's true that is mistrusted" (2.1.47), he is merely convincing himself of an inverse truth-guarantee. When he asks, "Is whispering nothing?" (1.2.184), he is confident that he knows it is not. He reasons that *if* all the signs of his wife's adultery are nothing, *then* "the world and all that's in't is nothing" (1.2.293). However vehemently denied, the *conditionality* of his hypothesis – the inescapable uncertainty that accompanies the eternal open-endedness of signs and their interpretation – creates the vortex of his crisis. One could argue that, like Posthumus in Act 2, Scene 4 of *Cymbeline*, Leontes convinces himself that his jealousy is justified as a means of evading the alternative interpretation, which is that he cannot know. Shakespeare's portrayal of Leontes' behavior matches Cavell's assertion that "failure of knowledge is in fact a failure of acknowledgement, the result of which is not an ignorance but an ignoring, not an opposable doubt but an unappeasable denial, a willful uncertainty that constitutes annihilation" (1987: 206).

I wish here to emphasize that Leontes is not driven to distraction by any outside force or person. His mistaken mistrust and his ensuing crisis are not caught like a disease from without or enforced upon him by external forces such as destiny or divinity. Leontes' crisis necessarily indicates a form of choice – a response to the challenge of doubt that misfires. He deliberately goes "angling" for evidence (1.2.180), encouraging Polixenes and Hermione to conduct themselves according to their "own bents," declining to join them when invited to do so, and then determining their actions as proof of his cuckoldry (1.2.191). His interpretation of their actions is determined by his preconceived suspicions. He jumps to conclusions bred of hysteria, losing the ability to weigh the evidence presented by different modalities, inventing hypotheses that deepen his mistrust.

As the cognitive neurologist Antonio Damasio avers, reaching advantageous decisions necessitates emotional engagement or "emotional intelligence." Reason enables us to reflect upon and control our emotions; yet since reason itself relies on emotion, its controlling capacity is sometimes very limited (Damasio 1999: 58). When Leontes senses his grip on realty slipping away, and when the abyss of skepticism gapes before him, he latches on, with his nails as it were, to the sturdiest rock he can find: the rock of reason. Paradoxically, it is because Leontes (like Othello) is so overwhelmed by his emotions (fear, jealousy, anger) that he mistrusts them, hoping that reason will prove an anchor for truth.

Francisco Varela and his co-authors, Evan Thompson and Eleanor Rosch (in Varela *et al.* 1991), warn that "to deny the truth of our own experience in the scientific study of ourselves is not only unsatisfactory; it is to render the scientific study of ourselves without a subject matter" (Ibid.: 13–14). Seen from this angle, it becomes apparent that for Leontes to suspect Hermione of adultery with Polixenes, he must ignore his long-term love relations with her and his long-term friendship with Polixenes; he must mistrust their history of virtuous, loyal, and loving behavior towards him, deny the affections they still express toward him, and instead imagine an intricate web of lies and deception. Logically, of course, this is not wholly impossible. As Leontes himself is quick to acknowledge, "There have been [. . .] cuckolds ere now" (1.2.190). But for Leontes to doubt Hermione – as

for Othello to doubt Desdemona – is for him to make the mistake of following the possibilities afforded by logic while effacing all evidence to the contrary. Leontes' doubt arises from an internally generated, willful solipsism
and intellectual short-circuiting of the multiple, alternative information
sources that could have led to different conclusions. Reason is here superim-
posed over a basic suspicion, which neutralizes all other considerations, preventing Leontes from assessing the situation in an emotionally intelligent
way.

Shakespeare dramatizes the benefits of alternative forms of knowing
through his treatment of Leontes' greatest critics. For instance, Camillo
defends the queen with an unflinching certainty that "recalls a medieval and
chivalric sense of loyalty grounded in tradition and decorum rather than
logic and intellect" (Landau 2003: 11). This axiomatic, unconditional faith
is also extended by Paulina, who does not rely on the physical resemblances
between Leontes and his daughter (to which she calls his attention) but sides
with her mistress intuitively, drawing her certainty from prior knowledge of
Hermione's character. Thus, Camillo and Paulina avoid the mistake Leontes
makes. Meanwhile Leontes' denial of embodied knowledge is expressed in
his desire to halt the proliferation of meanings as well as its physical analogue: human fertility and procreation. Poetic (or philosophical) justice dictates, therefore, that the initial shock of truth, which begins the process by
which Leontes is cured of the malady of reason, comes with the death of his
son Mamillius. This is the darkest point of the play's representation of
Leontes' skeptical crisis.

One way of circumventing this potentially paralyzing skeptical view of
truth is offered by the philosopher Richard Rorty. Rorty claims that binary
oppositions are misleading and that, accordingly, the values of true and false
are only a "supposed antithesis" (Rorty 1984: 5). Paradoxically, he explains,
the two sides of any binary depend on each other, define each other, and are
in fact inextricably linked by a gradient that stretches from one to the other
and does not allow for a clear-cut distinction.

Although his philosophical pragmatism ultimately contributes to anxieties regarding the allusiveness of meaning and truth – a consequence I aim
to mitigate in this essay – I find Rorty's concept of the gradient particularly
useful in defusing the supposed threat of skepticism.[12] The idea of gradience
has been reinforced by Cavell and Spolsky, who suggest that despite lacking
guarantees for absolute truth, humans do possess means of determining a
gradient of truths that ranges from less probable to plausible to apt or useful,
and so on. Cavell claims that "it is possible to live an intelligent, satisfying,
and even moral life with the mental equipment which is our inheritance"
and "recover ... from the tragically debilitating skepticism that rejects
'good enough' knowledge in a vain struggle for an impossible ideal" (quoted
in Spolsky 2001b: 2). Spolsky, advancing a cognitive-evolutionary argument, goes further, asserting that perfection is not only unattainable but
would be counter-productive.

I suggest that not only does *The Winter's Tale* convince us that human knowledge is "good enough," but that the play unfolds a *gradient* view of skepticism. While the play encourages doubt in the form of intelligent questioning that counterbalances blind faith, dogmatism and tyranny – i.e., in the form of healthy, prudent skepticism – it also, at the same time, fights off the destructive lure of abandoned or unqualified skepticism, which in its extremism encourages radical pessimism. *The Winter's Tale* demonstrates that unqualified skepticism leads to self-betrayal: the destruction of both family and kingdom. But it is a matter of wisdom and measure to understand that skepticism of the *prudent* kind is not only reasonable but *productive*.

Moreover, I suggest here that skepticism is deceptively overwhelming when it relates to a world in which the only human faculty that may "know" anything about that world is reason or logic. There are, however, multiple ways of knowing, ways that also include kinesics, sense-perception, emotional responsiveness, imagination, memory, and intuition. These ways of constructing or gathering knowledge are defined as *embodied* because they are governed by the laws of biology rather than by logic. Indeed, despite the philosophical traditions that, from Plato through to Descartes, have located the site of knowledge in the mind, cognitive scientists are today increasingly convinced that knowledge is *distributed* throughout the body. Bodies cannot be set aside or ignored during the processes of mental or imaginative contemplation. As Andrew Brook and Robert J. Stainton describe it, the "mind" is a complex system of relationships between brain, body, and environment (Brook and Stainton 2000: 203).

Spolsky's claim that "in the period just before Descartes, the entanglements of brain, body and culture were felt by some to be a sickening disappointment" (Spolsky 2001a: 4) provides not merely background but indicates the kind of existential questions that Shakespeare seems to have been considering at the time he wrote *The Winter's Tale*. Shakespeare seems to have known something that took theorists and scientists almost four subsequent centuries to fully grasp: that trust – skepticism's antithesis – is derived from embodied understanding. *The Winter's Tale* indicates an affiliation with alternative strains of medieval and Renaissance thought, among them medicine, alchemy, and socio-religious practices, which considered the body to be integral, if complexly related, to individual identity and personhood.[13] I argue that literature and particularly drama afford Shakespeare the tools with which to articulate this alternative philosophical position. The combined effect of the thematic, structural, and performative aspects of *The Winter's Tale* – through the activation of living bodies – proves not only the possibility but the benefits of reconstituting faith in and trust of the body and the knowledge the body provides. Drama thus (re)creates the trust of which philosophy deprives us.

In the second half of the play, we learn that the best control against error – and against endlessly self-perpetuating doubt – is faith. However, faith is not presented as an escapist abdication of responsibility for assessing one's environment. Faith does not equal unquestioning adherence to higher powers (whether fate, God, tradition, the law, or any others). Moreover, faith is not positioned as antithetical to reason. In *The Winter's Tale*, faith is a form of informed and conscious *choice*: a show of confidence in one's own embodied knowledge.

As a phenomenon, human faith is grounded in a variety of sources. As Damasio notes, even if in the future we will have the machinery to scan other people's sensual input, no amount of knowledge will suffice to obtain the very same experiences that other people have. Experience is so subjective and multilayered that it is forever a matter of "individual ownership and individual agency" (Damasio 1999: 306). Leontes simply cannot be sure of his wife's true experiences unless – and this will shortly prove crucial – he both takes her word for it and trusts his own embodied knowledge. I use the terms *faith* and *trust* here somewhat interchangeably. This is because my reading of *The Winter's Tale* suggests that Shakespeare's use of "faith" does not indicate conviction of the truth in a particular system of religious beliefs but, rather, expresses faith in the possibility of achieving satisfying knowledge and in the possibility of fostering trust-relations among people as opposed to doubt, suspicion and hate. At bottom, it is a matter of *confidence*, both in oneself and in others. Abstract reason is, on the whole, insufficient to convince one person to trust another. Conjecture and speculation, however systematic, must be supplemented by simulation, by employing one's capacities in a way that parallels those of the others, and by acknowledging that affective empathy is a legitimate and often subtle source of *knowledge*. Moreover, empathy is not dependent upon language and may thus bypass some of the pitfalls presented by the gaps between words and world(s).

However, as Henderson and Horgan explain, the off-line processes of simulation are informed by "discursive information," which plays a role in determining what cognitive processes to call into play when making decisions (Henderson and Horgan 2000: 123). Faith is grounded in a mutually beneficial "mix of strategies," "jointly providing multiple modes of epistemic access," which complement and compensate for one another (Ibid.: 123). In other words, by zigzagging back and forth from empathy to discussion, from intuition to assessment, and from action through feedback to refinement, we gradually progress, while continually monitoring and qualifying that progress. This advancement through dialogue and supplementation embodies the creative process by which brain, body, and world collaborate in producing meaning.

The pastoral cure

How then are we to come by this collaborative mixture between intellectual and embodied knowledge? One way is through learning from the long tradition of pastoral art and literature. Spolsky asserts that the function of the pastoral genre is to "correct an imbalance between an overdeveloped mental and an impoverished sensual life" (Spolsky 2001a: 17). She argues that the tremendous appeal of this sensual genre in the early modern period lies in its power to provide "bodily knowledge, and even more important ... confidence in that knowledge" (Ibid.: 16). As Spolsky points out, the conventions of the genre dictate that the hero(ine) spends a curative period in nature in order to "leave behind (temporarily) just the sophistication the high culture valued, and to abandon abstract knowledge in search of the satisfaction of learning that feels good, like a sunny day, good food, and sex without guilt" (Ibid.: 17). The hero(ine) then returns to city society, where his or her real destiny is to be fulfilled. This period away has provided the hero(ine) with a knowledge of nature and self through channels that are either unavailable or shunned in the world of the city, where the values are tilted towards those of the mind.

In keeping with the conventions of the pastoral genre, it is in retirement – far away from the court – that the characters of *The Winter's Tale* are brought in contact with the natural stimuli that encourage embodied knowledge. Perdita is brought up in the pastoral idyll of Bohemia; Hermione takes refuge at Paulina's residence.[14] However, if we seek a pastoral interpretation for *The Winter's Tale* as a whole, we discover a problem: Leontes never actually leaves court. Martha Ronk even offers a psychological interpretation of the play, in which the whole Bohemian interlude (Act 4) is but a dream or a metaphorical representation of Leontes' private journey to peace, a visible dramatization of his invisible "internal struggle" (Ronk 1990: 56). Have Leontes' 16 years of self-flagellation and repentance served as his pastoral retreat? Can nature be so easily substituted? It is one thing to claim that this period serves as a time of punishment so that he may emerge "worthy" to win back his wife and daughter; it is quite another to claim that he has thereby learned the invaluable lessons that the body (aided by the pastoral genre) teaches.

An entirely different interpretation of the function of the passing of time is offered by Valerie Traub, who argues that Leontes is driven mad by the fear of his wife's potential for erotic betrayal: that is, not by skepticism in general but by a specifically gendered and misogynistic anxiety. She reasons that Leontes must show devotion to his dead wife and be delivered from the exigencies of female erotic life before he can re-enter marriage with any degree of psychic comfort. Meanwhile, Hermione's sexuality – "too hot, too hot!" (1.2.108) – must be metaphorically contained and physically disarmed. Her silence toward Leontes in the last act of the play, according to Traub, bespeaks her submissiveness. But Traub's reading, focusing so forcefully on women's subjugation, fails to take into account the generic choice of the playwright. Traub implies that Hermione is presented as a chaste statue in order to lessen the threat of her sexuality. But sexuality is one of the embodied sources of knowledge that Spolsky has shown the pastoral genre encourages. If we accept Traub's interpretation (and it may be said to complement New Historicist claims for the early modern theatre's dynamics of containment), then it renders Act 5 a canceling out of Act 4. According to Traub's reading, both Hermione and Perdita return to court not to supplement its deficiencies but to be contained and nullified by them. This implies that the lesson Leontes has learned is how to successfully dominate women and how to suppress both his own and his wife's sexual desire. Are we then to assume that Shakespeare chose the pastoral genre only to discredit its power?

The pastoral, as I read it, teaches just how we may mitigate skepticism through trust. Leontes does not leave the court, but he learns the value of embodied knowledge through those he casts out: Hermione and Perdita. Cavell claims that "skepticism is a male business," for the masculine response to the passion of knowledge is doubt, while the female response is love.[15] Accordingly, the only way the hyperbole of doubt can be countered is by love – "skepticism under a reverse sign" (Cavell 1987: 16–18). Hermione personifies love. Her feminine power is not rejected as a form of wantonness but is recognized as the creative force of love. Her silence at the end of the play is, according to this reading, a sign not of submission but of triumph and regeneration. This interpretation is consistent with the advice that Cleomenes gives Leontes before Hermione returns: "Do as the heavens have done, forget your evil;/With them, forgive yourself" (5.1.5–6). Neither Hermione's nor heaven's forgiveness can substitute for self-forgiveness; Leontes cannot be fully cured until he forgives himself. This is not only a foregoing of weddedness to nothing (the skeptical abyss), or merely a renewed marriage to love (Hermione); it is also a profound acceptance of an imperfect self.

In the final scene of the play, Leontes is re-united with love and issue – the two things he most fiercely denied – and with the genuine embodied individuals who personify those abstractions for him. He learns that he is not only a mind, connected by laws to his subjects, spouse, and children, but also and predominantly a body connected by blood and love relations to a *family*. In Act 5 he is re-united with this family and thus with himself. This also represents a rather complex allegorical union of nature-to-be-refined-by-schooling (Perdita), love-enriched-by-forgiveness (Hermione), and (masculine)-reason-supplemented-by-these-two-(feminine)-forces and at peace with itself (Leontes). Why then does Shakespeare bend the conventions of pastoral? Might his refusal to be tied by genre conventions betray his discomfort with inflexibility? Like Leontes, many of Shakespeare's contemporaries sought to fend off the threat of uncertainty through increased religious dogmatism and scientific positivism. In *The Winter's Tale*, I argue, Shakespeare is trying a different strategy: He is ignoring strict generic categorization.[16]

In order for the human mind to reach a level of understanding about something that is in any way satisfactory, a process of supplementation must take place. Just as, according to pastoral conventions, city life and its sophistication are supplemented by the wisdom of nature, so in this play the conventions of the pastoral genre are themselves supplemented by those of romance and tragicomedy. A conventional romance structure typically unfolds a tale in which the hero is limited in his ability to control his destiny. In *The Winter's Tale*, the hero's destiny is subject to a strange mix of Christian and pagan divine powers, borrowing from both ancient mythology and the tradition of the medieval miracle plays. This lends a theological character to the romance action and subjugates it to the tragicomic message.

Tragicomedy was famously dubbed "mongrel" by Sir Philip Sidney because it merges the sublime with the ridiculous, joy with sadness, and an unflinching awareness of darkness with optimism. Similarly, Shakespeare insists that life cannot be neatly categorized into (literary) generic units. Illogicality, discontinuity, coincidence, frustration, and surprise are elements that abound in life. Therefore, it is fitting to represent these elements in art by using a "mixed mode" of expression.[17] As Stephen Greenblatt observes, this mixed mode "exposes the instability and uncertainty of human judgment. . . . It forces the reader to call into the open and examine consciously those standards by which he judges experience. . . . For the mixed mode, to resolve is to lie" (Greenblatt 1973: 351, 355).

Shakespeare's mixed mode, when viewed as a philosophical attitude, may provide an interesting vantage point from which to consider a dilemma facing contemporary philosophy of mind. Theorists are currently divided between two supposedly antithetical models for describing human cognition: Theory–Theory (hereafter TT) and Simulation–Theory (hereafter ST). Humans regularly understand the behavior of others by attributing mental states to their actions. This capacity was believed until recently to rely upon a particular conceptual system that develops as a child grows, known as a "Theory of Mind" (hereafter ToM).[18] The proponents of TT hold that humans gradually acquire an implicit, naïve commonsense theory of mind to which they refer while interpreting others; while proponents of ST hold that we are born with a biological, pre-linguistic capacity for empathy that allows us to relate to others on a far more basic level.[19] TT is thus a conscious, intellectual process, ST an automatic, intuitive one.[20]

I am convinced that were he alive today, Shakespeare would eagerly join David Henderson and Terence Horgan in calling for (re)conciliation between TT and ST. Henderson and Horgan hold that neither pure theoretical analysis nor our natural capacity for simulation is sufficient in itself for attaining reliable knowledge since each has "significant blind spots" (Henderson and Horgan 2000: 130). Instead, "we do well epistemically to employ simulation and theoretical modeling as complementary processes – and to employ hybrid processes" (Ibid.). "Hybrid" is indeed an adjective that accurately describes *The Winter's Tale*. The play expresses a conviction that it is not through binaries but through supplementation that we mitigate our limitations and secure knowledge that is – at the least – "good enough."

A (winter's) tale of embodiment

Human knowledge may be limited, but humans have also developed tools for bypassing their biological limitations and extending their cognitive abilities. One of these ways is through the telling of stories.[21] Moreover, it is not only the ubiquity of story-telling but its openness to reinterpretation that teaches, inspires, and contributes to both individual and cultural flexibility. The status of tales and their relation to truth(s) are at the very heart of *The Winter's Tale*. The phrase "an old tale" is repeated twice in Act 5, Scene 2 (30, 65), echoing the title of the play. The second gentleman says, "This news, which is called true, is so like an old tale that the verity of it is in strong suspicion" (5.2.30–1). Walter S.H. Lim maintains that Shakespeare foregrounds classical mythology in *The Winter's Tale* not simply to facilitate the demands of plot but also to "accentuate his interest in the status of different generic forms: the ballad, the ghost story, classical myth, and even the Bible itself" (Lim 2001: 317). The site of interest becomes not theology but the representational space of literary production, the Bible becoming just one of – rather than *the* – source text.[22]

Cavell holds that the activity of telling denotes "reconceiving, reconstituting knowledge, along with the world" (Cavell 1987: 204). To speak, he argues, "is to say what counts" (Ibid.: 205). Telling, therefore, implies accounting for what matters. Because the value of events is worked out in the telling, in tales the act becomes one of *re*counting. Cavell notices that Hermione's somewhat erotic pleasure in having tales told in her ear (II.ii.34: "Come on then, and give't me in mine ear") must be known to her husband and may therefore be one of the causes of his exaggerated suspicion of her whispering with Polixenes and then with Mamillius. Retelling tales in this context implies the sensuality of proliferation and unbounded fertility. Cavell also detects a competition between Leontes and his son over who has the right to tell this tale and suggests that the play unfolds a reversed Oedipal conflict: not one in which the son wishes to replace the father but one generated by "the father's wish to replace or remove his son" (Cavell 1987: 199). In his mad state, Leontes wants there to be no counting or recounting; in other words, he wants there to be nothing. And that is what he achieves: his son dies, his daughter is lost.[23]

Even more valuable than the tales themselves, however, are the forms of their telling. Reading engages the intellect and affects the emotions, but performance co-opts embodied knowledge to a far greater extent. Theatre is, therefore, a particularly successful means of conveying varied layers of meaning because it presents these meanings in verbal-intellectual *and* embodied forms. I have argued that Shakespeare's use of the pastoral genre emphasizes the importance of embodied knowledge. His decision to convert a prose-romance into drama, I suggest, allows him to combine as many bodily, sensory stimulants as possible to add to the otherwise verbal (and what we also think of as textual) tale. This need not be understood as a flaunting of the superiority of theatre over a more verbal and textual experience like reading. Rather, I assert that theatre is a means of advocating the *supplementation* of narration by performance. The most fantastical events in *The Winter's Tale* – a courtier is eaten by a bear,[24] the king's lost daughter is found, and the queen is miraculously resurrected (either from death or retirement) – are all expressed as events that have to be seen to be believed, since experience of them "lames report," "undoes description," and lies beyond the capacity of "ballad-makers ... to express it" (5.2.26–7).[25] The scene in which Perdita is "found" is *reported*, related by successive gentlemen, while the scene in which Hermione is "found" – lacking the naturalistic explanations accompanying her daughter's recovery – is *shown* in the most spectacular, super-theatrical manner.

It appears that performance finally overrides words when Shakespeare instinctively follows Aristotle's advice that "as far as possible, [the poet should] also bring [his plot] to completion with gestures" (*Poetics* [trans. 1987] I.xvii.4.3.2). After her "resurrection," Hermione is expressly asked by Paulina not to spoil the atmosphere by troubling their joys with "like relation" (5.3.130). Thus, Hermione's silence may, after all, signal neither submission (Traub) nor love (Cavell) but rather the power of theatricality. There is a time for intellectual explanations, but in the midst of reconciliation, such explanations would only spoil the mood. Silence allows the departing theatre audience to leave with a visual (and therefore unmediated) tableau imprinted in their minds. Though discussion will surely follow, the last image of the performance is that of a gesture. What, then, is the difference, in terms of what Henderson and Horgan have defined as "epistemic competence" (Henderson and Horgan 2000: 121), between reporting and enacting a scene? And what is the difference, in terms of emotional value and knowledge, between describing and staging it?

A tale performed: theatrical spectacle as revelation

The neuroscientific work of researchers such as Vitorrio Gallese has shown that understanding the potential meaning of an action and being able to forecast its consequences are enabled by the agent's motor equivalence. According to Gallese, much of what we ascribe to the minds of others depends on a "resonance mechanism that our actions trigger in us" (Gallese 2001: 47). In the process of simulation, we adopt another agent's perspective by "tracking or matching their states with resonant states of one's own" (Gallese and Goldman 1998: 493), creating a "correspondence" (Ibid.: 497). This enables the mind-reader to "retrodict" as well as predict-allowing both forward and backward inferences.

A collection of single neuron recording experiments conducted upon monkeys has proven that there is a special cortical sector of the brain (known as the Broca's Area) that is selectively activated by bodily movement and is particularly responsive to goal-related behaviors. The neurons in this area do not respond to random movements but only to apprehension interaction that is meaningful to the human species. Moreover, the neurons "appear to generalize across different ways of achieving the same goal," suggesting susceptibility to an "abstract type of action coding" (Gallese 2001: 36).[26] A set of 'Canonical neurons' is activated by the execution of a goal-related activity, and a set of 'Mirror neurons' (hereafter MNs) does the same but is also, crucially, activated by merely observing another individual execute a purposeful activity. This indicates that primates have "an action observation/execution matching system" (Ibid.: 36). In effect, MNs allow us to attribute intention to observed movements of others. This form of *representation,* argues Gallese, is made possible by establishing a link "constituted by the *embodiment* of the intended goal, shared by the agent and the observer" (Ibid.: 36; italics in original). In other words, in order to interpret the actions or intentions of another, the observer must share the motor schema of the agent – share a bodily knowledge. Equally interesting for the present study is the discovery that when we observe an action, our MNs actually activate the visual areas that observe the action and, concurrently, recruit the motor circuits used to perform that action. As Gallese notes, "action observation implies *action simulation*" (Ibid.: 37; italics in original).[27] This simulation involves neither overt knowledge nor conscious inference but is achieved by *physically participating* in the observed actions. The role of abstract theorizing in ascribing mental states to the actions of others is largely overtaken by attention to the *embodied mechanisms* of cognition. Mirror-matching, Gallese argues, is "a basic organizational feature of the brain" (Ibid.: 46).

These discoveries have far-reaching implications for theatre studies. By facilitating intersubjective communication, mind-reading, and empathy, our innate matching system is also responsible for our readiness to engage with fictional agents. Indeed, Gallese and Goldman define ST as "incorporating an attempt to replicate, mimic, or impersonate the mental life of the target agent" (Gallese and Goldman 1998: 497), which is exactly what we do when we engage with fictional agents. Because this ability is so clearly embodied, its study through the interaction of audiences with actor-characters in performance becomes all the more pertinent.

Lisa Zunshine has demonstrated how "our ability to navigate multiple levels of intentionality present in a narrative" (Zunshine 2003: 8) both extends and challenges our ToM capacities, making literary texts a source of valuable training and knowledge. I would like to go further and suggest that drama bypasses the constraints posed by the fact that the reader's analysis is always reliant upon the author's description of the character's behavior; drama has the added advantage of affording the theatre audience first-hand experience of the events performed. At the theatre, we are able to observe for ourselves the behavior of the characters embodied on stage. Even if the story it stages is fictional, a live performance enables the audience to witness the events it unfolds as tangibly *as if* they were really taking place. Despite there being a level of symbolic understanding that invites the audience to infer multiple levels of meaning in a play *as a play*, the audience nevertheless also benefits from having embodied knowledge and relies heavily on this knowledge to discern meaning as they watch the play.

Precisely this level of embodied engagement is required in order to make sense of *The Winter's Tale*. The meaning of Hermione's resurrection scene is left unresolved; Hermione is not permitted to reveal her secrets – to tell the tale. By this point in the play, "such a deal of wonder is broken out" (5.2.25) that the theatre audience is made to feel uncertain as to whether it ought to believe that this scene professes to represent a statue being brought to life, or whether it is intended to be interpreted as a trick – a performance. And, in either case, is this performance meant to convince or fool the play-characters to the same extent as the audience? Are we then to believe what we are *told* by Paulina, or are we to be wholly skeptical? Does the audience believe more or less because they have *seen* this scene?

Critics point out that the play continually undercuts its own symbolism, refusing to allow the audience to rest secure on a single interpretation.[28] For instance, Perdita, displaying no knowledge of the contemporary religious controversy over iconoclasm, kneels before the statue seeking its blessing, an act that (were the statue real, as she thinks it is) constitutes idolatry. Paulina swiftly prevents her from kissing the statue's hand with the excuse that the paint on the statue is not yet dry. Aaron Landau argues that Perdita's superstitious sense of piety gives away Shakespeare's allegedly Catholic confidence in the positive power of images (Landau 2003: 16). Another reading might find that Perdita, yet unschooled and knowing no better, is corrected by the wiser priestess Paulina.

My contention is that the audience's experience of the discovery of the statue is an instantaneous realization, comparable perhaps to the sudden shock Leontes experiences when hit by his skeptical realization. The instant the statue is uncovered, the audience experiences an immediate gestalt: because we know at once – quite possibly owing to the swift firing of our mirror neurons – that *this is the queen*, we begin to reorganize the information of Acts 3 and 4, recategorizing the tale in order to reach a new interpretation that allows for her having remained alive all this while. I argue that, in determining this new, retroactive interpretation, we are not relying upon sophisticated theoretical or literary skills but upon our most basic perceptual, embodied understanding.

This claim is corroborated by the director Nicholas Hytner, according to whom *performance* does away with many of the questions that seem unresolved in the text (Hytner 2002: 22). In every performance he has either directed or attended, writes Hytner, no one in the audience ever doubts that Hermione is alive. While reading the text justifiably encourages multiple possibilities for interpretation, performance takes place in the present and must necessarily foreground one interpretation. However, this interpretation cannot justifiably rest upon the whims of a particular production. Instead, by engaging embodied experience, performance of *The Winter's Tale* shows that it is the "tale" of Hermione-as-statue that is wholly unbelievable, while her living body is immediate and undeniable testimony that she is the same Hermione we saw in Act 1.[29] The only ones who are fooled by the tale of the statue are the characters on stage (though performance also determines the extent to which they appear to perceive that some clever trickery is being practiced, or to which they believe that a supernatural miracle is taking place). This fooling of the other characters is crucial: The presence of the queen's body on stage – the unequivocal realness of the flesh – sufficiently dispels doubt. The fact that in Shakespeare's day a boy would have performed the part of Hermione does not affect this argument, as it is the *life* of the *body* that gives away the lie. Even if the actor or actress is very skillful, the audience knows, by virtue of having bodies themselves, that this is not a lifeless statue. Clearly, then, Shakespeare is making deliberate use of his audience's embodied knowledge.

Spectators not only know the queen is alive, they also empathize with the performer's physical challenge (remaining motionless for so long). Thus, empathy – or simulation – works on a number of levels in this scene: the audience is invited to engage with the emotions of the major characters but also, at the same time, to engage with the physicality of performance. Accordingly, though the audience is wholly aware that this is a performer pretending to be a queen, pretending to be a statue – an entirely artificial and extra-theatrical situation – the success of the scene nevertheless relies upon very real and immediate bodily sensations.

As the discovery of mirror neurons and Gallese's motor equivalence theory would suggest, and as Hytner's theatrical experience shows, the resurrection scene in *The Winter's Tale* is made believable and therefore meaningful through attention to the physicality of the characters. Hytner asserts that noting that Mamillius's nose requires wiping (1.2.121) and later that Hermione's skin has wrinkled (5.3.28) both emphasize that *The Winter's Tale* is about "flesh-and-blood people" (Hytner 2002: 22). This makes the case of a man who gets jealous for no reason and tears apart his family – though strictly speaking a fictional tale – one that is based in embodied reality. Hytner's attention to realism also provides an explanation for Hermione's silence: she is still stunned by her own actions (Hytner 2002: 22).

Carol Chillington Rutter confirms this hypothesis when she distinguishes between reading of the performance-text and the playtext of a play. The former, she argues, involves an opening up of one's self to the play's "supplementary physical, visual, gestural, iconic texts." It also, interestingly, "mak[es] more space for the kind of work that women do in plays (particularly as Shakespeare situates their roles to play off men)" (Rutter 2001: xv). In almost every Shakespeare play, observes Rutter, men are given more lines, while women express themselves through actions; women's centrality to their respective plays is revealed, therefore, in performance. Thus, attending to the body means attending to "theatre's 'feminine' unruliness and the unpredictable, not to say promiscuous, theory-resisting effects performance generates" (Ibid.: xv).

As Hermione's final silence in this play demonstrates, silences are not only potentially pregnant with meaning but also connote action. Hermione dominates this scene by virtue of her positioning at center-stage (probably elevated on a pedestal). She need not speak to command the attention of those on stage, as it is for the purpose of seeing her that they have come to Paulina's gallery; while the other characters must rely more heavily on words to be noticed. This makes it clear to me that the "resurrection" of Hermione reveals not only the miraculous power of (divine) forgiveness but the impressive ingenuity of Paulina's theatrical skills and, thus, the creative power of theatre at large. Paulina and her art of careful concealment and timely revelation are a case of masterful stage-directing: of performance.[30]

In performance, we are also more likely to note that the only words Hermione utters in this scene are spoken to Perdita:

> . . . I
> Knowing by Paulina that the oracle
> Gave hope thou wast in being, have preserved
> Myself to see the issue.
>
> (5.3.126–9)

The second syllable of "Myself" is stressed at the beginning of the line and was most probably stressed by the actor in performance. This indicates that it is neither a miracle nor Paulina who is responsible for Hermione's return but rather Hermione herself. Additionally, her speech indicates that she has preserved herself not for Leontes but for her daughter and her grandchildren – for the prospect of issue, for the proliferation that Leontes had once tried to obliterate. In retrospect, the second gentleman recalls that Paulina "hath privately, twice or thrice a day, ever since the death of Hermione, visited that removed house" (5.2.114–15), in which Hermione is finally revealed. This too suggests that Hermione has chosen to remain in hiding until the Oracle's prophecy should come true and her daughter is found. It seems to me that when Leontes says that he has "in vain said many/A prayer upon her grave" (5.3.140–1), he indicates that he now understands she was never dead but only "thought dead" (5.3.140).

Whether or not this evidence is considered sufficient, the one certainty Shakespeare undoubtedly allows us to draw from this scene is that theatricality goes hand-in-hand with revelation. Human knowledge is always subject to suspicion; human apprehension and the interpretation of reality are necessarily unreliable. The status of truth can be, at best, as Cavell articulates it, "the status of opinion, educated guesswork, hypothesis, construction, belief" (Cavell 1987: 8). However, this belief is neither wholly random nor any form of blind faith but an informed species of decision-making, which takes account of – and trusts – embodied knowledge.

It is trust in bodily knowledge, then, that grounds the leap of faith we are required to make at the end of the play. The status of miracles is never fully clarified, but Shakespeare delights in the possibility that putting one's faith in miracles entails believing events that are in fact displays of artistic creativity. Whether or not this creativity is a sign of divine power or is independent of it also remains unresolved. Paulina's trick, or Hermione's craftiness, effectively moves the audience to faith. Mary Thomas Crane has rightly complained that preoccupation with the representational and philosophical implications of a play, especially its truth-value and its participation in dominant discursive structures, though valuable in themselves, can obscure what performance makes clear. Performance *does* things. Crane claims that performance incorporates, in its very definition, the concept of "turning something immaterial (a duty, a promise, a contract, the pattern of a ceremony) into a material thing" (Crane 2001: 173). I suggest that the resurrection scene in *The Winter's Tale* is a literal embodiment of this idea, giving it flesh and personifying its effects.

But it also complicates the ontological status of performance. Crane asks whether performance is a process or a material thing that can be "kept" or whether it is fraudulent, "pretending to produce something out of nothing" (Ibid.: 174). To answer this question, I ask whether anything is created by Hermione's performance in Act 5 and by the performance of *The Winter's Tale* as a whole. My answer is yes: both create greater intersubjective understanding and trust in embodied knowledge. Performance is a material process, by which actors and audiences participate in the process of making meaning. And as Cavell asserts, by answering Paulina's command of "It is required/You do awake your faith" (5.3.95), the audience members graduate from being spectators to participants. This faith that we are called upon to exercise is anchored in kinetic knowledge, intuition, memory, inference, imagination, experience and creativity. All these should be the means of attaining knowledge that is "good enough" to form the basis of healthy trust-relations with our fellow human beings.

Finally, if, as the mirror-neurons hypothesis suggests – that by observing action or attending a performance, we activate both neural and motor circuits in our bodies, thus initiating both intellectual and physical stimulation – then going to the theatre is a form of active knowledge acquisition that is not as different from other experiences as was once believed. In fact, because drama is designed for a purpose and is created deliberately in order to stimulate, and because our emotional engagement with the action is (at least) once removed, it may be argued that we learn more easily from theatre than from life.

Conclusion: performing the body

The current state of research in cognition casts doubt upon the commonly held assumption that human beings are free to act upon rational reasoning and should even strive to proceed according to hypotheses reached through theoretical understanding alone. It appears instead that isolated intellectual contemplation is an idealized fallacy: our mental faculties cannot be disengaged from the brain and mind in which they are formed or from the body in which the brain and mind function. Our search for answers will be forever limited, and ultimately self-defeating, if we refuse to acknowledge the embodied processes that necessarily partake in our search. It would be misleading, however, to assume that our natural capacity for empathy is in itself sufficiently complex to enable us to fully understand others. In any decision-making process, we draw upon emotion as well as reason, memory, physical sensations, imagination, intuition, and many other of our faculties.

As cognitive scientists are now claiming, human minds do not, strictly speaking, produce meaning but, rather, process the relationships between brain and world.[31] These relationships are not simple cause-and-effect connections or on/off functions but systems of implications. These systems and their implications differ from individual brain to brain because they are formed by active, creative – and thus personal – participation. One of the best means of stimulating the operations by which we process meaning, thereby making the world a more intelligible and a less threatening place, is through simulation at the theatre. This works so successfully because drama, theatre, and performance engage both the body and its embodied mind.

The optimistic ending of *The Winter's Tale* is not, then, a contrived forgetting of uncomfortable events and their inherent violence; rather, it suggests a solution to the threat of radical skepticism. Indeed, by witnessing murder desired and forestalled on stage, we experience the identification with violent impulses and then the cathartic release and containment of those impulses. Particularly, if this violence and disowning of knowledge and issue are a natural response to skepticism, as Cavell suggests they are, then the play fulfils the function of enlightening us, confronting us with this knowledge, and at the same time purging us of its negative effects. If we may learn from a play without having to make the mistakes it recounts, without having to suffer ourselves, without inflicting terrible damage upon others, and without having to wait 16 years, then Shakespeare has succeeded in demonstrating the genuinely miraculous power of art.

The Winter's Tale calls for skepticism to be pondered as a solution rather than a problem, an opening of multiple possibilities rather than a threat to knowledge. Prudent skepticism leads to the realization that it is counterproductive to seek absolute truth. Instead, the knowledge that emerges from performing *The Winter's Tale* is invaluable: in order to overcome the pain of the knowledge of skepticism and its potentially tragic implications, and in order to convert this knowledge into a productive force, Leontes – and the audience – must "awake [our] faith," faith in the generative and curative powers of performance. As we watch the performance, we witness the fertility of the creative act, which, far from being detached from the body, is rather enriched, even facilitated by the body. It is through trusting our bodies that we may best defy radical skepticism.

Notes

1 This understanding is not new in universal terms. For instance, Richard Schechner describes two very different tribal ritual-cycles among the Australian Aborigines and the Elema of New Guinea, both of which are "founded on the same belief in multiple, valid, equivalent, and reciprocating realities" (Schechner 1988: 49). However, the acceptance of multiplicity in Western philosophical thinking is relatively recent.

2 I am not referring to specific skeptical arguments of particular thinkers but using the term "skepticism" to denote a condition of conscious doubting that is often accompanied (unnecessarily, I argue) by an existential crisis. By "existential crisis" I refer to a range of pessimistic, nihilistic and existential philosophies as well as individual people's depressive states that emphasize the wretchedness of the world, the beastliness of human nature, and the necessary suffering of existence. I also have in mind such relativist-pragmatist positions as expressed in recent times by Nelson Goodman or Richard Rorty, which deny that any gradient of values exists and eschew the possibility that there exists an independent reality beyond interpretation expressed through language.

3 Cavell compares Leontes' laments that knowledge is like a poisonous spider (2.1.40–5) with the philosopher David Hume's sense of being "cursed, or sickened, in knowing more than his fellows about the fact of knowing itself" (Cavell 1987: 197), which Hume calls the "malady" of knowledge. I deliberately use the term *reason* because it is precisely the mistake of limiting "knowledge" to logic that breeds the malady.

4 Robert Greene, *Pandosto, or The Triumph of Time* (1588). King Pandosto's wife Bellaria, "to show how she liked him whom her husband loved" (159), attends to and entertains Egistus, King of Sicilia, with such "familiar courtesy" that she could perhaps be suspected. For instance, she "oftentimes came herself into his bed-chamber to see that nothing should be amiss" (159). This is not given as justification of Pandosto's "flaming jealousy" (160). However, Bellaria and Egistus are described as "silly souls" (160) who, though innocently, may have lacked a certain measure of tact or propriety, spending too much time in one another's company, allowing Pandosto's "disordinate fancy" to "misconstrue of their too private familiarity" (160).

5 *The Winter's Tale*, asserts Cavell, "questions the universality or radicalness of skepticism altogether" (Cavell 1987: 15).

6 King Leontes (Everyman), by rejecting Grace (Hermione), killing Childhood (Mamillus) and banishing natural Innocence (Perdita), is left bereft, lonely and on the verge of despair. He is, however, taught humility through suffering but is not finally denied heaven's grace. See Milward (1964).

7 The issue of Hermione's "resurrection" is discussed at length below. Suffice it to say that I side with those who do not believe that she dies in prison and is later brought back from the dead but that she has been in hiding. As for lying: Gallese and Goldman cite experiments that indicate that not only is the attribution of mental states and intentionality basic to us primates but so is deception (Gallese and Goldman 1998: 499).

8 Polixenes commands Camillo: "If you know ought which does behoove my knowledge/Thereof to be inform'd, imprison't not/In ignorant concealment" (1.2.395–7). Yet both Leontes and Polixenes are weakened by inform'd knowledge and restored by concealment. Camillo, Florizel, Perdita, Autolycus, Paulina, and Hermione each in turn conceals knowledge, thereby correcting the faults of others (Palmer 1995: 335).

9 Shakespeare's evident fear and rejection of religious dogmatism has led some scholars to conclude that he was anti-Puritan if not actually Catholic (Landau

2003). I believe, however, that his anxiety in relation to growing religious extremism was not indicative of a particular religious persuasion but of his philosophy of art. Intolerance – religious, moral, or political – is the site of Shakespeare's criticism and not specifically Protestant behavior. Alternative political contexts to the religio-political theme are offered by Donna B. Hamilton's reading (1993), which reminds us that the play was written just as King James' proposal to unify England with Scotland was hotly debated, noting that Shakespeare deploys the literary trend of using a pastoral setting for political commentary and thereby replicates the particular rhetoric of the Union controversy in *The Winter's Tale*. Daryl W. Palmer explores the connections between this winter's tale and that of Richard Chancellor who "discovered Russia" in 1553. The ensuing diplomatic ties with the Muscovites were apparently accompanied by proliferating tales of strange customs, jealousies, and violent deeds that fueled the English imagination, and it is by no random chance, argues Palmer, that Shakespeare chooses for Hermione "The Emperor of Russia" for a father (3.2.119). In Shakespeare's source it is not Pandosto's wife Bellaria but Egistus' wife who is the daughter of the Russian emperor (*Pandosto* 164), thus providing Egistus with powerful alliances that dissuade Pandosto from waging war on Sicilia. The fact that Pandosto cannot effectively reap his revenge upon Egistus is given as the prime reason for his turning all his anger towards Bellaria (*Pandosto* 164).

10 Spolsky has considered the unreliability of spectral evidence through a reading of *Othello*. She argues that "the tragedy emerges from various forms of sense entanglement, particularly from the ease with which we incorporate (the pun is productive) different kinds of visual knowing, in spite of the difficulties of making their conflicting messages produce non-contradictory and satisfying understanding" (Spolsky 2001a: 1).

11 Once again, the verity of the report of Hermione's death depends on the interpretation of Act V. The present reading holds the report of her death to be untrue.

12 The preference for a gradient may be traced back to Heidegger (1927) as he ardently resisted closed dualities and criticized Plato's use of binaries.

13 For which see Bynum (1995: 33).

14 Unless one argues that she was dead for 16 years, etc.

15 Cavell explains that men and women are equally capable of "masculine" doubt or "feminine" love; his distinction refers to "the masculine and the feminine aspects of the human character generally." If this is the case, he should perhaps have described these traits in less gendered terms. His advice is in any case that we marry the two – figuratively as well as physically. For Cavell's theory of the reinvention of marriage as revision of religion, see Cavell (1987: 216–20).

16 Stephen Orgel (1991) speculates that a rigidity underlies Shakespeare's and other poets' eagerness to celebrate the mysterious opacity of poetry and to show up absolute interpretations as dangerous.

17 Robert W. Corrigen has argued that this hybrid genre is endemic to times of unrest (Corrigen 1979: 222), but it may be argued that almost every period in history has included elements of unrest. Indeed, Stephen Greenblatt (1973: 348) argues that as an artist, Sidney was not concerned with re-establishing the stability that his times seem to have lost but rather was a "connoisseur of doubt" (351). This I believe was also Shakespeare's aim.

18 According to this theory, humans assume that others have a mental and emotional life more or less comparable to their own and thereby infer other individuals' intentionality. For more on ToM, see Carruthers and Smith (1996).

19 For the historical evolution of the concept and its part in contemporary debates, see the long and detailed introduction to Kögler and Steuber 2000. They write

that "empathy" is a later English translation of the German word Einfühlung, originally introduced by Theodore Lipps (*Grundlegund der Aesthetik* 1903) into the vocabulary of aesthetic experience to denote the relationship between an artwork and the observer, who imaginatively projects him/herself into the contemplated object. Husserl's phenomenology further emphasized the role of the acting body in perception. The term "empathy," argue Kögler and Steuber, has evolved since Romantic times to become a laden term in both philosophy and the social sciences.

20 See also Davies and Stone (1995a, 1995b).

21 See Andy Clark (1998) about "mental scaffolding." See also Young and Saver (2001) about storytelling as essential to the construction of self.

22 In a parodic version of faith, Leontes believes in, even though he has not directly witnessed, Hermione's infidelity. Nothing that comes by way of council can convince him of the fallacy of that belief, and his obdurate blindness foregrounds the gulf separating conviction from truth. Translated into the discourse of religious conviction, belief in things unseen does not necessarily add up to possessing the truth (Lim 2001: 321).

23 This is of course far from traditional interpretations of the death of the son, for which see R.G. Hunter (1965: 186–203). On the connection with the ongoing conflict between King James and his son Henry, see Palmer (1995: 331). As for Perdita being "lost," Frances E. Dolan argues that *The Winter's Tale* is most "like an old tale" (5.3.117) because it replicates an all-too-familiar story of infant abandonment. She insists that we do not efface the fact that Perdita was never "lost" but was cast out by her violent father. By dwelling on the language of loss, argues Dolan, "the play prepares for forgiveness by sparing Leontes the direct, criminalized agency ... helping us to repress our knowledge of his crucial role in 'losing' his children" (Dolan 1994: 167). Moreover, in order to allow forgiveness at the end, the figure of the mother must be both silenced and shaped into a fantasy – a statue.

24 See 3.3.90–100 where Antigonus is reported by the clown to have been eaten by a bear. It is a matter of directorial choice whether or not the audience sees or merely hears of this event. In the 2003 RSC production, a huge bear devoured him on stage.

25 Lim notes that this scene further stresses the premise that representation in language is "defined by a gap that always exists between literary portrayal and the object portrayed" (Lim 2001: 328).

26 Interestingly, 18-month-old babies already distinguish between action performed by a human agent from that performed by a machine, even a hand-held tool (Gallese 2001: 36).

27 This suggestion is reinforced by Fadiga, *et al.* (1995) and Fadiga and Gallese (1997), who have demonstrated that human matching systems activate the same muscle groups of those utilized by the observed target. Clinical evidence of a similar phenomenon is also found in so-called "imitation-behavior" (Lehrmitte, *et al.* 1996), according to which, humans observing another agent in action "generate a plan to do the same action, or an image of doing it, themselves," whether or not this is translated into actual motor movements.

28 Stephen Orgel argues that, in reading or watching Shakespeare, we must remember that at his time, the mysterious opacity of poetry was celebrated, while absolute interpretations were seen as dangerous. Incomprehensibility was in fact considered "a positive virtue," so that radical indeterminacy and symbolic discontinuity between words and images were believed to contribute to the sense of mystery – and it is in the mystery, rather than its rational or clear explanation, that the early moderns found satisfaction because it assured them of the existence of a higher meaning (Orgel 1991: 437).

29 It is interesting to note that this is the opposite argument from that offered by McGuire (1985). McGuire corroborates Hytner when he insists that "a play is not identical with its words" but comes to life in performance, where actions and silences can override words (McGuire 1985: xxvii). However, he argues that the printed playtext is fixed, while the creative freedom of performance creates variety. In my view, playtext and performance-text are equally contingent. What performance dictates is that, in a particular production, choices must be made regarding the interpretation that is to be staged, while the text can enjoy greater ambiguity and multiplicity. Crucially, however, as Hytner shows us, these choices are less random than "creative freedom" may suggest. They are in fact anchored in human embodied experience, which may be overlooked while reading the playtext but which becomes the primary criterion for interpretation when attending its performance.

29 This renders the story of the Roman artist simply untrue unless Paulina is thereby confessing her own theological leanings, which seems rather inappropriate at a moment when it is she, rather than God, who is astounding the audience.

30 There is no reason to deny Landau's claim that Paulina's continual apologies for the seeming "unlawful business" (5.3.96) at hand are "to secure herself against the eminent forces of official, and/or popular, censure and repression" (Landau 2003: 18). But I believe it is natural for the dramatist Shakespeare to defend the theatre against its enemies and that this has no bearing on guess-work concerning his religious preferences. One must keep in mind that the event on which the entire Christian religion rests is the Incarnation. Protestant or Catholic, opposed to or supportive of ritual, everyone in Shakespeare's audience (bar perhaps a few individuals who kept their mouths shut) believed in *that* miracle. The religious message of Hermione's resurrection cannot, therefore, be a singularly Catholic one.

31 This approach has been dubbed "externalism" as opposed to "internalism," the traditional notion that meanings are processed in the head (Brook and Stainton 2000: 203).

References

Aristotle (1987) *Poetics*, trans. R. Janko, Indianapolis, IN: Hackett.

Brook, A. and Stainton, R.J. (2000) *Knowledge and Mind: A Philosophical Introduction*, Cambridge, MA: MIT Press.

Bynum, C. (1995) "Why all the fuss about the body? A medievalist's perspective," *Critical Inquiry*, 22: 1–33.

Carruthers, P. and Smith, P. (eds) (1996) *Theories of Theory of Mind*, Cambridge: Cambridge University Press.

Cavell, S. (1987) *Disowning Knowledge in Six Plays of Shakespeare*, Cambridge: Cambridge University Press.

Corrigen, R.W. (1979, 1981) "Tragicomedy," *The World of the Theatre*, Glenview: Scott, Foresman. Rpt. in Corrigen, R.W. (ed.) *Comedy Meaning and Form*, 2nd edn, New York: Harper & Row, 222–8.

Clark, A. (1998) "Where brain, body and mind collide," *Daedalus*, 127(2): 247–80.

Crane, M.T. (2001) "What was performance?" *Criticism*, 43(2): 169–87.

Damasio, A. (1999) *The Feeling of What Happens: Body and Emotion in the Making of Consciousness*, New York: Harcourt.

Dolan, F.E. (1994) *Dangerous Familiars: Representations of Domestic Crime in England, 1550–1700*, Ithaca, NY: Cornell University Press.

Davies, M. and Stone, T. (eds) (1995a) *Folk Psychology*, Oxford: Blackwell.

—— (1995b) *Mental Simulation*, Oxford: Blackwell.

Fadiga, L., Fogassi, L., Pavesi, G., and Rizolatti, G. (1995) "Motor facilitation during action observation: a magnetic stimulation study," *Journal of Neurophysiology*, 73: 2608–11.

Fadiga, L. and Gallese, V. (1997) "Action representation and language in the brain," *Theoretical Linguistics*, 23: 267–80.

Gallese, V. (2001) "The 'shared manifold' hypothesis: from mirror neurons to empathy," *Journal of Consciousness Studies* 8, 5(7): 33–50.

Gallese, V. and Goldman, A. (1998) "Mirror neurons and the simulation theory of mind-reading," *Trends in Cognitive Sciences*, 2(12): 493–502.

Greene, R. [1588] (1963) *Pandosto, or The Triumph of Time. The Winter's Tale*, Kermode, F. (ed.), Harmondsworth: Penguin.

Greenblatt, S.J. (1973, rpt. 1986) "Sidney's *Arcadia* and the mixed mode," *Studies in Philosophy*, 70(3): 269–78. Rpt. in Kinney, A.F. (ed.) *Essential Articles for the Study of Sir Phillip Sidney*, Hamden: Archen.

Hamilton, D.B. (1993) "*The Winter's Tale* and the language of union, 1604–1611," *Shakespeare Studies*, XXI: 228–50.

Heidegger, M. (1927, 1993) "The Exposition of the Question of the Meaning of Being," in Krell, D.F. (ed.) *Basic Writings*, 2nd edn, London: Routledge.

Henderson, D. and Horgan, T. (2000) "Simulation and Epistemic Competence," Kögler, H.H. and Steuber, K.R. (eds) *Empathy and Agency*, Boulder, CO: Westview, 119–41.

Hunter, R.G. (1965) *Shakespeare and the Comedy of Forgiveness*, New York: Columbia University Press.

Hytner, N. (2002) "Behold the swelling scene: the theatrical consequences of Shakespeare's addiction to truth," *TLS*, 1(11): 22.

Landau, A. (2003) " 'No settled senses of the world can match the pleasure of that madness': the politics of unreason in *The Winter's Tale*," *Cahiers Elizabethains*, 64: 29–42.

Lehrmitte, F., Pillon, M., and Serdrau, M. (1996) "Human autonomy and the frontal lobes: 1. imitation and utilization behavior: a neuropsychological study of 75 patients," *Ann. Neorology*, 19: 326–40.

Lim, Walter S.H. (2001) "Knowledge and belief in *The Winter's Tale*," *Studies in English Literature 1500–1900*, 41(2): 317–34.

McGuire, P.C. (1985) *Speechless Dialect: Shakespeare's Open Silences*, Berkeley, CA: University of California Press

Milward, P. (1964, 1991) "A theology of grace in *The Winter's Tale*," *English Literature and Language*, 2, 27–50. Rpt. in *The Medieval Dimension in Shakespeare's Plays: Studies in Renaissance Literature*, 7, New York: Edwin Mellen, 102–24.

Orgel, S. (1991) "The poetics of incomprehensibility," *Shakespeare Quarterly*, 42(4): 431–7.

Palmer, D.W. (1995) "Jacobean moscovites: winter, tyranny, and knowledge in *The Winter's Tale*," *Shakespeare Quarterly*, 46(3): 323–39.

Ronk, M. (1990) "Recasting jealousy: a reading of *The Winter's Tale*," *Literature and Psychology*, 36(1–2): 50–77.

Rorty, R. (1984) "Deconstruction and circumvention," *Critical Inquiry*, 11(1): 1–23.

Rutter, C.C. (2001) *Enter the Body: Women and Representation on Shakespeare's Stage*, London: Routledge.

Schechner, R. (ed.) (1988) *Performance Theory*, New York: Routledge.

Shakespeare, W. (1610–11) *The Winter's Tale*, Kermode, F. (ed.) Harmondsworth: Penguin.

Spolsky, E. (1993) *Gaps in Nature: Literary Interpretation and the Modular Mind*, Albany, NY: State University of New York Press.

—— (2001a) *Satisfying Skepticism: Embodied Knowledge in the Early Modern World*, Aldershot: Ashgate.

—— (2001b) "Darwin and Derrida: cognitive literary theory as a species of post-structuralism," *Poetics Today*, 23(1): 43–62.

Traub, V. (1992) "Jewels, Statues, and Corpses: Containment of Female Erotic Power in Shakespeare's Plays," *Desire and Anxiety: Circulation of Sexuality in Shakespearean Drama*, New York: Routledge, 25–50.

Varela, F.J., Thompson, E., and Rosch, E. (1991) *The Embodied Mind: Cognitive Science and the Human Experience*, Cambridge, MA: MIT Press.

Young, K. and Saver, J.L. (2001) "The neurology of narrative," *SubStance*, 30(1–2): 72–84.

Zunshine, L. (2003) "Theory of mind and experimental representations of fictional consciousness," *Narrative*, 11(3): 270–91.

Section 3

Acting and cognition

6 Neuroscience and creativity in the rehearsal process

John Lutterbie

Two actors from very different backgrounds use a similar metaphor to describe their work in rehearsal. Each of them talks about suspending certain aspects of the self so she can be surprised by the discoveries made in improvisational, creative play. For one actor, it is silencing the critical voice, removing the clutter, so that she can be open to her interaction with other actors and the text. The second speaks of not following the brain, of letting the body suggest images and going in the directions in which they point. In each there is a sense of setting aside cognitive functions that we know cannot be deferred because that is not how the body works; and yet we know what they mean. Indeed, in everyday life as well as the theatre, we have all had the experience of trying to quiet the voices inside our heads, of trying to get rid of distractions so that we can focus our attention. While these are common locutions, there has been no concentrated effort in theatre studies to understand this experience or to investigate the metaphors of suspending or emptying the self so that it can be filled with fresh contents. Advances in neuroscience and cognitive philosophy provide tools that allow us to think through these tropes so that we may better understand the creative process in acting.

The prevalence of the desire in theatre to separate cognitive thought from noncognitive exploration is almost universal; it found its fullest expression in Descartes' mind/body split. Traces of this division can be found in virtually every discussion of the theatre. Even Bertolt Brecht, the theatre practitioner most associated with the use of the intellect in acting, encouraged actors to physicalize an idea through improvisation and then analyze its usefulness – a process that required continued refinement of the experiential to achieve precision as a form of social critique. However, it is most clearly present in the writings of Antonin Artaud and in the work of Jerzy Grotowski. Both, in their different ways, try to negate the power of the mind in order to tap the resources of the body. Artaud seeks "a meticulous and unremitting pulverization of every insufficiently fine, insufficiently matured form ... to let the spirit take its leap ..." (Artaud 1958: 51). Similarly Grotowski uses a *via negativa* to break down resistances to the direct communication of the actor's impulses. But there is, at the same time, a resistance to thinking of the body and mind as separate states of being. The desire to tap into "primal" energies is not irrecoverably anti-intellectual. Artaud, for instance, seeks a "deeper intellectuality," while Grotowski sees acting as "involving [the actor's] whole being from his instincts and his unconscious right up to his most lucid state" (Grotowski 1968: 57). Neither Brecht nor Artaud nor Grotowski are invested in maintaining Descartes' mind/body split. They conceive of the body organically, as an interconnected web of potentials that can be exploited differently for different aims.

Why, in contemporary discussions about acting, does the binary between mind and body, between intellect and emotion, persist? Some practitioners argue that people who are too intellectual do not make good actors because they are not sufficiently in touch with their emotions; while others maintain that the emotionalism of contemporary acting styles should be avoided in favor of a more detached approach to performing. Elly A. Konijn, author of *Acting Emotions* (2000), begins to address one side of the binary by exploring the emotions actors experience in performance and the relationship of these feelings to the portrayal of the character's emotions. But by focusing on the emotive, she does not attend to the role of the intellect in acting, although it is not clear if she believes the mind to be subsumed in the play of emotions or if the intellect is irrelevant to the discussion of feelings. Furthermore, by focusing on emotions in performance, Konijn does not explore the relationship between the rehearsal process and performance or the interaction between the diverse discoveries arising from investigations and technique. By questioning first the tropes of "emptying" the self and the immanence of discoveries that "fill" the space, and second the relationship between emotion and rational thought, I show the inadequacies of these binaries. In so doing, I hope to shed some light on the creative process, not to destroy its mystery but to better understand where the mystery lies.

The journey begins with the two actors introduced above. A brief biography of each is offered to acknowledge their very different approaches to the theatre and training as performers. Despite their clear differences, in interviews they use remarkably similar terms to discuss their approach to the rehearsal process. Understanding the metaphors they use and grounding that understanding in recent discoveries in neuroscience helps us to see that the complexity of the experiences gained in a rehearsal depends on the kind of questions the actor asks as she or he engages the process. The findings of Mark Johnson and George Lakoff, cognitive philosophers who argue for a foundational relationship between metaphor and consciousness, converge with those of neuroscience in underlining the centrality of associative cognition to an understanding of the acting process.

The findings of Mark Johnson and George Lakoff, cognitive philosophers who argue for a foundational relationship between metaphor and consciousness, converge with those of neuroscience in underlining the centrality of associative cognition to an understanding of the acting process (Lakoff and Johnson 1999).

Emptying the self

The two actors, both women, come from very different backgrounds and have distinctly different approaches to the art of acting, and yet the metaphors they use to describe their rehearsal process are strikingly similar. Deborah Mayo grew up in a theatre family that moved from the United States to England when she was a child. By the age of nine or ten she was playing lead roles, mostly britches parts because of her height; she eventually grew to almost six feet tall. In high school after playing one of the fathers in John Gay's *A Beggar's Opera*, she was asked to play the part of Richard II in the next year's production, but her family moved. Despite losing the role, Mayo said it gave her confidence to know that an English director considered her ready to play the role. While attending school, she was exposed to a steady diet of English acting. "So it was pretty clear that was what I loved doing pretty early on, I guess. During the time I was living in London, all those years I saw Lawrence Olivier and Maggie Smith, and Robert Stephens and Peggy Ashcroft and Ralph Richardson. So I was hooked" (Mayo 2003). After returning to America and attending Wheelock College, she went to graduate school in acting at Yale. She describes her training at the Drama School as:

> Hodge-podge (laughter). We weren't taught *a* technique, we were exposed to different teachers, different ideas. So I would characterize my training as three years of being in the trenches, acting all the time in different venues. That was the value of it for me. That we . . . not that we were self-taught . . . we learned by doing. Because 24 hours a day, we were in plays. That may be unkind to say to my teachers; we had good teachers for sure, but the focus was on the doing.
>
> (Mayo 2003)

She is not comfortable describing her approach to acting, saying that actors tend to latch on to techniques that work regardless of the source. However, Mayo recognizes that her training can be characterized as "traditional" in the sense that there was little emphasis on improvisation and that she was not exposed to alternative training methods, such as those of Joe Chaikin and The Open Theatre. Mayo continues to work primarily in text-based theatre, working regularly in regional theatres and doing some work on Broadway.

Margarita Espada-Santos was born and raised in Puerto Rico where her initial training in performance came from work in the martial arts, specifically Karate. Less interested in the fighting aspects of the form, she fell in love with the *Kata*, a set sequence of moves where the emphasis is on the specificity of each gesture and the fluidity of the sequence. "I was very curious about how you manipulate energy, how you can really play with timing – and play with the audience" (Espada-Santos 2003). Her introduction to theatre came when she saw *La vida es Sueño* by Calderón de la Barca, in sixth grade. Until that time she was unaware of theatre, coming from a working-class background in a poor country. "And when I saw it I knew, 'I want to be there'" (Espada-Santos 2003).

Her first formal training in theatre came in 1984 when she entered Puerto Rico University. The training was traditional conservatory and based on the precise execution of exercises. Her work on the *Kata* prepared her well for this approach to training in courses such as mime. However, she found the strictures of repetition-based techniques frustrating – "This structure bothers me. Like, 'Stay here on the line.' I need to jump" (Espada-Santos 2003) – and she joined an alternative theatre company founded on the popular theatre principles of Boal's *Teatro Oprimido*. The improvisatory nature of this work created a tension with the precision demanded by her formal university training that began to be reconciled when she attended an international theatre festival in Cuba. There, for the first time, she encountered Eugenio Barba. It was a turning point for her because she began to see the possibilities of combining specific, physical work with a more improvisational approach to the making of theatre. She runs her own company, *Teatro yerbabruja*, based in Puerto Rico, with a second home on Long Island.

Espada-Santos' process begins with the generation of images, which are then structured into a performance and rehearsed until ready for an audience. In the early stages she prefers to go into the rehearsal space alone to center, focus, and quiet the voices of the day. Once she has achieved the right degree of silence, Espada-Santos begins to move, seeking a deep relationship between herself and the images that are generated. She attends to the feelings and images that arise from the physical experience of moving, letting each movement suggest the next and acknowledging the sensory effects that arise. At this point, she is less interested in what the experiences mean than the unanticipated associations that arise seemingly unbidden from her subconscious. As she moves and recognizes images without judging or evaluating them, she is also aware of the feelings that are evoked, allowing them to spur the next emotion, to underscore the next association. This feedback loop – from movement to image to feeling to movement – carries forward particularly strong images, while allowing others to dissipate or recede into the background. "I don't want to think, just to see what comes. Suddenly I have an image of someone walking. Then other images open up. Suddenly there is a flood of different images, and I have to work with them to get a clean image" (Espada-Santos 2001). In this way, material accrues, each with its own potential. The concepts, as they arise, do not, however, maintain a neat sequence; rather, as their contents become clearer they fold back on each other or suggest alternative directions to explore. As she works with the material, certain images gain intensity and become more insistent, defining a basic structure that may or may not find a place in the final performance; that may or may not appear in the particular form that arises during the exploratory process.

The two qualities that are central to the generation of material are the suspension of judgment and responsiveness to the changing dynamics of the body. The moving body goes through a series of gestures that reflect past experiences and certain pleasures, pains, and anxieties. But while she is moving and focusing on the initial image, impulses or other images arise that suggest different kinds of movement. As the work proceeds, the dynamic proliferation of subsidiary images intensifies and transforms the original concept, enriching its potential or giving rise to unexpected and divergent possibilities; or if it fails to find the impetus to continue, the process stops. Another end to the exercise is the surfeit of material, when judgment can no longer be suspended, when concentration is broken either by the singularity of an image or the overload of the senses – when it is not possible to clarify a "clean image." Most difficult to describe is the suspension of judgment, which it is not conceptually difficult but is far from easy to achieve in the process and to define:

> Where everything is blank. I try to get to this point where I am just pure energy. No past, no present, just here, now. Not necessarily Zen – the neutral mask of LeCoq. What it means to carry a neutral mask. Almost impossible.
>
> (Espada-Santos 2002)

The distinction between Lecoq's concept of neutrality and a Zen state is one of movement. Zen is associated, rightly or wrongly, with a passive, meditative state, while the creative act in the theatre is active. In drawing the parallel between Lecoq and Zen, Espada-Santos is creating an interesting binary between passive and active states, suggesting that the two qualities can exist simultaneously.

Mayo works primarily with texts and the development of character. She goes to rehearsal with a certain amount of homework done – a relatively clear idea of her character's objectives, a breakdown of the actions, and as many of the words learned as possible. When entering the rehearsal space, she has a set of structures that guide her explorations, but equally important is what she does *not* bring to the rehearsal. She refers to these negative aspects as "clutter," which she defines as "judging, self-judging, any mental activity, in other words, focused on anything other than the given circumstances, any ego concerns, ideas of right and wrong choices" (Mayo 2001b). The value of this avoidance of the cognitive is what it allows to happen: "being loose enough to let [the character] in, it is so gratifying. There is an awareness that it happens, but that is what the 'uncluttering' is: standing back and letting that happen" (Mayo 2001b). Mayo knows that the idea of the character taking over sounds like "hocus-pocus"; nevertheless, "it feels like you empty yourself.... It's not that you are making but responding. There is a moment when [the character] seems to take over and does what she wants to do" (Mayo 2001b). However, it is not work done in isolation. Much of the discovery process comes from the presence of the other actors:

> It is almost always the other actors that are the stimuli. The way they listened or the way their characters were reacting to me that somehow bolstered or affirmed my going out on the limb I was going out on. So much is response and attentiveness.

> (Mayo 2001a)

The rehearsal process requires being open to the moment, investing in the given circumstances without concern for what might happen or has happened. What am I being given now? What is the response I make? After the response has happened it is possible to reflect on what this tells her about the character or the action of the play and whether or not the response was appropriate. But at the time there needs to be openness to what is happening, an attentiveness that is not interrupted by cognitive oversight. In common acting parlance, you have to be in the moment.

The idea of "being in the moment" is important to both actors and, I suspect, is one of the more universal concepts in acting. It is constituted, at least for these two actors, by avoiding the intrusion of discursive thought, which is seen as a negative influence that interferes with the actor's availability to unexpected images, as clutter that disrupts the reciprocal exchange between actors. For Mayo and Espada-Santos, it involves a suspension of the intellect in favor of attending to the physical and emotional impulses that arise from the flow of images in one case and the exchange of responsive behavior defined by the structure of the script in the other. Reflection and decision-making happen later, after the exercise is completed, whether in an improvisation or scene work.

It is interesting that two artists from such different backgrounds and dissimilar approaches to training describe their work using the same primary metaphors – metaphors that are central to understanding the creative process. First is the binary of intellect and emotion. Rational thought needs to be put on hold so that the experience of images and emotional responses can play freely across and through the body. It is only *after* the improvisational experience that a process of reflection allows for a rational evaluation of the images and emotions evoked in the rehearsal. A second binary perceives the self as a container that can be emptied and filled with fresh contents. The self is perceived to be a force of containment that impedes the creative process; to be productive in rehearsal thus requires a relaxing of the boundaries, a move into a neutral state. Linking these binaries is the need to be in the moment. The assumption is that subjectivity and rational thought take you out of the moment (if such a thing is possible) and that when concerns about the past and the future are bracketed, artistry becomes most compelling and vibrant. Two very different actors rely on the same metaphors – negation/affirmation, emptying/filling, and being in the moment – to describe the states necessary for making theatre. In the remainder of this essay, I explore these metaphors in light of discoveries in neuroscience and advances in cognitive philosophy to shed a different kind of light on the acting process.

Being in the moment

Speaking from the perspective of phenomenology or, for that matter, animate being, we are never *not* "in the moment," responding to the life world in which and with which we exist. Sleeping or waking, perceptual systems are aware of changes in the environment. In the middle of the night, I wake up because I am cold and seek another layer of covers; as I write this and retreat into thought to determine the next step in the argument and how to phrase it – how to word this example – I am, nonetheless, aware of the sounds around me, the cluttered landscape that surrounds the computer screen. I may be no more than peripherally cognizant of this extraneous information because the ability to concentrate privileges certain perceptual experiences, relegating others to the background. But I am still, quite literally, "being in the moment." Since "being in the moment" is descriptive of being itself, to grant it literal status is a tautology or at best identifies a quality of what it means *to be*. The phrase, then, has status as a metaphor used to define a *way* of being that – at least in the sense it is used in the discussions of the acting process – privileges attendance to perceptual data over the self-isolating ruminations of thought.

The implication is that I can, to a certain extent, control my ability to focus on certain perceptions and cognitive functions. When I feel my mind drifting, I close my eyes to shut out distractions, and I breathe deeply and slowly to give myself the chance to refocus on the subject at hand. As I describe this process, I become aware that it is not merely a mental exercise, but that it requires the cooperation of the body not only in the process of blocking out distracting perceptions but in evaluating my readiness to focus on the particular problem. I know it is time to stop writing for the day when I *feel* a state of homogeneity set in, when it becomes too difficult to isolate a particular thought among the various potentials that have a legitimate claim to consideration. I recognize it as fatigue, as a diminution of the kind of energy I need to pursue writing. When this happens, I need to do something else. But each of these states is still "being in the moment" even if I think of one as being more so than another. What is at stake is the state most appropriate to the kind of work I need/want to be doing at a particular moment. So "being in the moment" refers to an ability to concentrate or focus on a particular set of experiences – it is defining "the moment" in terms of a certain class of perceptions that I understand to be vital to what occupies me.

Mayo and Espada-Santos describe being in the moment as a neutral state or one that is uncluttered. It is the ability to bracket certain kinds of perception to the exclusion (however temporary) of others that tend to distract from their particular needs as they pursue their art. It seems paradoxical that a conscious decision is made to enter the rehearsal space in a state that suspends cognitive practices. "If I go in thinking 'I'm going to try this in this moment,' I'm already out of it. What can I do to be in the moment, there in that day, that moment?" (Mayo 2003). "It can never be what you have in your head – your body will go a different way. But the brain keeps trying to push the body" (Espada-Santos 2002). Cognitive thought, it seems, establishes expectations for a type of behavior that truncates, at best, a process that can open deeper, more complex insights into the questions being asked. Philosophers, I expect, would find this a difficult conclusion because, for them, the exercise of rational thought *allows* you to arrive at a deeper understanding of a problem than one that is based on the emotions. Yet both would argue, I suspect, that they are engaged in creative practices – although philosophers might prefer to claim that they are increasing our understanding of the life-world and our relationship to it "objectively" rather than creatively, that they are engaging what is there rather than inventing. However, the theory developed here argues that the distance between emotionally based creativity and rational objectivity is minimal; the paradox that an intellectual choice is made to avoid being intellectual is to a large extent illusory; and what really matters are the kinds of questions being asked and the bracketing undertaken to explore the issues under consideration to arrive at understandings that are complex and empowering.

We are engaged in the world as animate beings from infancy, and as Maxine Sheets-Johnstone has argued, in that engagement we are undivided. It is only in processing experience that we begin to devise an architecture of understanding through categories of differentiation. When we navigate a crowded street, we do not distinguish between thought and movement but think *in* movement.[1] It is only when we stop to reflect that we articulate what Artaud calls the "body without organs" (Sontag 1976: 571) into abstractions such as reason and emotion. We accept the divided body because it helps us give meaning to and communicate experience. But as neuroscience is beginning to confirm, we are not segmented creatures with separate systems for thinking and feeling but one organism that is able to know the world concretely and abstractly. The natural and cultural environments in which we live, by and large, determine the ways in which we define these structures, but they are abstractions whose value lies in our ability to use them to live our lives successfully. The knowledge that we glean – what we are able to think about at a particular moment – is dependent on the integrated matrices of the body. Without the complex interdependency of what we differentiate into body, brain, and mind, we would not recognize ourselves or know what we feel.

Emotion and rational thought

As far back as Plato, the division between the mind and the body, the emotions and rationality, creative inspiration, and philosophical thought have been taken as givens. Stereotypes of gender have rested on the difference between cool thought and passionate responses. Leaders are respected for their ability to resist giving into the heat of the moment in favor of a calm calculation of risks. One is a sign of weakness, the other of strength. Recent developments in understanding the physiology of the brain and its interconnectedness with the rest of the body indicate that such differences are unsupportable and that decision-making processes are indebted as much to emotional as to rational input.

The binary is maintained, in part, on a mid-twentieth-century model of the tripartite brain: brain stem, cerebellum and neo-cortex. In this structure, the brain stem, called the reptilian brain by Paul MacLean, functions according to simple cause-and-effect impulses such as fight or flight and is described by James Papez as the "stream of movement" (quoted in Turner 1988: 161). It operates by instinct and does not require considered decision-making but is based in reflex action. The cerebellum or "old-mammalian brain," the next stage in evolution in MacLean's taxonomy, is the seat of voluntary movements (for instance, control over where one looks), homeostatic functions (such as responding to hunger), and the objective of the moment (locating food). Papez characterizes it as the "stream of feeling." The neo-mammalian brain, "the stream of thought," and the most recent in the evolutionary continuum, is the center of long-term memory and higher mental functions (such as language and rational thought) that define us as higher, conscious beings (Ibid.: 162). Furthermore, the neo-mammalian is divided between the right and left hemispheres, with one side dedicated to rational consciousness and the other to creativity. As long as these three parts of the brain were understood to serve distinct functions, the separation of intellect and emotion seemed at least theoretically possible if not an absolute. But current research using new imaging techniques and the study of the effects of brain injuries indicates that this theory does not fit the evidence.

While the evolutionary development of the brain is not in question, the discrete functions thought to belong to each part are. Research indicates that the brain is not so easily divided into regions linked to distinct operations; rather, it is better understood as consisting of interlocking systems:

> In short, there appears to be a collection of systems in the human brain consistently dedicated to the goal-oriented thinking process we call reasoning, and to the response selection we call decision making, with a special emphasis on the personal and social domain. This same collection of systems is also involved in emotion and feeling, and is partly dedicated to processing body signals.
>
> (Damasio 1994: 70)

Antonio Damasio, a neuroscientist, studies people who have suffered brain impairments, either through injury or disease. His preferred way of thinking is to identify how different areas of the brain interact to create two kinds of consciousness: core and extended. Core consciousness "provides the organism with a sense of self about one moment – now – and about one place – here" (Damasio: 1999: 16). Extended consciousness, on the other hand, of which there are many levels and grades, provides the organism with an elaborate sense of self – an identity and a person, you or me, no less – and places that person at a point in individual historical time, richly aware of the lived past and of the anticipated future, and keenly cognizant of the world beside it.

(Ibid.: 16)

Core consciousness, in the earlier theory of the brain, is connected to the functions associated with the brain stem and cerebellum, that is, instinctual movement and voluntary responses to the demands of particular circumstances. Extended consciousness, which previously had been associated with the neocortex, includes higher reasoning functions, the use of language, long-term memory, and the functions linked to concepts of the self. Damasio believes that the evolution of the brain was not a process of creating organs that took responsibility for certain needs and opportunities but one that developed to assist the existing brain in responding to more complex situations.

In doing so, Damasio inverts the Cartesian dualism that would privilege extended consciousness over core consciousness (the former associated with the mind, the latter with the body) when he finds that higher reasoning depends on simple and foundational forms of consciousness: "When core consciousness fails, extended consciousness fails as well. On the other hand, when extended consciousness is disrupted ... core consciousness remains intact" (Ibid.: 122). Our ability to perform as rational beings depends on the proper functioning of the "stream of feeling."

His point is not to denigrate higher reasoning. After all, it is these functions that allow him to write the book. Instead, Damasio argues that Descartes simply had it wrong; that it is impossible to separate the mind from the body because the well-being of any person is dependent on the cooperative interrelatedness of the body's systems. While extended is dependent on core consciousness, without the former we could not survive in the complex environments we have created. However, the ability to cope with modern life is equally dependent on the information we receive from the internal monitors of the physical body and the accuracy of the perceptions we receive from the external world. And perceptions are not objective representations but are felt by the body (although most of the time they form a continuous flow of feelings relegated to the background[2]) and in the process of being interpreted engender feelings and emotions linked to previous experiences and current body states that cannot be simply dismissed when engaging higher thought. Indeed, he makes a convincing argument that were emotions excised from reasoning, we would never come to any decisions because rationality demands the consideration of every possible outcome. Patients impaired emotionally have a very difficult time coming to effective decisions in situations that require cognitive rather than emotive responses. Damasio's theory is that we limit the range of possible interpretations because we *feel* that certain avenues are more productive than others:

The lower levels in the neural edifice of reason are the same that regulate the processing of emotions and feelings, along with global functions of the body proper such that the organism can survive. These lower levels maintain direct and mutual relationships with the body proper, thus placing the body within the chain of operations that permit the highest reaches of reason and creativity. Rationality is probably shaped and modulated by body signals, even as it performs the most sublime distinctions and acts accordingly.

(Damasio 1994: 200)

Our ability to reason depends, in part, on how we feel – the degree of stress, fatigue, for instance, or the noise level of the environment or number of interruptions or, more significantly, the choice that feels most right in the situation.

The point is that the emotions and feelings we experience are integral to our intellectual processes. Emotions, far from undermining rational thought, are important if not necessary to the process. If Damasio and others working on this problem in neurobiology who concur with him are right, when actors say that they do not want to be too intellectual and prefer to trust their emotions, they cannot be speaking literally. The question is: How can we understand their metaphors?

Lateralization and zones of convergence

Recent discoveries in neuroscience raise questions about the right-brain/left-brain theory without discounting it. While there is evidence that in certain instances one hemisphere of the neo-cortex is activated more than the other, findings indicate that the use of the brain's resources is less differentiated. The idea that there are discrete areas for specific functions has given way to the concept of networks that link different parts of the brain to deal with different aspects of a problem. (Evidence indicates that remembering a person's face combines several images stored in different parts of the brain, for example.) Different perceptual inputs converge in the same cortices, locations in the brain where numerous neuron nuclei are gathered in "bunches." For instance, the same convergence zones may be used to process texture/touch and surface/vision perceptions, suggesting that our ability to predict the texture of a surface is possible because of the proximity of neurons associated with tactility and vision. The implication is that a degree of cross-modality occurs; for instance, memories of how velvet feels may be activated even though we are looking at rather than touching the fabric. The significance of discoveries about lateralization and convergence zones in understanding the art of acting requires further development.

A recent exploration of lateralization attempted to prove the hypothesis that the body receives a stimulus that is then divided into constituent parts and directed to specific areas in the brain depending on the kind of response needed. The assumption was that regardless of the question being asked about the object, a singular stimulus representing all aspects of the object being experienced would be apprehended, dissected, and the data sent to relevant areas of the brain for interpretation. The experiment looked at the distinctly different processes of (a) recognizing a word and (b) making a visuospatial judgment about the location of a letter in the word (Klass *et al.* 2003: 384–6). The findings did not support the hypothesis. Instead, the evidence suggests: "the functional split between the left and right hemispheres of the brain depends on what must be done with an incoming stimulus (the task), rather than the nature of the stimulus itself" (McIntosh and Lobaugh 2003: 322). In other words, the stimulus we receive from the world and where that information is processed depends on the question we ask – how we frame our expectations rather than what is available to be perceived in the life-world. This does not mean that only one part of the brain is used given a particular point of view. Instead, the "results emphasize the cooperative nature of brain activity, where areas rapidly exchange information when engaged in mental operations" (Ibid.: 323). The indications are that the way we focus attention determines what we perceive and which regions of the brain are activated.

The implication is that the question an actor asks going into rehearsal has a significant effect on the kind of information that is gleaned from the experience. When Mayo wants to avoid "judging, self-judging, any mental activity, that is focused on anything other than the given circumstances, any ego concerns, ideas of right and wrong choices," or when Espada-Santos says, "I don't want to think, just to see what comes," they are recognizing, albeit in different terms, that the question, the frame of mind with which they enter the rehearsal space, is of tantamount importance to the gathering of useful information. Their focus is designed to elicit a range of perceptual inputs that create unexpected associations rather than attempt to answer a specific question. It is at this point that the idea of convergence zones becomes pertinent.

Convergence zones are areas of the brain where there is a high concentration of neuron nuclei, the center of cellular activity. Stimulations to the cell are processed in the nucleus and responses sent through the axon, or cell body, to dendrites or stellates, depending on the type of nerve cell. This information is then transmitted to other neurons or non-neural parts of the body, such as the muscles or viscera. This movement of information results in physical activity, emotional experience, creation of memories and cognitive thought. The discovery of these areas containing a high density of neurons has raised questions about the potential for communication between cells that are linked to disparate operations of the organism and about what they mean for cognitive practices.

The potential for cross-activation among nerves representing different senses has gained strength in studies of synaesthesia, defined by V.S. Ramachandran and E.M. Hubbard as a "condition in which an otherwise normal person experiences sensations in one modality when a second modality is stimulated" (Ramachandran and Hubbard 2001: 4). The subjects they investigate have "grapheme-color synesthesia," in which the shape of certain numbers or letters induces color experiences, such as seeing the number five as red, while the number two might be green. Their conclusion, based on tests in conjunction with brain-imaging technologies, is that there seems to be a cross-activation occurring between neurons and areas of the brain that are usually linked to discrete functions, i.e., are related to word *or* color recognition but not both at the same time. Ramachandran and Hubbard go on to argue, based on the increased frequency of synesthesia in artists, that metaphor may also be based on the cross-activation of neurons. Such conclusions are also supported by findings from another study:

> Neighboring areas of the cerebellum often receiv[e] inputs from disparate regions of the body and with areas that [are] far apart being represented next to one another in the cerebellum.
>
> (Bower and Parsons 2003: 55)

The fragmentation of sites of representation in the cerebellum suggests that our everyday experience of the world, our ability to maneuver successfully in time and space, may be an effect of the integration of information from different parts of the sensate body made possible by neural proximity. If this is the case, then the cross-modality experienced by the synesthete may be an extreme form of a general ability.

Convergence zones exist throughout the brain and, Damasio believes, provide a locus for activating memories linked to certain types of stimuli, that is, how we responded in a similar situation in the past, the effectiveness of that response, and alternative possibilities for responding. The information generated through such activation includes emotional as well as high-order cognitive strategies. The decision-making process involves the interaction of the responses generated. Because experiences are seldom, if ever, identical to previous occurrences, it is likely that the responses to events are generalized, activating memories, emotions, and strategies that are approximate or similar. Only in extreme circumstances that require instinctual responses will the decision-making process be circumvented. In normal, that is non-life-threatening situations, the responses are complex, allowing us to consider a number of options prior to making a choice, even if the decision is to defer deciding.

Metaphorical structuring of consciousness

For Ramachandran and Hubbard, metaphors such as "Juliet is the sun" indicate a tendency toward synesthesia, but for cognitive philosophers Mark Johnson and George Lakoff, it is a creative expression of processes that underlie all consciousness. Using information gleaned from a number of different disciplines in the sciences, social sciences, and humanities, Lakoff and Johnson come to the conclusion that consciousness operates, in large measure, through the use of a finite number of metaphors that can be utilized singly or in complex combinations to provide nuanced understandings of the expansive field of human experience. Johnson argues that these structures derive from basic experiences and that they "are embodied and give coherent, meaningful structure to our physical experience at a *preconceptual level . . .*" (Johnson 1987: 13; italics in original). Although they predate the acquisition of language, these experiences are culturally reinforced, becoming "shared cultural modes of experience" that "help to determine the nature of our meaningful, coherent understanding of our 'world'" (Ibid.: 14).

> These primary metaphors are "creative," in the sense that they create an analogy linking two phenomena through similarity; they do not rely on the recognition of an inherent, objective similarity between two phenomena. Because these and numerous other primary metaphors link everyday experience to sensorimotor phenomena, most conceptual thinking cannot occur without metaphors.
>
> (McConachie 2003: 13)

Lakoff and Johnson have identified 24 such metaphors that exist in many languages. These basic metaphors, such as whether something is contained (in or out) or complete (empty or full), derive from our earliest experiences and limit the ways in which we make meaning. Or to put this another way, our understanding is constrained by the application of these tropes although "constraint" implies more limitation than is actually the case, given that these metaphors can be used in conjunction with each other and allow for combinations that exceed 6×10^{23} possibilities without taking into account irony, double entendre, etc.

Even if the arguments of Lakoff and Johnson are only partially correct, the prevalence of metaphors that translate physical experience into linguistic tropes for describing complex situations suggests the centrality of our ability to juxtapose experiences from different sensory operations in the creation of complex concepts. Many of the current discourses on the boundaries and mapping of identities are based in the trope of containment – are we in or out, centered or de-centered, whole or fragmentary?

Mayo and Espada-Santos want to "empty" themselves so they can be "filled" with alternative contents. This trope voices the desire to enter into an "unfocused," "open-ended" exercise that circumvents the "limits" of a "focused" exploration, "freeing" them to engage in the "play" of associations that "arise" from the evocation of memories while "attending" to the emotional/cognitive, phenomenological experience of animate, sensate beings. They seek associations that support and disrupt their preconceived notions of what comes next. But in order to find these associations, they need to pose a "question" for which there is no simple, concrete answer. Nonetheless, it is a question that allows for the proliferation of possibilities making use of images that arise from neural cross-modality and from our ability to combine metaphors in interesting and powerful ways.

As Lakoff, Johnson, and others argue, the play that allows for associative thought is not a discrete mental operation. Metaphors already structure our understanding of and interactions with the world. Indeed the distinction between emotion and reason is based on metaphors, some of which have to do with containment and tactility: reason is hard-edged and bounded, while emotion is soft and open-ended. Where you or I position ourselves in relation to this binary depends on the side of the boundary with which we identify. This is not to say that identity is relative. To say, "I am being emotional" indicates a state that we consider to be the exception rather than the norm. Recognizing this difference is responsive to our immediate circumstances and does not mean that we consider ourselves more or less intellectual.

Were this set of metaphors to lose currency in the society, we would not be left in limbo as to how to understand the experience but would simply use a different set of metaphors. How Mayo or Espada-Santos understands her approach to acting depends (a) on the metaphors available in our particular society to describe the experience of creating a performance, and (b) on the metaphorical relations that evolve in the rehearsal process. At stake is not whether metaphorical thought is desirable but which metaphors current in the culture best describe the creative process.

Some tentative conclusions

What are actors saying when they argue against depending on the intellect in favor of the emotions? was the question asked at the beginning of this essay. We have found that the claim cannot be taken literally because emotion and rational thought are inextricably linked. Thought gives rise to emotion – anyone who has felt the joy or despair of arriving at a conclusion will recognize this – but emotion also gives rise to and directs rational thought by encouraging consideration of phenomenal experience and by limiting the possible understanding of what "feels" right. Emotion permeates cognitive processes. If the binary between thought and feeling is false, then we need to look elsewhere to understand what actors are doing when they create this distinction.

In current research on the brain and how it operates, the two areas of exploration that seem most valuable are lateralization and cross-activation, particularly as it sheds light on creativity and metaphor. The study of lateralization indicates that (a) there is some validity to the right-brain/left-brain theory, but a more accurate image is of a series of interacting networks that are activated differentially based on how we bracket the world; and (b) the stimuli perceived or, perhaps more aptly put, privileged in the perceiving are determined to some extent by the attitude of the perceiver. Synesthesia, the shifting of sensory modalities in the apprehension of certain objects, is quite likely the effect of cross-activation between neurons, a phenomenon that leads Ramachandran and Hubbard to hypothesize about the relationship between the sharing of neural information across functional boundaries and creativity through the associations of metaphor. Cross-modality in people who are not synesthetes in the clinical sense seems possible, albeit to a less dramatic degree, given the prevalence of what Damasio calls convergence zones, areas of high concentrations of neural nuclei, and the fragmented structure of sensory processors in the brain. The prevalence of sensory information from different parts of the body found in proximate areas of the cerebellum allows for a more comprehensive understanding of experience than would be possible if taste were experienced without the visual, tactile, and kinesthetic components. Lakoff and Johnson, from very different points of departure, support this hypothesis by arguing that the meanings derived in consciousness are constructed through the manipulation of paradigmatic metaphors.

We are, then, in a better position to appreciate the distinction being made when actors seek to differentiate between the intellect and emotion. They associate intellectuality with a sharply focused attention, one that approaches a situation looking for a specific type of information ("Is this how my character behaves in this moment?") and a more open-ended investigation that seeks, through systems of association, to gain information that can later be interrogated for its value in the development of performance. They see a hard focus as letting cognitive functions lead and as calling for self-judgments; whereas, they understand a softer focus to be placing trust in the emotional, suggesting ways of behaving that are not immediately obvious in the initial context – i.e., the point of view arrived at through pre-rehearsal preparations. On the one hand, the "intellectual" approach activates parts of the brain that seek specificity and therefore limit the type of information discoverable through pre-selection of the kind of stimuli allowed in the decision-making process. On the other hand, the "emotional" approach places boundaries on what is perceived and in doing so utilizes a more general form of investigation; this in turn allows for a deferral of the moment of decision-making and the entertainment of a greater – if less specific – variety of stimulation.

What needs to be questioned in discussions about acting is the dichotomy between reason and passion. Espada-Santos defines herself as a scholar-performer, while Mayo's process is based in her emotional availability to the text and other actors. Both, however, ask similar questions in the process of creation – questions that are open-ended and allow for a proliferation of competing images. By seeking richness and complexity in the material they craft into their performances, they are not valuing intellect over emotion or vice versa but understanding the framing that needs to be in place when they enter the space of rehearsal. Instead of depending on an easy and divisive binary, we need to embrace the fundamental value of associative and metaphorical processes in the complex art of acting.

It can be argued that if all thought is metaphorical, then this discussion merely replaces one set of metaphors with another, and that if the separation of feeling from reason works in practice, there is no need to rethink the art of acting. These terms are not merely descriptive, however, but reflect values that impinge on how actors are perceived culturally. Emotional people are generally viewed as less strong, less reliable in the decision-making process. It is perhaps not surprising that these are the same terms traditionally used to define the feminine and to keep women from assuming positions of authority – both in and out of the theatre. This may explain the difficulty women have establishing themselves as directors and why actors are seldom considered for positions as producers or artistic directors. This bias also affects how actors are treated in the rehearsal space, from the kind of information they are to be given about the cultural background of the play to who makes decisions about character interpretation. The cost of this binary is the understanding that creativity is an associative process, an inter-weaving of the affective and the rational. In subjugating one side of the binary to the other, we are, in effect, limiting the creative potential of those who bear the greatest burden in giving life to the theatre. Perhaps we would have a more satisfying theatre if we accepted the importance of the intellect in acting and encouraged actors to explore their full creative potential.

It is true that I am merely replacing one set of metaphors with another. The question is whether or not this succession enhances our understanding of the creative process. As Herbert Blau writes at the end of *To All Appearances*, "as long as we are in the theat[re] there is some point in improving the quality of our illusions" (Blau 1992: 199). A better understanding of the cognitive processes can improve our illusions, helping us to better understand the art of acting and the act of making theatre.

Notes

1 See "Thinking in Movement" in Sheets-Johnstone (1999: 483–516).
2 Damasio argues that in addition to the feelings of which we are aware, there is a continuous field of background feelings related to the status of bodily functions. He claims, for instance, that "The background feeling is our image of the body landscape when it is not shaken by emotion" (Damasio 1994: 151); and that "[B]ackground feeling is mostly about body states. Our individual identity is anchored on this island of illusory living sameness against which we can be aware of myriad other things that manifestly change around the organism" (Ibid.: 155).

References

Artaud, A. (1958) *The Theatre and Its Double*, trans. M. Richards, New York: Grove Press, Inc.

Blau, H. (1992) *To All Appearances: Ideology and Performance*, London and New York: Routledge.

Bower, J.M. and Parsons, L.M. (2003) "Rethinking the 'lesser brain,'" *Scientific American*, 289: 50–7.

Damasio, A. (1994) *Descartes' Error: Emotion, Reason, and the Human Brain*, New York: Avon Books.

—— (1999) *The Feeling of What Happens: Body and Emotion in the Making of Consciousness*, New York, San Diego, CA, London: Harcourt Brace and Co.

Espada-Santos, M. (2001) Interview with John Lutterbie, Stony Brook University, 12 November.

—— (2002) Interview with John Lutterbie, Stony Brook University, 4 February.

—— (2003) Interview with John Lutterbie, Stony Brook University, 30 June.

Grotowski, J. (1968) *Towards a Poor Theatre*, New York: Simon and Schuster.

Johnson, M. (1987) *The Body in the Mind: The Bodily Basis of Meaning, Imagination, and Reason*, Chicago, IL and London: University of Chicago Press.

Klass, E.S., Marshall, J.C., Friston, K.J., Rowe, J.B., Ritzl, A., Zilles, K., and Fink, G.R. (2003) "Lateralized cognitive processes and lateralized task control in the human brain," *Science*, 301: 384–6.

Konijn, E.A. (2000) *Acting Emotions*, Amsterdam: Amsterdam University Press.

Lakoff, G. and Johnson, M. (1999) *Philosophy in the Flesh: The Embodied Mind and Its Challenge to Western Thought*, New York: Basic Books.

McConachie, B. (2003) *American Theater in the Culture of the Cold War: Producing and Contesting Containment, 1947–1962*, Iowa City, IA: University of Iowa Press.

McIntosh, A.R. and Lobaugh, N.J. (2003) "When is a word not a word?" *Science*, 301: 322–3.

Mayo, D. (2001a) Interview with John Lutterbie, Stony Brook University, 7 November.

—— (2001b) Interview with John Lutterbie, Stony Brook University, 5 December.

—— (2003) Interview with John Lutterbie, Stony Brook University, 3 July.

Ramachandran, V.S. and Hubbard, E.M. (2001) "Synaesthesia – a window into perception, thought and language," *Journal of Consciousness Studies*, 8: 3–34.

Sheets-Johnstone, M. (1999) *The Primacy of Movement*, Amsterdam and Philadelphia, PA: John Benjamins Publishing Company.

Sontag, S. (ed.) (1976) *Antonin Artaud: Selected Writings*, trans. H. Weaver, Berkeley, CA and Los Angeles, CA: University of California Press.

Turner, V. (1988) *The Anthropology of Performance*, New York: PAJ Publications.

7 Image and action

Cognitive neuroscience and actor-training

Rhonda Blair

In the spring of 2003, I directed Rebecca Gilman's *Boy Gets Girl* for Echo Theatre, a professional theatre in Dallas. The script presented particular challenges, and we were an eclectic group with widely varying training and experience. I knew the leading actor, Ellen Locy, but knew none of the other performers prior to auditions, though I had seen the work of two; I had directed none of them before. We had a standard three-week, three-hour-a-day rehearsal period prior to opening. The script, a seven-character, two-act play with nine scenes in each act, tells the story of Theresa Bedell, a magazine writer whose world is thrown into upheaval as she is increasingly terrorized by a blind date who turns out to be a stalker. There are multiple settings (including a magazine writer's office, her apartment, a couple of restaurants, a pornography filmmaker's office, a hospital room), with rapid scene changes that require actors (especially the central character, who is in all but one of the scenes and has a costume change for each one) to shift gears quickly from scene to scene. While plot is central to this piece (particularly in the sense of a classically melodramatic "What's going to happen to Theresa?"), its successful enactment is dependent upon a sense of richly embodied characters and their relationships unfolding through the course of the evening.

A primary goal for actors in conventional Western theatre is to make strong, emotionally charged, and specific choices through the process of embracing language and action, leading to compelling characterizations. Actors also must integrate their work with that of the other company members. The processes by which actors move the language of the script off the page and into their bodies, so that it can be shared with the audience, have historically existed on contested, inexact, and often mystified ground. Contemporary approaches to this problem began most significantly with Konstantin Stanislavsky, the father of twentieth-century Western acting. He described successful acting variously as "the creation of [the] inner life of a human spirit," "living the part," "reaching the subconscious by conscious means," and "the artistic embodiment of inner emotional experience"; phrases such as these occur throughout Stanislavsky's *An Actor Prepares* (1964) and Vasily Toporkov's *Stanislavski in Rehearsal* (1998). In the final incarnations of Stanislavsky's work, the method of physical action and the method of active analysis, the goal is to create an embodied, coherently articulated being; this is done by closely engaging given circumstances (i.e., the facts of the script – "who," "where," "when," "what," the specific language – and the production), and by manipulating behavior, imagination, attention, emotion, and memory so that the actor is fully engaged. At the heart of acting is the concept of a complex consciousness that suffuses the entire body, in which voluntary and involuntary processes and behaviors are not cleanly separated from one another. For those not involved in making theatre, it can be useful to understand the actor's process as having similarities to that of a musician's or a dancer's; the notes or steps may be unchanging in the written score of a piece, but the way in which these are executed will vary greatly from artist to artist. The performances that are most successful are those in which each note, gesture, or word feels fully inhabited and fully connected to the overall flow of the piece.

On the face of it, *Boy Gets Girl* is a very straightforward script. This is a blessing, for the narrative is accessible; and it is a curse, for it makes it easier to remain formulaic in playing received tropes of realism rather than fully exploring the play's action and unfolding relationships. At our first rehearsals, after laying out the general ground for the play and for the accumulating movement over each scene and in the play as a whole, I required the actors to be word-specific in memorizing and working with the text, and to "treat it like Shakespeare, even though it wasn't Shakespeare." This prepared the way for working with them on very particular and personal images in constructing the unfolding action. The link between specificity in language and specificity in image/action is crucial; if the language changes or is unclear, the image, and therefore the action, is more likely to be unclear, certainly in the preparation of the piece. (Here I'm referring to most traditional, scripted theatre, and less to improvisational, interactive performances.) Throughout the process, along with the many amendments and changes that normally happen in any rehearsal, we continually refined the work so that each moment became increasingly articulated in the actors' bodies and heads. They needed to have a specific stream of images to carry them through each scene as well as specific images in mind prior to entering for any scene. This was an explicitly technical approach, so the actors who were used to being more "personal" or improvisational in their rehearsal process were initially challenged, but they were ultimately successful. (Three of the seven actors were nominated for "best actor" in their categories in Dallas' major theatre awards event – one won.)

I "debriefed" Ellen about her experience working on this show, and she confirmed what I had thought was true. She felt the big difference in our process was the degree to which she was challenged to be specific with what this conventionally realistic text meant – word by word, image by image. Ellen described how, over the course of rehearsals and the run of the show, this process became "deeper and fuller and richer" for her as the stream and cascade of images in her mind – an idea to which I will return – increasingly filled up and drove the action. She felt the need to see absolutely everything she was talking about. This ranged from getting specific with images (visual, aural, experiential, etc.) about things ranging from Kuala Lumpur, sandwiches, William Dean Howells, Terre Haute, to the layout of the offices outside of her door. (This required library and Internet research, but it also meant watching a bit of soft porn – one of the characters is a Russ Meyer type – and bad made-for-TV stalker movies.) Besides this, her construction of images of the character's memories, based on information in the play's text, was crucial to activating and driving her interactions with the other characters; these character-memory images provided color and urgency to her engagements with her fellow actors.

From her perspective as a TV/film/commercial/stage actress who comes out of non-academic training grounded in American psychological realism, Ellen summed up her experience in the production as follows: she realized that the key for her was being sure each referent or line had personal meaning for her as actor/character in order to anchor the referent and action of the moment. She noted that the work with images regularly led to very unexpected line readings, because the specificity of the image took her away from pedestrian and mundane interpretations. Ellen closed by saying, "The specific images in your head open you up to more possibilities to what can be happening in a scene or a performance, into the unexpected because it comes from a very personal engagement with the script" (Locy 2003). It could be argued that, for Ellen, the process was essentially a rich integration of her Strasberg-influenced background with Shakespeare-influenced close readings, and I wouldn't need to disagree with her in terms of the actor's application of technique.[1] I am sure my work with her would not have been as rigorous without the insight gathered from research I have been doing for the past few years in cognitive neuroscience as it relates to acting.

What I was doing through much of the process was guiding Ellen to create a very detailed stream of mental images, connected to the script and to her fellow actors, so that as many moments as possible were not just about "telling" but about feeling in the sense of being present to the character's story and immediate world.

Cognitive neuroscience

Issues of consciousness, feeling, and action/behavior are central to both acting and cognitive neuroscience.[2] Cognitive neuroscience's linkage of "perception, attention, memory, and thinking to underlying mechanisms in the brain" (LeDoux 2003: 23) allows us to move beyond binaries splitting mind-body and reason-emotion that have, since at least the time of Descartes, hampered our ability to understand what it is that we do when we act. There is an organic, biological ground out of which self, character, sense of narrative, and hence acting grow. Specifically, Stanislavsky-based approaches to acting – basically, those focusing on the actor's engagement with character and story, with a sense of something significant being lived in the present moment in front of an audience – are connected to our biological being (Blair 2000: 201–18; 2002: 177–90). In considering how brain structure and function are materially related to the nature of consciousness and self, we can move toward a more concrete sense of how the actor works. The focus here is on aspects of the neurocognitive ground of memory, feeling, imagery, and representation, and questions of emotional authenticity and self.

My use of the science is integrative, rather than reductive or essentialist, since the interplay among biology, environment (which includes culture), and psychological phenomena is highly dynamic. To quote feminist theorist of science Elizabeth Wilson, "if biology can be adequately articulated as a site of play, then we have come some way toward neutralizing the effect and domination of biologically reductionist principles in psychology" (Wilson 1998: 96) and can responsibly engage the material grounds of consciousness. Similarly, psychologist Jerome Kagan describes the simultaneously contingent and constrained nature of human development: we must resist thinking that there is "a strict determinism between biological events and the emergent psychological phenomena of thought, emotion, and behavior," even though "biological processes bias humans to develop a particular set of cognitive, affective, and behavioral forms in very particular ways" (Kagan 2001: 177). That is, each temperament constrains "a certain *family* of developmental outcomes" (italics added). Psychological development can be seen as "a sequence of cascades involving large numbers of events. Each event decreases, or limits, the probability of developing some outcomes, while determining no specific outcome" (Ibid.: 187). Similarly, for biological anthropologist Terrence Deacon and his co-authors, "evolution doesn't just build things up like a recipe. It sets up a stage of competition and then lets that competition set up another stage of competition, which then sets up another stage; in a sense, this is evolution inside of evolution inside of evolution" (Harrington 2001: 248). This resonates on a species scale with Kagan's "cascade" metaphor for the development of the individual's self as a persistent interaction between organism and environment. Neuroscientists Antonio Damasio and Joseph LeDoux point in similar directions in defining mind, consciousness, and cognition. For Damasio mind is "a process, not a thing" (Damasio 2003: 183); further, consciousness and mind are not synonymous – since aspects of mind function pre- and sub-consciously – though consciousness and *conscious* mind are (Ibid.: 187). Similarly, LeDoux distinguishes between cognition and consciousness: "Consciousness can be thought of as the product of underlying [unconscious] cognitive processes" (LeDoux 2003: 191); mind is "an integrated system that includes, in the broadest possible terms, synaptic networks devoted to cognitive, emotional, and motivational functions. More important, it involves interactions between networks involved in different aspects of mental life" (Ibid.: 258).

LeDoux's self is "not real, though it does exist," for it is "the totality of what an organism is physically, biologically, socially, and culturally. Though it is a unit, it is not unitary. . . . [T]he self is a 'dramatic ensemble'" (Ibid.: 31). (Theatrical metaphors are common in cognitive research.)

From the perspective of acting as "doing" rather than "being," all of this resonates with how an actor engages a role and a performance – it is inter-active, relational, and biological. It is ultimately about processes, rather than entities, that manifest in memory, feelings, and emotions.

Neural pattern development

Some neuroscientists maintain that who we are and how we function are based upon, among other things, potentials for specific neural patterns – or connections – and how they develop. Wilson's connectionist models "figure cognitive processing as the spread of activation across a network of intercon-nected, neuron-like units. . . . It is the connections between these units, rather than the units *per se*, that take on the pivotal role in the functioning of the network" (Wilson 1998: 6). In a postmodern sense, "None of the ele-ments in the network (the units and the connections) can be thought of as present and locatable," since "their effect is constituted through the spatial arrangement of the connectionist architecture and the temporal vicissitudes of the activation rules" (Ibid.: 162). In *Synaptic Self: How Our Brains Become Who We Are*, LeDoux asserts that we are our synapses, the product of neural patterns, the potential with which we are born and which we develop over a lifetime, since "synapses are changed every time our brain records an experience" (LeDoux 2003: 68). The brain's plasticity allows neurons and neural pathways to be altered by experience, so that "repeated delivery of a brief electrical stimulus to a nerve pathway [can] alter synaptic transmission in that pathway" (Ibid.: 137). Neural nets are changed, and the actual size of cortices can increase with stimulation. Not surprisingly, the size of string musicians' cortices devoted to their hands is significantly larger than those of non-musicians (Kandel and Squire 2001: 128).[3] That is, the neural biology with which we are born interacts with our environment and experi-ences to determine the particular way our individual set of neural paths – and, hence, our self – develops.

Culture and the construction of feeling

Given that biology and culture are simultaneously constrained and provi-sional (Wilson 1998: 65), Jerome Kagan's four types of psychological struc-tures in humans describe one way of understanding how consciousness and language grow out of biology. These are: (1) representations of bodily activ-ity, or visceral representations, that contain information about physiological states; (2) representations of motor sequences, or sensorimotor schemes, i.e., "reports" about movement (this makes it possible for dancers and musicians to do what they do); (3) schemas about external events, such as those mediated by sight and hearing, i.e., pre-linguistic "reports" about the sensory environment; and (4) "semantic structures that combine lexical representations with [schemas] to form networks that are logically constrained, hierarchical, and used for both thought and communication," i.e., semantic or symbolic systems that allow us to process the first three categories, or our experiences (Kagan 2001: 178–9). It is in the last category that culture comes most into play, since "biological constraints are weakest on semantic structures" because these structures vary across cultures and among individuals.[4]

Kagan goes on to say that differing semantic categories of social values and of metaphors for cultures and individuals impinge upon how, growing out of biology, we construct our sense of identity and self (Ibid.: 180–2). Conscious awareness of who we are depends on our linguistic interpretations of experience (cf. LeDoux's notion of a narrative self (LeDoux 2003: 20, 199); and Damasio's autobiographical self (Damasio 2003: 271–2)). Actors and acting teachers benefit from dealing rigorously with the cultural contingency of language structures and the way a presumption of "truthfulness" or "universality" about a particular framework can unnecessarily limit an actor's creativity and engagement. Becoming more conscious of the values imbedded in a particular culture's semantic structures is a starting point for the work (this has been a project of postmodernism from the start), but it is insufficient to stay at the level of culture. It is the interrelationship of biology and culture that is key; bodily schemas are an element of this interrelationship.

The concept of bodily schemas describes the way neural networks, the body, and culture are integrated. Wilson describes a bodily schema as

> a postural model of ourselves that is dynamic and which determines the *psychological* parameters of bodily posture and movement. New movements are assimilated into one's schema, change that schema, and then become part of the general determining force of bodily posture and movement. Incoming stimuli are always interpreted according to the already existing schemata; thus the registration of every sensation is always influenced by what has gone before.... Specifically, these schemata are organized chronologically (rather than spatially) and according to various laws of association, and they are mediated by appetite, instinct, interest, and ideals.... [T]he pattern of interconnections between schemata forms what is called temperament or character. Schemata are also intrinsically social.... [C]ognition cannot be simply the possession of an individual, but is the effect of a web of determination between individuals, and between an individual and the social.
>
> (Wilson 1998: 171–2)

Feeling and consciousness, conditioned by culture, grow out of bodily schemas, which are the product of neural networks, which are themselves the result of various kinds of experiential and cognitive memory, including, for want of a better term, neural memory.[5]

The fluidity and reciprocity of the processes linking brain, mind, culture, and behavior, and the questions these raise about consciousness and self, make it necessary to reconsider what it is we do when we're acting (or teaching/coaching actors). If teaching, training, and rehearsal are in fact "brain modification" working on biological and cultural fronts, this must change our sense of what acting is. Longer rehearsal periods and runs of a play allow actors more time to "pattern" the work into their bodies; an actor can develop richer, stronger synaptic patterns by having a longer engagement with a piece of material. This insight also pertains to Kabuki actors who might play a role for decades or the Wooster Group that rehearses and works on plays for months, often reviving/revising them over years. In the summer of 2002, I saw Ian Richardson recite from *Hamlet*, a role he first played in his 20s, in a master class with John Barton. Richardson, then 69 years old, did nothing but sit in his chair and speak the "To be or not to be" soliloquy. I was struck by the way craft, culture, life experience, and time came together in this simple, moving moment. Beyond Richardson's conscious skill, the work was supported by a deep, synaptic patterning in the body-brain of the performer.

Memory

From the perspective of neural patterning as a process of experience, neural function can be viewed as various kinds of learning and memory, both conscious and unconscious; e.g., synaptic, kinesthetic, sensory, and cognitive. According to LeDoux,

> Learning, and its synaptic result, memory, play major roles in gluing a coherent personality together as one goes through life.... Learning allows us to transcend our genes.... Our knowledge of who we are ... is in large part learned through experience, and this information is accessible to us through memory ... learning and memory also contribute to personality in ways that exceed explicit self-knowledge. The brain, in other words, learns and stores many things in networks that function outside of conscious awareness.
>
> (LeDoux 2003: 9–10)

Further,

> [M]uch of the self is learned by making new memories out of old ones. Just as learning is the process of creating memories, the memories created are dependent on things we've learned before. [... Memory is] a reconstruction of facts and experiences on the basis of the way they were stored, not as they actually occurred.
>
> (Ibid.: 96)

Memory can be explicit or implicit. Explicit, or declarative, memory is "the ability to consciously recollect, to remember what happened" (Ibid.: 97). It is divided into episodic memory (personal experiences, "things that happened to you at a particular time and place") and semantic memory (facts – things you know but have not necessarily experienced) (Ibid.: 108). Explicit memory is *relational*, so that "activation of a declarative memory leads to the activation of other related memories. As a result, declarative memories can be activated independent of the context in which they were established, and by stimuli other than those that were initially involved in the learning" (Ibid.: 115). The significance of this relational (or conjunctive) characteristic of explicit memory for actors will become clearer when I discuss image streams. Implicit memory is "reflected more in the things we do, and the way we do them, than in the things we know" (Ibid.: 116); for instance, learned motor and cognitive skills, such as walking and talking, and conditioned responses (Ibid.: 117). Regardless of the kind of memory, reconsolidation is involved in memory retrieval, i.e., "if you take a memory out of storage you have to make new proteins (you have to restore, or reconsolidate it) in order for the memory to remain a memory.... [In other words] the brain that does the remembering is not the brain that formed the initial memory" (Ibid.: 161).

Memory's provisional nature is directly connected to emotion and feeling. While emotionally competent stimuli (i.e., those that trigger an emotional response) "can be actual or recalled from memory," and nonconscious conditioned memory can lead to a current emotion, and thence to a feeling, in the manner of an actor's use of emotional or sense memory (Damasio 2003: 57), the memory is not a retrieval of an object but, in LeDoux's phrase, *"an imaginative reconstruction, or construction, built out of the relation of our attitude toward a whole active mass of past experience"* (LeDoux 2003: 177, italics added):

> So memory neither produces something completely new, nor simply reproduces something that already exists. Instead, memory is "literally manufactured" ... within or between already existing schemata. Memory is never the re-presentation of an element stored elsewhere; it is always an "imaginative reconstruction," a constant variation without a discrete origin.
>
> (Wilson 1998: 173)

This makes concepts such as emotion memory and sense memory not false but more complex than they might seem. Actors regularly draw on past emotional and kinesthetic experiences (emotion memory and sense memory) to help them connect more immediately with a character's situation. In much standard actor training this is often seen as reliving an experience or "truthfully" reconstructing an emotional or sensory state. However, though neural patterns are indeed activated when we have memories, they are new events. In fact, "memories of emotional experiences are often significantly different from what actually happened during them. . . . [M]emories are constructions assembled at the time of retrieval, and the information stored during the initial experience is only one of the items used in its construction" (LeDoux 2003: 203). This requires us to re-evaluate traditional approaches to acting and memory, especially as they relate to feelings. If we can view memory as neither an accurately retrievable truth nor an object (in the sense of being a fact) but as a trace, a neurochemical reconstruction whose nature is affected by the given moment and context of retrieval, we might more effectively manipulate memory as a tool for the actor. It would move us toward increased specificity and nuance in observations, with an increased emphasis on present-ness and imagination rather than "retrieval" or "fact." There is an interpenetration of physiological and psychological factors going beyond the level or kind described by Stanislavsky, Strasberg, and others but which is certainly continuing in the direction implied by their systems.

Particular kinds of "memorization" – conscious and unconscious, verbal/vocal, physical – occur depending on the rehearsal/cultural context's interaction with the individual actor. This has significant implications for the processes we set up for the acting class and the rehearsal studio. One could argue that, since all conscious memory is false in the sense that it is always a selective reconstruction of a past event, it might be productive to think of the "memory" used by actors as a specialized kind of fictive memory, a focused "imagining" that activates selective visceral, sensorimotor, and semantic schemas. For an actor, what matters is not recapturing the most authentic or truthful memory (sensory or emotional) but understanding that memory is a phenomenon of the moment, of the now – a tool to be used to forward the work. What matters is that it is a re-imagining of something that has a cognitive, affective, neurochemical utility, which is only provisionally autobiographically or historically "accurate." The science frees us from conventional approaches to sense or emotion memory that emphasize "reliving" a "true" past experience. It allows us to acknowledge both the importance of the actor's personal history and the centrality of feeling and memory to the human experience, so that the power of imagination can be tapped fully to make the actor's range of expression as wide and deep as possible.

Feelings and emotions

As far back as Meyerhold's work with biomechanics (influenced by the James–Lang theory of psychology) and Stanislavsky's methods (influenced by Ribot, Pavlov, and other research psychologists), the material bases of actors' emotional lives have been a subject of theorization and study.[6] Explorations have often been hampered by imprecise or overly subjective vocabularies, so I want to lay out some specific definitions to distinguish various levels at which emotional life functions, using Damasio's framework. In his terminology, emotions are basically biological responses, while feelings are conscious mental formulations of the former. Both emotions and feelings are connected to the struggle for homeostasis, in that their first function is to help us detect threats or benefits and thereby negotiate our environments effectively (Damasio 2003: 53). Distinguishing between aspects of – for want of a better term – emotional life clarifies human experience and articulates more specifically what an actor does.

As Damasio emphasizes, an emotion is a change in the body state and in brain structures that map the body and support thinking. Emotions are neural or chemical patterns produced when the brain detects an emotionally competent stimulus (or ECS, an actual or remembered object whose presence triggers a given pattern). They are automatic, based on inherited and learned repertoires of action; like any bodily processes, they are continually in flux (Ibid.: 63). When emotions rise to consciousness, feelings result, based on adaptive adjustments to the internal and external environment (Ibid.: 49). Feelings "translate the ongoing life state in the language of the mind" (Ibid.: 85). A feeling is *"the perception of a certain state of the body along with the perception of a certain mode of thinking and of thoughts with certain themes"* (Ibid.: 86, italics in original). Simply put, "Emotions play out in the theater of the body. Feelings play out in the theater of the mind" (Ibid.: 28). This framework begins to provide a way of distinguishing between physical and mental elements of the actors' work, while also describing the continuum on which they exist. Because they are conscious, feelings allow the possibility of non-stereotypical response (Ibid.: 80); i.e., choice and decision-making come into play. The powerful degree of interpretation involved in translating emotional/body states into feeling reinforces the idea of the actor's freedom to think creatively in imagining a role.

Over time, associative learning links emotions with feelings, thoughts, and body in a multivalent network, in which any of the three can "lead" at any given moment; i.e., a body-state, thought, or gesture can initiate a sequence of experience.[7] There is measurable neurological evidence that emotion and feeling sometimes follow "doing." Damasio in fact states, "In the beginning was emotion, but at the beginning of emotion was action" (Ibid.: 80). LeDoux's slightly different definitions are also useful. For him, emotion is a "process by which the brain determines or computes the value of a stimulus"; while, feeling emerges following taking action based on the emotion; for example, "The feeling of fear came after you jumped and after your heart was already pumping – the feeling itself did not cause the jumping or the pumping" (LeDoux 2003: 206–8). One might thus think of feeling as being the interpretation of the response to the stimulus. Both perspectives give credence to elements of Meyerhold's biomechanics and to Stanislavsky's methods of physical action and of active analysis: physical behavior – adjusting the body-state – can lead to or at least affect emotion and feeling.

This is only one argument against traditional separations of "reason" or "cognition" from "emotion" and "viscera" in actor training (as in acting teachers' exhortations to actors to "get out of your head"). Another is that research reveals that the higher the state of emotional arousal, the higher the number of brain systems activated; thus, "because more brain systems are typically active during emotional than during non-emotional states, and the intensity of arousal is greater, the opportunity for coordinated learning across brain systems is greater during emotional states," as LeDoux puts it (Ibid.: 322). The implications of this for acting include the wisdom of engaging the actor as fully as possible across as full a range of experiencing as possible. The mood-congruity hypothesis further links emotion and explicit memory; it holds that "memories are more easily retrieved when the emotional state at the time of memory formation matches the state at the time of retrieval. . . . [T]he more similar the pattern of activation is during learning and retrieval, the more efficient the retrieval is likely to be" (Ibid.: 222). (This provides concrete support for using sense and emotion memory, though it also must be placed in the context of the provisional and imaginary nature of memory. It is relative and "authentic" in various ways that may or may not be pertinent to the work. The point of the emotion or sense memory work is ultimately not to retrieve the memory but to support the life lived in the moment of performance. The point, in other words, is about a present, not the past.)

Neural function, cultural construction, memory, and feelings and emotions can be negotiated around the idea of imagination and imagery, specifically "image streams." This is one point at which the science can be applied concretely by the actor.

Image streams

From Plato through Diderot and on to today's approaches to acting, the intersections of "fiction" and "reality," "feeling" and "reason," the "imaginary" and the "real" in the Western actor's process have been endlessly contested. Stanislavsky and Lee Strasberg focused their work on engaging the actor "truthfully" with imaginary circumstances. A crucial chapter in Stanislavsky's *An Actor Prepares* is "Imagination." For actors, image, imagery, and imagination remain key terms. While imagination and imagery can function at the level of semantic memory ("things you know but haven't necessarily experienced," i.e., facts or cognitive "information"), the actor must evoke or fabricate episodic memory (personal experiences, "things that happened to you at a particular time and place," i.e., things experienced by the body) as much as possible. For cognitive neuroscientists, psychic images are always of the body since they are generated only within a body. Images of our bodies – unconscious and conscious – are the basis for how we negotiate our world. The actor's work does not happen without a sense of the body. The ground out of which our psychic images grow is our body image, a kind of body schema that is "the product (and producer) of the space between self and other, between sensations over time, between the inside and the outside, between and through bodily movements ... a living, constantly developing organization of knowledge" (Wilson 1998: 173–4). It is "not locatable as delineated and static cognitive structures," but "a dynamic system regulated by social and intrapsychic forces" (Ibid.: 173–4). This view manages to be material and fluid, personal and social – like the best acting.

Damasio connects body image, i.e., mappings of body-states, with emotions and feelings by means of his somatic-marker hypothesis (Damasio 2003: 148). There are two kinds of body images – from the body's interior and from sensory probes such as the retina and cochlea (Ibid.: 195), i.e., information regarding our internal state and external environment. There is a stream of foundational images in the mind that are "images of some kind of body event, ... [their basis being] a collection of brain maps, that is, a collection of patterns of neuron activity and inactivity (neural patterns, for short) in a variety of sensory regions" (Ibid.: 197). The images we experience are "brain constructions *prompted* by an object, rather than mirror reflections of the object" (Ibid.: 200, italics in original). That is, like a memory, the image is a thing unto itself, just as real as – but *not* the same as – the object that triggered it. The body images "that flow in the mind are reflections of the interaction between the organism and the environment.... The mind exists for the body, is engaged in telling the story of the body's multifarious events, and uses that story to optimize the life of the organism" (Ibid.: 206). In short, mind exists because there is a body to furnish it with contents. Consciousness arises when the flow of sensory images – the movie-in-the-brain – is accompanied by the images of a self (Ibid.: 215). Further, body-sensing areas of the brain reflect not only actual body states, but they can also deal with "false" or "as-if" body states (Ibid.: 118). These can be thought of as imaginary states, essentially based on memory, i.e., recollections and reconstitutions of conscious and somatic experiences.

We have some control over these states and can manipulate them to opportunistic ends. The actor is constantly engaged in the manipulation of various kinds of body-states through the manipulation of imagination and environment in order to embody certain conditions. There are, in fact, direct analogies between Stanislavskian and current neurocognitive terms. Character and its relationship to given circumstances (the "facts" of a play and its situation) mirror the idea of a self or organism in relationship to an environment, while action can be aligned with the organism's attempts to interact successfully with the environment, based on the "movie-in-the-brain." All human beings rely on image-manipulation – a core element of the actor's work – to survive. When we act or teach acting, we are involved in creating and shaping responses to emotionally competent stimuli, i.e., stimuli that lead to specific emotional and hence behavioral outcomes. We create the right physical and imaginational environments to lead to an efficacious stream of images that lead to the desired behavior and feeling. For example, actors would tend to focus on images connected to episodic, rather than semantic, memory, for actors in performance are typically more concerned with personal experience – "things that happened to you at a particular time and place," things experienced by the body – than with facts or cognitive information.

Application: a (very) small example

> Okay. When I was a freshman in college, I dated a guy who was a bartender. I would go and sit at the bar and wait for him to get off work. And there was this old man there who was always drinking alone and I always felt sorry for him. One night, he started talking to me, telling me all about his life and how he had lost his wife and how his children didn't speak to him anymore, and I felt really sorry for him and I told him I felt bad for him and he told me it would make him feel better to kiss a pretty girl. So I let him kiss me. On the mouth. *(Beat.)* I didn't want to at all. He was an old drunk and it made me sick. But I did it anyway because it's what I thought I was supposed to do. I was supposed to be nice.
>
> (Gilman 2000: 85)

This is the beginning of a speech in Act II, scene iii of *Boy Gets Girl*, in which Theresa is trying to figure out why she is nice, rather than honest and self-respecting, in situations with men. An approach grounded in a typical American psychological realism might guide the actor to create a general imaginary memory and feeling about this narrative, sometimes as part of a detailed character biography that the actor would develop far beyond the specifics of the script. The moment would also regularly be connected to elements of the actor's personal life. This can work, but it sometimes leads actors to focus on a feeling *about* what they are doing rather than on feeling *what* they are doing. These are radically different things. Another way to describe this is to say that the actor can be busier feeling the (character's or her own) feelings than being present to the feeling that arises in the moment of the acting.

In the approach I'm proposing, Theresa's speech, a response to a story just told by another character, is an attempt to understand the other character's point that, when we find ourselves in bad situations, "we can't always tell how much is us and how much is the world around us" (Ibid.: 84). Without deliberation, Theresa immediately returns to her freshman year, to an incident she hypothetically hasn't thought of in two decades; this in itself indicates that it has weight or emotional "charge" for the character. The images to work with include herself as a freshman (the actor would possibly "remember" clothing, vulnerability, hair, sensory specifics related to the bartender-boyfriend), the bar (where she sat, how long she'd been waiting, where the old man sat, time of year, time of night, the smell, the crowd or lack of it, how much she had to drink), the old man (hair, skin, clothing, smell, hands, face, voice), the kiss (his mouth, along with the preceding). These images – a very few of what could be generated for this brief passage – are for the purpose of feeling, of vitality, not for "fact" or information, and they narrow in on the feeling of the intimate interchange between the girl and the old man, and then on the woman's realization of her participation in her violation. The language's punctuation also provides cues for the physical, and hence psychic, feeling of the movement of the language. There is a short, full-stopped "Okay," followed by two brief, descriptive sentences – a set-up for sharing something difficult or perhaps Theresa reconstructing things in her head. The next sentence begins with "One night" and ends with "pretty girl," broken only by two commas. When I read this straight through without stopping or taking a significant breath, I feel a bit "run over" and not completely in control. The important thing here is not the information of the man's story but the feeling Theresa has as she is recollecting the event, including, for example, the way he sounded, looked, and smelled when he said "kiss a pretty girl." The impact (for actor and audience) on "So I let him kiss me. On the mouth" is dependent on the actor having very specific kinesthetic and olfactory images of that moment – of the old man's smells, lips, the feeling on her mouth, her nausea and physical tension – and of Theresa's reaction to it in the now. Again, in performance, the "information" of the story is incomplete dramatically without the feeling of the awful, intrusive kiss. The actor does not "play" these choices but merely reacts to the stream of images she has set up as they arise. The images do not need to make "logical" or even "biographical" sense, any more than the images that pass through our heads at any given moment of the day make sense. Their purpose is to have psychophysical *efficacy* in engaging and moving the actor and thereby the audience.

Conversations with a master acting teacher

The head of our Acting programs, Michael Connolly, is a Stanislavsky-based professional actor, director, and a superb acting teacher and coach. He works primarily with Shakespeare and other classic texts of the Western canon. A central concern of his work is to make the actor's work emotionally full, intellectually specific, and physically compelling (Connolly 2003). Michael is drawn to the research I have been outlining here because it is based in the genuinely organic: it acknowledges how we actually function in the world and provides a clear picture of how all aspects of the actor's being are integrated. The neuroscientific perspective critiques twentieth-century approaches that compartmentalize different aspects of the actor's being, e.g., separating acting from voice, voice from movement, and all of this from research and critical thinking. This approach refigures the sequence of events that leads to the embodiment of analysis, of research, text work, and personal history in the service of performance. Michael and I appreciate that this approach frees us from conventional notions of affective and sense memory as "retrievals of past truths" and objectified notions of the self since it allows the actor to work from the perspective that there is no "objective" authentic self, past or otherwise, to engage but only the self-in-the-now of the rehearsal or performance. From this perspective, we guide the actor not to be more "honest" or "connected to her truth" but to be more adept at psychoemotional improvisations related to the scene or play.

Michael noted that, though imagination is central in Stanislavsky's writing, there isn't much "microscopic" detail about how this might be used by the actor. The idea of image streams fills a lacuna in Stanislavsky's work, running counter to kinds of US training that focus on the actor's personal "material" at the expense of imagination. Michael has recently been working with this in two arenas: in teaching his senior BFA acting class, focused on Shakespeare, and in directing Timberlake Wertenbaker's *Our Country's Good*. In the class, students perform sonnets as a kind of character monologue; in previous years Michael would require students to develop a complete "discursive" paraphrase/narrative for the sonnet before moving on to more "poetic" aspects. This time he has moved more directly to word-by-word questioning of the actor to be sure he or she has a connection to each moment and image in the sonnet, with the idea that the narrative will fill itself in as the images become articulated. What he has observed is an immediate payoff in terms of the actor's personalization of the material (I believe this is precisely what is described by Ellen Locy above). For *Our Country's Good*, he spent more time on getting actors to "see" specific images related to their work, setting up what he describes as "an imaginative technical rehearsal in their heads." He required the actors to locate themselves as completely as possible in the world of the play and its givens in images and to create givens and images where there were gaps in the project.

For many years Michael has been involved in recruiting for strong acting programs. His thinking about what is raised for acting by cognitive neuroscience and his beginning experiments with what it might imply are leading him to redefine his definition of "talent," that thing that has led him to say, "Ah, there's an actor." He proposes that we might set up new parameters, that talent might more accurately – and simply – be defined as "the ability to embody what is imagined." The issue becomes not how vulnerable or "expressive" or passionate an actor is but how easily and fully he or she enters into a theatrical or performative world, how free his or her imagination is to allow him or her to embody it.

Conclusion

The reframing of the actor's process allowed by cognitive neuroscience moves us past some counter-productive historical and cultural conventions (or habits of thought) related to acting. It has nothing to do with a preordained sense of an "ought to be" but rather works with the intertwining of the cultural and biological in a way that acknowledges the contingency and fluidity of what it means to be human, without denying basic material (or mortal) limits. It is based on our current best sense of how we, as organisms, function. If we operate from the provisional biological and cultural perspective I've been describing, we might more productively work with the actor to construct image streams. We could operate on at least two fronts: emphasizing episodic, rather than semantic, connections; and reinforcing neural patterns and responses that break free of culturally and personally habituated framings of the "problem" of the character or the moment. We could liberate actors' image-inations by guiding them *consciously* to create a vivid string of both cascading and "anchoring" images, sensory and affective, connected where appropriate to explicit memory, in combination with a clear kinesthetic score that supports the body-mapping of those images. The applications of this research should be as varied as the artists employing them, for it is more about basic principles than about rules or formulas. The point is to find strategies and ways of working as actors or working with actors to *activate* them. As with other approaches, one engages in defining and discovering given circumstances and creating a vital sense of unfolding embodiment. What this approach can do is liberate us from formulaic approaches to genre, style, and technique.

I don't believe actors necessarily need to know a great deal about cognitive neuroscience. However, reframing their sense of self and "emotional truth," not to mention theatricality, in light of a more nuanced and specific grasp of the interrelationship among the physical, cognitive, and emotional, and recontextualizing their sense of action and image-ination by divorcing it from limiting vocabularies of twentieth-century psychology and cultural production expand our capacity for both exploring and embodying theatrical material. For example, what may sometimes be defined as an emotional or psychological issue in acting is actually, on a deeper level, better understood as a physical or body-state issue. It is about the actor's habituated interpretations of homeostatic and autonomic symptoms, as well as his or her relationship to emotion and cognition and how both of these manifest in (or are "interpreted into") conscious feelings. The "mistranslation" of somatic and sensory representations at the semantic-cultural-"psychotherapeutic" level has led to a great deal of boring, self-conscious acting, often having to do with the exertion of trying to "live the role" or "become the character" within a narrow range of personal or cultural "authenticity."[8]

Finally, from the perspective of neurocognitive processes, it is possible to get around arguments about how "split" or how "merged" actor and role are, as well as whose "truth" or "feelings" are being experienced or witnessed at any given moment, not to mention how "authentic" that expression is. We can move beyond Descartes' body-mind split and Diderot's paradox. A new vocabulary based on neurocognitive views of memory, feeling, image streams, their embodiedness, and their basis in basic biology and evolution provides a way of talking about the acting phenomenon rather as an evolution of a single organism in a very specific, very material way. Issues of "taking on a character" or "imbibing the reality" are recontextualized as strategies for *performance*, because the character becomes a set of choices and behaviors – a process rather than a discrete entity – supported by what the actor brings to the role in terms of imagination, voice/speech, body, and intellect. Questions of what belongs to the "character" and what to the "actor," what is "real" and what is not, become moot. There is no character in any objective sense; there is only the process and behavior of a particular individual in a particular context.[9] What the actor is doing becomes simply – and complexly – that: what the *actor* is *doing*.

Notes

1 Samuel Beckett's, Harold Pinter's, and David Mamet's scripts are examples of how "mundane" language can be carefully crafted – like poetry – to provide a powerful rhythmic and imagistic impetus for the actor's embodiment. The feeling and discovery come fully only with a specific engagement with the words and punctuation on the page. The same can be true for almost any well-written modern play.

2 Sometimes also called neurocognitive science or computational neuroscience.

3 The biology of socialization specifically looks at how experience organizes and is conditioned by brain circuitry (Posner 2001: 208). This is determined by epigenetic rules, "largely unconscious heuristics that are the results of culture and genetics that operate to determine the way people filter or explore their environments. At the most elementary level they are things like the restricted portions of the electromagnetic spectrum that influences our visual system. It limits the range of information to which we are sensitive.... Selection of information by attention involves more complex epigenetic rules that select information based on both an automatic and a voluntary basis" (Ibid.: 213).

4 For example, while both Americans and Caroline Islanders tend to classify emotional names according to the categories of "pleasant/unpleasant," the second parsing for Americans is intensity, while for Caroline Islanders it is whether another person was the origin of the feeling state. These tendencies have to do with differing social structures (Kagan 2001: 179–80).

5 One of the things that occurs with experience and synaptic patterning is habituation, "a form of learning in which repeated presentation of a stimulus leads to a weakening of response – you jump the first time you hear a loud noise, but if it is repeated over and over you jump less" (LeDoux 2003: 138). This raises a seeming paradox in relationship to acting, in which we rehearse and repeat, often in order to achieve the illusion of the first time. On this point, it is important to distinguish between two things going on in rehearsal and performance: the repetition of a set score within a generalized range of consistency, and the truly spontaneous and immediate variation within that score in any particular rehearsal or performance, similar to the way in which a musician might hit the same notes or a dancer do the same steps, "the same but different" every time.

6 Study continues in the development of technologies such as positron emission tomography and functional magnetic resonance imaging (PET scans and fMRIs), which allow us to see the processes of the brain at work. As Richard Davidson states, "Experiential shaping of the brain circuitry underlying emotion is powerful. The neural architecture provides the common pathway through which culture, social factors, and genetics all operate together" (Davidson 2001: 191). We can take pictures of where and how emotion happens in the brain.

7 The most notable studies in this regard are Paul Ekman's work on facial muscle movement, which demonstrates that changing the body-state changes the feeling state at least in part because of what we cognitively associate with a particular body-map (cited in Damasio 2003: 71). See also Ekman (2003).

8 I am reminded of misunderstandings of Stanislavsky and mistranslations of one of his key terms, *perezhivanie*, which is literally "living *through*," not "living," the role, and implies something more dynamic and vital than is typically understood.

9 From this view, perspectives such as that described in Konijn (2000), which examines the difference between the actor's and her character's feelings during performance, are limited because they stop at the level of conscious mind and selective physiological measurements and are on the verge of viewing emotions as entities rather than processes. Such approaches, overlooking the deeper neurobiological ground of what the actor is doing, do not address the genuine "blur" between actor and character, for instance, the not-me/not-not-me of Winnicott *et al.* involved in play.

References

Blair, R. (2000) "The Method and the Computational Theory of Mind," in Krasner, D. (ed.) *Method Acting Reconsidered: Theory, Practice, Future*, New York: St. Martin's Press, 201–18.

——— (2002) "Reconsidering Stanislavsky: feeling, feminism, and the actor," *Theatre Topics*, 12(2): 177–90.

Connolly, M. (2003) Private conversation, 29 August.

Damasio, A. (2003) *Looking for Spinoza: Joy, Sorrow, and the Feeling Brain*, Orlando, FL: Harcourt, Inc.

Davidson, R.J. (2001) "Toward a Biology of Personality and Emotion," in Damasio, A.R., Harrington, A., Kagan, J., McEwen, B.S., Moss, H., and Shaikh, R. (eds) *Unity of Knowledge: The Convergence of Natural and Human Science*, New York: The Academy of Sciences, 191–207.

Ekman P. (2003) *Emotions Revealed: Recognizing Faces and Feelings to Improve Communication and Emotional Life*, New York: Times Books, Henry Holt and Co.

Gilman, R. (2000) *Boy Gets Girl*, New York: Faber and Faber, Inc.

Harrington, A., Deacon, T.W., Kosslyn, S.M., and Scarry, E. (2001) "Science, Culture, Meaning, Values: A Dialogue," in Damasio, A.R., Harrington, A., Kagan, J., McEwen, B.S., Moss, H., and Shaikh, R. (eds) *Unity of Knowledge: The Convergence of Natural and Human Science*, New York: The Academy of Sciences, 233–57.

Kagan, J. (2001) "Biological Constraint, Cultural Variety, and Psychological Structures," in Damasio, A.R., Harrington, A., Kagan, J., McEwen, B.S., Moss, H., and Shaikh, R. (eds) *Unity of Knowledge: The Convergence of Natural and Human Science*, New York: The Academy of Sciences, 177–90.

Kandel, E.R. and Squire, L.R. (2001) "Neuroscience: Breaking Down Scientific Barriers to the Study of Brain and Mind," in Damasio, A.R., Harrington, A., Kagan, J., McEwen, B.S., Moss, H., and Shaikh, R. (eds) *Unity of Knowledge: The Convergence of Natural and Human Science*, New York: The Academy of Sciences, 118–35.

Konijn, E.A. (2000) *Acting Emotions*, Amsterdam: Amsterdam University Press.

LeDoux, J. (2003) *Synaptic Self: How Our Brains Become Who We Are*, New York: Penguin Books.

Locy, E. (2003) Private interview, 20 August.

Posner, M.I., Rothbart, M.K., and Gerardi-Caulton, G. (2001) "Exploring the Biology of Socialization," in Damasio, A.R., Harrington, A., Kagan, J., McEwen, B.S., Moss, H., and Shaikh, R. (eds) *Unity of Knowledge: The Convergence of Natural and Human Science*, New York: The Academy of Sciences, 208–16.

Stanislavski, K. (1964) *An Actor Prepares*, trans. Elizabeth Reynolds Hapgood, New York: Routledge/Theatre Arts Books.

Toporkov, V.O. (1998) *Stanislavski in Rehearsal: The Final Years*, trans. Christine Edwards, New York: Routledge.

Wilson, E.A. (1998) *Neural Geographies: Feminism and the Microstructure of Cognition*, New York: Routledge.

Section 4

The spectator and cognition

8   See the play, read the book

Howard Mancing

There is a fundamental difference between reading a text such as a novel and watching any sort of collaborative, multi-media display such as the performance of a play. My basic thesis in this essay is that seeing and knowing is not the same thing as reading and knowing.

Textualizing the world

Because we have literalized the reading metaphor – we say that we "read" television, "read" fashion, "read" a situation, or "read" a mind – we have blurred the line that separates two basically different processes. We do *not* "read" films, television programs, or theatrical performances: we perceive them both visually and aurally. During and after both kinds of experience – reading a text and perceiving a play – we interpret or creatively and imaginatively understand text and performance using cognitive processes that are very similar if not identical and that necessarily involve language and symbolic thought. But the nature of the interpretive activity should not obscure the fact that the aesthetic activities of seeing and reading are two very different cognitive processes.[1]

One of the reasons we have tended to talk and write about "reading" performances is our continued reliance on an outdated structuralist theory of language and cognition.[2] Virtually no one in linguistics today conceives of language as a closed self-referential system of differences, believes that the terms "signifier" and "signified" are particularly meaningful or useful, places processes of coding and decoding at the heart of communication, or conceives of the listener (or reader) as a passive receiver of the speaker's (or writer's) message. Yet all these concepts are cornerstones of Saussurean and post-Saussurean linguistics, and all are crucial to semiotics, deconstruction, Lacanian psychoanalytical theory, poststructuralism, and much more. Ann Marie Seward Barry, in her excellent book *Visual Intelligence* (1997), consistently and appropriately distinguishes between visual and linguistic knowledge and laments the fact that "[t]he prejudice for the verbal and against the visual dominates and confuses almost all intellectual discussion on the visual image to date" (Ibid.: 139). Barbara Maria Stafford similarly makes the case against structuralism's "logocentrism," which she defines as "that cultural bias, convinced of the superiority of written or propositional language, that devalues sensory, affective, and kinetic forms of communication precisely because they often baffle verbal resolution" (Stafford 1999: 23). Stafford specifically, and correctly, relates this tendency to the linguistic theories of Saussure:

> The totemization of language as a godlike agency in western culture has guaranteed the identification of writing with intellectual potency. Ferdinand de Saussure, the early twentieth-century founder of structuralism, strengthened the biblical coupling of meaning with naming by formulating the opposition of signifier/signified. These verbalizing binaries turned noumenal and phenomenal experience into the product of language. Not only temporal but spatial effects supposedly obeyed an invisible system, the controlling structure of an inborn ruling *écriture*.
>
> (Ibid.: 5)

Research in linguistics today owes virtually nothing to the theories of Saussure, though of course Saussure continues to be acknowledged for his historical importance.[3] Rather, the contemporary study of linguistics begins with Noam Chomsky, whose book *Syntactic Structures* (1957) completely reoriented the study of language.[4] Although elements of the early Chomsky were still largely structuralist, from the beginning he based the study of linguistics in psychology and biology where it belongs.[5] Today the most significant work in linguistics always has this psychological (social) and biological foundation and is found in the areas of pragmatics, sociolinguistics, psycholinguistics, neurolinguistics, and cognitive linguistics, where language is viewed most often as a cognitive tool used by specific people in specific socio-historical contexts.[6] Such an approach owes nothing whatsoever to Saussure or any of his followers. Yet we in literary theory and criticism continue blithely to talk about signification, language systems, and decoding as if those were still meaningful concepts.

Although Jacques Derrida railed at the "logocentrism" of traditional Western metaphysics, no theory is more logocentric than one derived from structuralism, which makes all knowing into a reading of texts. "There is nothing outside the text" Derrida (1967: 158) has famously proclaimed: Everything is text; everything is to be understood as we understand text; everything is reading. In fact, structuralist-semiotic thinking often runs something like this:

1   language is a sign system that we understand by "reading" its codes;
2   language is the paradigm of all sign systems;
3   all sign systems can be "read" as is a language; and therefore
4   all understanding consists of "reading" the signs of the system.

Nonsense. The cat that sees a mouse and pounces has not read anything at all but knows (based on perception and instinct) what the situation is and what is to be done. The early pre-linguistic hominid who survived on the savannas of Africa used a perception-based cognition that still underlies modern thought (see below the brief discussion of Merlin Donald's "mimetic" stage of human evolution), even though human cognition also today makes significant use of symbolic processes.

The psychology of perception

Perceiving and knowing something is simply not the same thing as reading and knowing something. Perceptual understanding, the primary cognitive mode in nature, is not at all linguistic, and by definition it cannot involve "reading." Modern theories of perception and thought identify two fundamental ways of knowing: perception and symbolic thought.[7] Psychologist Allan Paivio summarizes the basic differences between visual and linguistic knowledge: "Picture-like representations are variously described as having analogue, iconic, continuous, and referentially isomorphic properties, whereas language-like representations are characterized as being non-analogue, noniconic, digital or discrete (as opposed to continuous), referentially arbitrary, and propositional" (Paivio 1986: 16).[8]

We can conceive of human cognition as taking place along a continuum, with perception at one pole and symbolization at the other. Most of what happens in our everyday cognitive processes involves some combination of the two (for the two processes are distinct but function in parallel, complimentary, and cooperative ways) and thus is located somewhere on the continuum between the two extremes. A theatrical performance, for example, draws simultaneously upon cognitive processes from across the spectrum, prominently involving both visual and auditory perception, on the one hand, and symbolic (that is, linguistic) cognition on the other. Essential for consideration of this question is Paivio's "dual-coding theory," the basic underlying assumption of which is that "there are two classes of phenomena handled cognitively by separate subsystems [of the brain], one specialized for the representation and processing of information concerning nonverbal objects and events, the other specialized for dealing with language" (Ibid.: 53). This distinction is fundamental to most of today's neuroscience and cognitive psychology.[9]

Consistent with Paivio's view is James J. Gibson's "ecological" approach to visual perception (1966, 1979). Gibson has proposed, first, that traditional psychological theories of external stimulus input and internal mental response are inadequate. Instead, he suggests, we have five active perceptual *systems*: the *orienting system*, which is basic to all the others, and the *auditory*, *haptic*, *taste–smell*, and *visual systems* (Gibson 1966). These systems are essential to an animal's ability to pick up veridical and invariant information from the environment and to make pragmatic use of the "affordances" of that environment. Affordances are the possibilities or opportunities that exist in the world, what the environment offers, provides, or furnishes for an animal. Our perceptual systems, shared to a large extent by other animals, do not in any way depend on language to function. Perception-based cognition, the most elemental and most fundamental kind of knowing that exists, in its purest and most ancient form has nothing to do with texts.

Gibson notes that although we normally say that vision depends on the eye, which in turn is connected to the brain, it is more accurate to say that "natural vision depends on the eyes in the head on a body supported by the ground, the brain being only the central organ of a complete visual system" (Gibson 1979: 1). Gibson is interested in the way we perceive the real world in real life, and this is the reason he uses the term "ecological" to describe his approach. Gibson distinguishes between direct perception and perception that is mediated: "Direct perception is what one gets from seeing Niagara Falls, say, as distinguished from seeing a picture of it. The latter kind of perception is *mediated*. So when I assert that perception of the environment is direct, I mean that it is not mediated by *retinal* picture, *neural* picture, or *mental* picture. *Direct perception* is the activity of getting information from the ambient array of light" (Gibson 1966: 147). All mediated perception, then, is a secondary process derived from and based on the primary (in both senses of first and most important) experience of direct perception.[10]

Perhaps the best detailed description of the biology of visual perception and of visual cognition is the one provided by Semir Zeki in his book *A Vision of the Brain* (1993) and extended to a biological approach to art and aesthetics in *Inner Vision* (Zeki 1999). His fundamental point in both of these works is that the visual brain's primary function is "the acquisition of knowledge about the world around us" (Ibid.: 8). Zeki both validates and updates Gibson's ecological theory, especially in light of the turn in cognitive science toward theories of embodied cognition, of which Zeki's argument itself is a very good example.

The evolution of human speech

Recent developments in evolutionary science further support the concept of two types of knowing. For example, Merlin Donald's book entitled *The Origins of the Modern Mind* (1991) is a subtle and convincing outline of human evolution that traces humanity's development through four broad evolutionary stages: the episodic, the mimetic, the mythic, and the theoretic. Other animals at best live in an "episodic" culture, one bound to the here-and-now and dominated by perception.[11] The first phase of human development beyond the episodic stage is what Donald calls the "mimetic" stage, a pre-linguistic, gesture-based mode of communication. For Donald,

Mimetic skill involves much more than imitation; but it must have started as an extension of primate imitative ability.... Although this capacity was a necessary cognitive bridge to the later evolution of language, it lacks certain key linguistic properties. Mimesis remains an *analog* representational strategy; driven largely by imagery, which refers by means of perceptual resemblance.

(Ibid.: 360)

From this developed the "mythic," or storytelling, phase of human development, a stage which is still very much with us today. Central to the mythic culture are language and narrative. As Donald says, "Viewed from an evolutionary perspective, the language system brought with it not only a new vocal apparatus but a *wholly new system for representing reality*" (Ibid.: 259; italics in original). Donald's fourth stage of human evolution (in which we now find ourselves) is that of "theoretic" culture, whose most distinctive characteristic, perhaps, is that we now store most of our memory outside our biological bodies.[12]

Complementing the approach outlined by Donald is Terrence Deacon's theory of the "co-evolution of brain and language." The physical, biological evolution of the brain was accompanied by the simultaneous evolution of language from its earliest gestural (mimetic) roots to its modern complex symbolic structures; all along the way, each process directly influenced the other, so that, in Deacon's words:

the evolution of language took place neither inside nor outside brains, but at the interface where cultural evolutionary processes affect biological evolutionary processes.... It is simply not possible to understand human anatomy, human neurobiology, or human psychology without recognizing that they have all been shaped by something that could best be described as an idea: the idea of symbolic reference.

(Deacon 1997: 409–10)

An understanding of the long, slow evolutionary process by which language came to be perhaps the single most distinctive characteristic of our species – that which most distinguishes human beings from other animals – makes all the more abundantly clear the fundamental distinction between symbolic cognition and perception.[13]

Mimesis and diegesis

One can find a parallel, I would suggest, between modern evolutionary science and cognitive psychology, on the one hand, and literary theory and criticism, on the other, and the place to begin is at the beginning: with Plato and Aristotle. Plato first distinguished between *mimesis* – representing or imitating – and *diegesis* – narrating (see Kirby 1991). The two great ancient philosophers

used these terms in different ways and with different emphases, as is only reasonable for people who lived in an age when most of what we today call "literature" was primarily a multi-media, perception-based activity. Epic poems
were recited/sung before a public; poetry, too, was normally read, recited,
sung, or declaimed; theatre was always a public performance. The solitary
reading of texts was very far from the norm and was not a major aesthetic issue
for Plato or Aristotle.[14] Certainly nothing existed at that time that was even
remotely comparable to a massive literate public and mass-produced printed
texts: the primary ingredients for the modern reading of literature.

But surely we can recognize the validity of the clear distinction between
the two concepts: I can mimetically act out a scene, or I can write it for you
to read. They are not at all the same thing. Theatre, I suggest, is essentially
mimetic, not diegetic (except in very special circumstances and in very
limited ways); while a written narrative text is essentially diegetic, not
mimetic (again, except in very special circumstances and in very limited
ways). When we watch a play in a theatre, we *see* the characters, their dress,
the scenery; and we *hear* the characters' voices, the sound effects, the music
(if any). But when we read a novel, we *see* only the symbols on the printed
page, and we *hear* nothing; we must *creatively imagine* the characters, their
clothing, their voice, other sounds, and the physical context. Take, for
example, the following scene from *Don Quixote*:

> The first to stir was Sancho Panza; finding himself next to his master, in
> a weak, plaintive voice he said:
> "Señor Don Quixote! Ah, Señor Don Quixote!"
> "What do you want, brother Sancho?" replied Don Quixote in a voice as
> feeble and pitiful as Sancho's.
>
> (Cervantes 2003: 104)

The reader can't *hear* either Sancho's "weak, plaintive voice" or Don
Quixote's "voice as feeble and pitiful as Sancho's." In a theatrical performance of this scene, the two voices would be heard directly, but in a written
text they can only be described (and imaginatively created by the reader). A
novel cannot be mimetic or perceptual; a play by definition is.

In literature, mimesis and diegesis can be combined in various ways, but
even when we have diegesis in the theatre, it is primarily mimetic. When a
messenger comes on stage and narrates what took place in an offstage incident (say, a battle in which an important personage was killed), we *hear* that
messenger's voice, tone, inflexion; we *see* the actor's gestures. The messenger
certainly is narrating, but he is also (and primarily) representing to us the
scene he is narrating. Similarly, even when we have a kind of mimesis in a
print text, it is primarily diegetic. The novelist can attempt to describe the
speaker's tone (as does Cervantes in the example above), but it is impossible
to represent it directly to us. We often speak and write of the narrative *voice*
in a novel or story, but (and the point is often forgotten) this can only be a

convenient metaphor or shorthand, for the *voice* is not literally represented or imitated in the text but must be imagined by the reader.

It is not possible to tell a story by means of perceptual perception; there is no narrative without language. The main reason for this is that a narrator is necessary to tell a story, and in the theatre (with but rare exceptions) there is no narrator (see Garner 1989). The same is true of photographs, paintings, or other graphic arts, and of (instrumental) music. Show someone a picture or play a piece of music, and the person can imaginatively construct a story, but that imaginative construct may be (and usually is) radically different from one person to another, and these people's reports of what they imagined may have nothing at all in common. When the same people read a text, however, they will all have had access to exactly the same story and will be able to summarize it in very similar ways.[15]

Perception in general, and vision in particular, are older in terms of evolution than is language, and they are more powerful (see below). As Donald (1991: 269–75) describes the shift from mimetic cognition to mythic (symbolic) cognition, the former is enfolded within the latter, forming its core and informing its structure. There would be no language if there were no perception, no myth without mimesis. Sometimes ontogeny recapitulates phylogeny; the individual develops according to the same pattern as the evolution of the species.[16] Theatre is older, more primitive, and more powerful than the novel. As Bakhtin says, theatre had its origin and was developed to its full capabilities in an ancient oral (perceptual) culture, while the novel came into being only after the invention of the printing press and in a literate (symbolic) culture.[17]

Reading as imaginative performance

When we read a text we creatively imagine a situation and construct an understanding of it. When we read *Don Quixote*, for example, we create mental images of the characters and the settings; we imagine the intonation of the dialogue; we regulate the rhythm of the prose; we relate events to our personal schemata, memory, values, emotions, feelings, and more; we understand within the limits of our specific location in space and time, our history, our culture, our circumstances. The characters and settings we imaginatively "see" are uniquely ours, not shared in detail by any other person. This cannot be said of something that we all actually "see" together. Everyone looking at an actor on stage is seeing and hearing almost exactly the "same" thing. Of course, some will pay attention to or notice some details that others will not (*notice* is not a synonym for *see*); of course, some will understand what is said or done in a way quite different from how someone else understands it; and, of course, the view from one side of the room is somewhat different from the view from the other side. But any individual's perception of the actor shares more with the perceptions of other people than can his or her imaginative creation of a character in a novel.

Richard J. Gerrig, a cognitive psychologist who has studied real people reading real texts in real contexts, reports that "readers are often described as *being transported* by a narrative by virtue of *performing* that narrative" (Gerrig 1993: 2). The degree to which Gerrig is correct and the experiences of being transported and performing are present in readers of a book is the degree to which the experience of reading a book is comparable not to the watching of a play but to participation in its performance. A written narrative creates a whole world (or, better perhaps, a version of the real world) into which the reader enters. The reader's imaginative powers bring the world alive. The reader can get "lost" in a book, forget about the passage of time, and experience another (virtual) reality.[18] For Norman N. Holland, also, reading is the creation of experience: "We craft, we perform, we construct a literary experience. We use poems and fictions to make experiences" (Holland 1988: 169). Empirical research involving readers of romance and "ludic" readers shows repeatedly that Gerrig's metaphors of *transportation* (or "escape") and *performance* are indeed at the heart of the aesthetic reading experience, whether the book being read is great literature or popular romance. As pioneering reader-response theorist Louise Rosenblatt says: "A specific reader and a specific text at a specific time and place: change any of these, and there occurs a different circuit, a different event – a different poem" (Rosenblatt 1994: 14). All recent research in the cognition of reading is consistent with these positions.[19]

We should never forget that reading is more difficult and more demanding than watching any visual (or, more generally, perceptual) medium.[20] Reading is not like visual perception or spoken language, which are functions of our evolutionary biology; reading is only acquired by conscious effort, over a period of time. Our brains were not designed for reading but are capable of adding reading to their more innate procedures (Klawans 2000: 97–9). It takes years to learn to read, mere seconds to "learn" to watch TV, and little more than that to participate in most other media: "unlike the difficulty of learning to read, the ability to view motion pictures is readily acquired. There is no special alphabet, no special language of film. We see and hear the characters and events of motion pictures directly" (Anderson 1996: 159; see also Messaris 1994). Reading is a slower process, demanding a higher degree of concentration than any perceptual medium. By comparison, most of the other media are fast, direct, simple, and exciting. But the rewards of the extra effort required by reading are great: complete control of pace (you can stop, reread a passage, contemplate its implications, put the book down and return to it later), absolute imaginative creativity, and incomparable richness of the experience.

Theatre as perceptual performance

When someone sees a performance of a play, she or he has an experience much more like actually seeing reality than that person could possibly have when reading a book. It is the illusion of reality (and the reality of that illusion) that gives theatrical performance its superior *vividness* in comparison with a book. What film director and theorist Joseph Anderson has said of film applies equally to a play in a theatre: "Because motion pictures can be constructed of the stuff of everyday experience, they can function as a surrogate for the physical world, not in the way that arbitrary symbols such as words may stand for physical objects, but as an actual substitute for the thing itself" (Anderson 1996: 164). In fact, the case for theatre is even more illustrative of this point, as a live performance *is* (a mimetic) reality and the act of viewing it *is* the direct perception of that reality. As George Bluestone states it in his classic study on novel–film relationships: "These distinguishing traits follow primarily from the fact that the novel is a linguistic medium, the film essentially visual." Bluestone elaborates:

> With the abandonment of language as its sole and primary element, the film necessarily leaves behind those characteristic contents of thought which only language can approximate: tropes, dreams, memories, conceptual consciousness. In their stead, the film supplies endless spatial variations, photographic images of physical reality, and the principles of montage and editing. All these differences derive from the contrast between the novel as a conceptual and discursive form, the film as a perceptual and presentational form.
>
> (Bluestone 1957: vi–vii)

Obviously, viewing a film and a theatrical performance are two very different activities, but they share one thing: actual visual perception, which is completely absent in the act of reading a book. Our mental images during the reading process are never as precise and detailed as our perceptual experiences: seeing is more vivid than imagining.[21] Actually being there is more vivid, immediate, and intense than imagining being there.

To talk of the "language" of visual media not only confuses the issue, it simultaneously overvalues and undervalues the uniqueness of the reading experience. If reading is overvalued as the highest form of knowing and understanding something – as it is in the structuralist-semiotic-poststructuralist paradigm – then devotees of other means of cognition often feel the need to strive for comparability and attempt to "elevate" the processes involved in perception to the same "height" as those involved in the "higher-level" process of reading, lest they be thought of as dealing with something inferior, something less academic and less respectable. Symbolic understanding is fundamentally different from perceptual knowledge, and it is a uniquely human process;[22] but this in no way implies that it is the only kind of human cognition that exists or that it is the most important human way of knowing. If all cognition is considered as reading, then reading is synonymous with perceiving, feeling, knowing, understanding, thinking, and so forth; there thus exists but a single process, and the uniqueness of reading – a matter of comprehending symbolic language that is radically different from perceptual knowledge – is devalued, its uniqueness lost in the amorphous act of knowing something. Similarly, if all cognition is like the reading of texts, we lose our ability to recognize the life-like, vivid, direct, perception of a play on the stage.

Reading vs. perception

The defining difference between the book and all perception-based media is that *the book has no analogue in direct biological perception*. Gibson makes this distinction explicit when he differentiates clearly between:

> perceptual cognition, or knowledge of the environment, and symbolic cognition, or knowledge *about* the environment. The former is a direct response to things based on stimulus information; the latter is an indirect response to things based on stimulus sources produced by another human individual. The information in the latter case is *coded*; in the former case it cannot properly be called that. . . . The process by which an individual becomes aware of what exists and what goes on around him is perception. The process by which a human individual is *made* aware of things outside his immediate environment is one stage higher. It is mediated perception. It involves the action of another person besides the perceiver. A man or a child can, as we say, *be told* about things, or *be taught*, or *be given to understand*, or *be informed*, or *be shown*. Speech, that triumph of the human species, is the earliest and perhaps the principal vehicle for this indirect apprehension.[23]
>
> (Gibson 1966: 91, 234)

Our senses of sight, hearing, touch, and so forth, are shared (to varying degrees and in varying ways) with other animals. As such, they are more primitive and more powerful than the products of our symbolic cognitive powers, which are possessed uniquely by our species: "Because vision developed before verbal language, images are a natural part of our primal sense of being and represent the deepest recesses of ourselves" (Barry 1997: 69).

In comparison with any other medium, the book provides virtually nothing to be directly perceived but arbitrary, conventional symbols. And by doing this, the book places the highest demand on the reader to create the interpretive performance, to interact imaginatively with the poverty of perceptual stimulation and bring into being the (virtual) reality that is evoked. As Christopher Collins notes:

> *Literacy shrank the perceived world in order to expand the imagined world.* Orality had permitted a central communicative space that might be perceived as a hundred meters across, but literacy narrowed its perceptual

space to one quarter meter – the distance between the page and the reader's eye. Yet as a means to prompt mental imagery, literacy made an immeasurably vaster world conceivable and eventually perceivable as well. Writing places the solitary reader at the center of the world that he or she imagines and, by imagination, seems to oversee.

(Collins 1991: 14; emphasis added)

We readily acknowledge the power of actual visual perception. Many media other than the book – including, specifically, the theatre – are often much more vivid than the creative imagination afforded by linguistic symbols. When one sees and hears something in real life, or on a television, movie, or computer screen, or on a stage, one can normally no longer imagine it in any other way. As Collins notes, "perceptual and imaginal visuality are mutually interferent. In any one-on-one competition for attention a percept will always win out over a mental image" (Ibid.: 4). Vision is the most powerful – the most vivid – sensory system human beings have;[24] it blots out the imagination and limits creativity. (It's a good thing it does, too, for if our ancient ancestors had permitted their imagination of a scene, say of a tranquil meadow, to take precedence over their perception, perhaps of a tranquil meadow also containing a hungry predator, they probably would not have survived long enough to pass on their genes to our generation.) Once we see an actor in the role of a character, we can normally no longer imagine anyone other than that actor when we read or think of that character. In contrast, the whole point of a print narrative is that the description may be elaborate, minimal, or even nonexistent, but we *experience* (we imagine, construct, create, even virtually *see*) what is described. We are *transported* there and *perform* it ourselves.

For the reality is that we go to *see* the play, but we *read* the book. My point is not that reading a novel and imaginatively performing it are superior to seeing the performance of a play; nor is it that the vividness of actually seeing a play is a superior aesthetic experience to the often-vague imaginative involvement with a novel. It is, rather, that the two processes are fundamentally *different* and that we should recognize and celebrate that difference, rather than make all the world a text to be read, thereby implicitly denigrating the perceptual activities involved in seeing a theatrical performance.[25]

Notes

1 See Solso (2003). Throughout his book Solso repeatedly makes the point that when we look at art we all *see* virtually the same thing, but what it *means* may be very different for all of us. Seeing – perception – is a human universal, while understanding is individual.

2 There is a growing body of works critical of the structuralist-semiotic-poststructuralist paradigm; among them: Cameron (1985); Graham (1992); Harland (1993); Hart (2001); Holland (1992); Jackson (1991); Mancing (2003); and Tallis (1988).

3 For strong assertions that this is the case, see Holland (1992: 141); Jackson (1991: 12–13); and Sperber and Wilson (1995: 7–8).

4 Critics of Chomsky often continue to take issue with his earliest formulations of his linguistic theories, ignoring the fact that those theories have developed and grown into something quite different in the four decades since he began to write. For a good, recent, articulation of Chomsky's approach to language, see Chomsky (2000). For a useful assessment of Chomsky's contributions in linguistic theory, see N. Smith (1999).

5 The case for language as a biological function is compellingly made by Anderson and Lightfoot (2002); Jenkins (1999); and Obler and Gjerlow (1999).

6 Contemporary literary critics and theorists tend to be completely unaware of the vast body of work in non-Saussurean, post-Chomskyan linguistics. Among the most important works in these areas are the following: Blakemore (2002); Cameron (1985); Clark (1996); Gibbs (1994); Harris (1981); Jackendoff (1983, 1992, 1994, 1997, 2002); Lakoff (1987); Lakoff and Johnson (1980); Langacker (1987, 1988); Levinson (1983); Pinker (1994, 1999); Sperber and Wilson (1995); and Toolan (1996).

7 The two major authorities I will cite in this section are Allan Paivio and James J. Gibson. Given that their fundamental research was carried out in the decades of the 1960s–1980s, it may seem outdated, especially in comparison with most of the others I cite throughout this essay. Perhaps because perception in general and vision, in particular, is so fundamental to human psychology, basic research in this area was carried out earlier and now thoroughly informs that in many other areas of psychology.

8 Paivio here refers specifically to vision, but in other places he makes it clear that the other senses – hearing, touch, smell, taste – also function in a similar non-symbolic manner.

9 That our evolved perceptual abilities, shared with other animals, especially primates, are of a different order than symbolic cognition is generally assumed in contemporary biology and psychology. For example, Deacon (1997) is built upon the fact that there is only one symbolic species on the planet. Deacon does not have to state explicitly that language is different from perception because the point is so obvious; see the third section of this essay, on the evolution of human speech. There is not space here to continue to document the fact that visual perception and reading are two different processes. For a variety of approaches to the subject, see Bermúdez (2003); Hoffman (1998); Jackendoff (1997); Solso (1994); Stafford (1996); and Weiskrantz (1988).

10 For a very nice assessment of Gibson's important contributions to the study of perception, see Reed (1988). For extensions and applications of Gibson's work, see Anderson (1996); Gibson and Pick (2000); and Reed (1996).

11 Animals as distinct as parrots, dogs, and chimpanzees can, for example, all watch television and understand that the visual display on the screen represents real-life actions. Direct perceptual cognition does not depend on symbolic thought.

12 For a review of Donald's theory of evolution and its implications for our understanding of human consciousness, see his more recent book, *A Mind so Rare* (2001).

13 In addition to Donald and Deacon, see the following important contributions to our growing understanding of how our species developed the capability of communicating symbolically: Armstrong (1999); Armstrong, *et al.* (1995); Bickerton (1990); Calvin and Bickerton (2000); Corballis (2002); Dunbar (1996); Lieberman (1984, 1991, 1998, 2000); Mithen (1996); Pinker and Bloom (1990); and Tomasello (1999).

14 Aristotle may at least take silent reading into consideration when he writes in

the *Poetics* (1987: 4.1.1.3) that "the plot should be constructed in such a way that, even without seeing it, someone who hears about the incidents will shudder and feel pity at the outcome." Some scholars believe that the phrase "even without seeing it" might refer to the reading of the playscript, while others think it more likely that Aristotle is referring to the listening to the reading of another person.

15 It is true that a series of pictures, a silent motion picture, or a mime perform-ance affords the viewer more of an opportunity to construct nearly the same narrative understanding. But this is true only to a minimal extent: the story may be something like "the wind blows off the clown's hat, he tries to pick it up but accidentally kicks it farther away, this is repeated several times ..." Try "telling" the story of Hamlet or Emma Bovary in pictures or music, without a narrator and without language.

16 Nelson (1996) brilliantly uses Donald's multi-stage model of the evolution of human cognition to describe the stages through which the developing child progresses as he or she acquires language; see especially the chapter entitled "Evolution and Development of the Hybrid Mind" (Ibid.: 59–88).

17 See Bakhtin's important essay entitled "Epic and Novel" (1981: 3–40) for the compelling argument that the novel is radically different from all other literary genres and that it emerged only in the Renaissance (sixteenth century). Bakhtin implicitly argues against both the tradition that holds that the modern novel first came into being in the unique circumstances of eighteenth-century England – see Watt (1957) for the paradigm statement nearly unanimously and uncritically accepted in nearly all contemporary Anglo-American scholarship – and the more recent argument that ancient prose fictions are not romances but novels in the fullest sense of the word; see Doody (1996) for the most complete exposition of this position. In basic agreement with Bakhtin's stance are theo-rists such as Alter (1975); Couturier (1975); Reed (1981); and Wilson (2000). For more on competing theories of the history of the novel as a genre, see also numerous entries in Mancing (2004).

18 See Nell (1988) and Radway (1991). See also Deacon (1997: 22) for a discussion of the "shared virtual world" that literature makes possible for the only species with language; he also discusses consciousness itself in terms of virtual reality (Ibid.: 452). See also Oatley (1992: 398) for a discussion of art as a "simulation that runs on our minds rather than on a computer."

19 Again, the relevant bibliography in this area is large, but the following offer a good introduction: Crawford and Chaffin (1986); Holland (1988); McCormick (1985); Olson (1994); Rosenblatt (1995); Rumelhart (1980, 1984); F. Smith (1994); and Spiro (1980).

20 For representative arguments on this point, see Barry (1997); Mankiewicz and Swerdlow (1978); and Winn (1977).

21 On mental imagery, denied or ignored by most current literary theory, see Arnheim (1969); Barry (1997); Esrock (1994); Harth (1993); Johnson-Laird (1983); Kosslyn (1994); and Scarry (1999).

22 It is so, in part because it is based on – it is a development from – perception and embeds perceptual cognition (Donald's mimetic cognition) within it.

23 Gibson was writing some four decades ago. Today, instead of privileging speech as the "triumph of the human species," we are more likely to write of symbolic communication (see Deacon 1997), which includes speech but also much more. Furthermore, note that Gibson says that speech is "the earliest and perhaps the principal vehicle for this indirect apprehension." In evolutionary terms, at least in scenarios such as Donald's, mimesis and then speech did in fact precede all other types of symbolic communication.

24 The occipital lobes, where vision is processed, are more self-contained and dis-

cretely modular than the other lobes and make up the largest area of the brain devoted to a single function, which is at least part of the reason why vision is the most powerful source of knowledge in the human brain (it has been estimated that up to 60 percent of the cerebral cortex is involved in visual processing in one way or another). Appropriately enough, Zeki (1993) uses his analysis of visual cognition as a metonym for all non-symbolic brain functions.

25 I would like to thank my friend and colleague John Kirby for reading this essay and making valuable suggestions for its revision, particularly in the section on mimesis and diegesis. I am similarly indebted to Catherine Connor and Charles Ganelin for their comments on this essay and for their willingness to engage with me in an ongoing discussion of nearly every conceivable aspect of cognitive science and literature.

References

Alter, R. (1975) *Partial Magic: The Novel as a Self-Conscious Genre*, Berkeley, CA: University of California Press.

Anderson, J.D. (1996) *The Reality of Illusion: An Ecological Approach to Cognitive Film Theory*, Carbondale, IL: Southern Illinois University Press.

Anderson, S.R. and Lightfoot, D.W. (2002) *The Language Organ: Linguistics as Cognitive Physiology*, Cambridge: Cambridge University Press.

Aristotle (1987) *'Poetics' I with the 'Tractatus Coislinianus,' a Hypothetical Reconstruction of 'Poetics' II, the Fragments of the 'On Poets,'* trans. R. Janko, Indianapolis, IN: Hackett.

Armstrong, D.F. (1999) *Original Signs: Gesture, Sign, and the Sources of Language*, Washington, DC: Gallaudet University Press.

Armstrong, D.F., Stokoe, W.C., and Wilcox, S.E. (1995) *Gesture and the Nature of Language*, Cambridge: Cambridge University Press.

Arnheim, R. (1969) *Visual Thinking*, Berkeley, CA: University of California Press.

Bakhtin, M.M. (1981) *The Dialogic Imagination: Four Essays*, ed. M. Holquist, trans. C. Emerson and M. Holquist, Austin, TX: University of Texas Press.

Barry, A.M.S. (1997) *Visual Intelligence: Perception, Image, and Manipulation in Visual Communication*, Albany, NY: State University of New York Press.

Bermúdez, J.L. (2003) *Thinking Without Words*, New York: Oxford University Press.

Bickerton, D. (1990) *Language and Species*, Chicago, IL: University of Chicago Press.

Blakemore, D. (2002) *Relevance and Linguistic Meaning: The Semantics and Pragmatics of Discourse Markers*, Cambridge: Cambridge University Press.

Bluestone, G. (1957) *Novels into Film*, Baltimore, MD: Johns Hopkins University Press.

Calvin, W.H. and Bickerton, D. (2000) *Lingua ex Machina: Reconciling Darwin and Chomsky with the Human Brain*, Cambridge, MA: Bradford Book/MIT Press.

Cameron, D. (1985) *Feminism and Linguistic Theory*, New York: St. Martin's Press.

Cervantes, M. de (2003) *Don Quixote*, trans. E. Grossman, New York: Ecco.

Chomsky, N. (1957) *Syntactic Structures*, The Hague: Mouton.

—— (2000) *New Horizons in the Study of Language and Mind*, Cambridge: Cambridge University Press.

Clark, H.H. (1996) *Using Language*, Cambridge: Cambridge University Press.

Collins, C. (1991) *A Poetics of the Mind's Eye: Literature and the Psychology of Imagination*, Philadelphia, PA: University of Pennsylvania Press.

Corballis, M.C. (2002) *From Hand to Mouth: The Origins of Language*, Princeton, NJ: Princeton University Press.

Couturier, M. (1975) *Textual Communication: A Print-Based Theory of the Novel*, London: Routledge.

Crawford, M. and Chaffin, R. (1986) "The Reader's Construction of Meaning: Cognitive Research on Gender and Comprehension," in Flynn, E.A. and Schweickart, P.P. (eds) *Gender and Reading: Essays on Readers, Texts, and Contexts*, Baltimore, MD: Johns Hopkins University Press, 3–30.

Deacon, T.W. (1997) *The Symbolic Species: The Co-Evolution of Language and the Brain*, New York: W.W. Norton.

Derrida, J. (1967) *Of Grammatology*, trans. G.G. Spivak, Baltimore, MD: Johns Hopkins University Press.

Donald, M. (1991) *The Origins of the Modern Mind: Three Stages in the Evolution of Culture and Cognition*, Cambridge, MA: Harvard University Press.

—— (2001) *A Mind so Rare: The Evolution of Human Consciousness*, New York: W.W. Norton.

Doody, M.A. (1996) *The True Story of the Novel*, New Brunswick, NJ: Rutgers University Press.

Dunbar, R. (1996) *Grooming, Gossip, and the Evolution of Language*, Cambridge, MA: Harvard University Press.

Esrock, E.J. (1994) *The Reader's Eye: Visual Imaging as Reader Response*, Baltimore, MD: Johns Hopkins University Press.

Garner, S.B., Jr (1989) *The Absent Voice: Narrative Comprehension in the Theater*, Urbana, IL: University of Illinois Press.

Gerrig, R.J. (1993) *Experiencing Narrative Worlds: On the Psychological Activities of Reading*, New Haven, CT: Yale University Press.

Gibbs, R.W., Jr (1994) *The Poetics of Mind: Figurative Thought, Language, and Understanding*, Cambridge: Cambridge University Press.

Gibson, E.J. and Pick, A.D. (2000) *An Ecological Approach to Perceptual Learning and Development*, Oxford: Oxford University Press.

Gibson, J.J. (1966) *The Senses Considered as Perceptual Systems*, New York: Houghton Mifflin.

—— (1979) *The Ecological Approach to Visual Perception*, Boston, MA: Houghton Mifflin.

Graham, J.F. (1992) *Onomatopoetics: Theory of Language and Literature*, Cambridge: Cambridge University Press.

Harland, R. (1993) *Beyond Superstructuralism: The Syntagmatic Side of Language*, London: Routledge.

Harris, R. (1981) *The Language Myth*, New York: St. Martin's Press.

Hart, F.E. (2001) "The epistemology of cognitive literary studies," *Philosophy and Literature*, 25(2): 314–34.

Harth, E. (1993) *The Creative Loop: How the Brain Makes a Mind*, Reading, MA: Addison-Wesley.

Hoffman, D.D. (1998) *Visual Intelligence: How We Create What We See*, New York: W.W. Norton.

Holland, N.N. (1988) *The Brain of Robert Frost: A Cognitive Approach to Literature*, New York: Routledge.

—— (1992) *The Critical I*, New York: Columbia University Press.

Jackendoff, R. (1983) *Semantics and Cognition*, Cambridge, MA: MIT Press.

—— (1992) *Languages of the Mind: Essays on Mental Representation*, Cambridge, MA: Bradford/MIT Press.

—— (1994) *Patterns in the Mind: Language and Human Nature*, New York: Bantam Books.

—— (1997) *The Architecture of the Language Faculty*, Cambridge, MA: MIT Press.

—— (2002) *Foundations of Language: Brain, Meaning, Grammar, Evolution*, Oxford: Oxford University Press.

Jackson, R. (1991) *The Poverty of Structuralism: Literature and Structuralist Theory*, London: Longman.

Jenkins, L. (1999) *Biolinguistics: Exploring the Biology of Language*, Cambridge: Cambridge University Press.

Johnson-Laird, P.N. (1983) *Mental Models: Towards a Cognitive Science of Language Inference and Consciousness*, Cambridge, MA: Harvard University Press.

Kirby, J.T. (1991) "Mimesis and diegesis: foundations of aesthetic theory in Plato and Aristotle," *Helios*, 18: 113–28.

Klawans, H. (2000) *Defending the Cavewoman: And Other Tales of Evolutionary Neurology*, New York: W.W. Norton.

Kosslyn, S.M. (1994) *Image and Brain: The Resolution of the Imagery Debate*, Cambridge: Bradford Book/MIT Press.

Lakoff, G. (1987) *Women, Fire, and Dangerous Things: What Categories Reveal About the Mind*, Chicago, IL: University of Chicago Press.

Lakoff, G. and Johnson, M. (1980) *Metaphors We Live By*, Chicago, IL: University of Chicago Press.

Langacker, R.W. (1987) *Foundations of Cognitive Grammar*, Vol. I: *Theoretical Prerequisites*, Stanford, CA: Stanford University Press.

—— (1988) "An Overview of Cognitive Grammar," in Rudzka-Ostyn, B. (ed.) *Topics in Cognitive Linguistics*, Amsterdam: John Benjamins, 3–48.

Levinson, S.C. (1983) *Pragmatics*, Cambridge, MA: Cambridge University Press.

Lieberman, P. (1984) *The Biology and Evolution of Language*, Cambridge, MA: Harvard University Press.

—— (1991) *Uniquely Human: The Evolution of Speech, Thought and Selfless Behavior*, Cambridge, MA: Harvard University Press.

—— (1998) *Eve Spoke: Human Language and Human Evolution*, New York: W.W. Norton.

—— (2000) *Human Language and Our Reptilian Brain*, Cambridge, MA: Harvard University Press.

McCormick, K. (1985) "Psychological realism: a new epistemology for reader-response criticism," *Reader*, 14: 40–53.

Mancing, H. (2003) "Rastier revisited: paradigms in conflict," *Semiotica*, 145: 139–49.

—— (2004) *The Cervantes Encyclopedia*, 2 vols, Westport, CT: Greenwood Press.

Mankiewicz, F. and Swerdlow, J. (1978) *Remote Control: Television and the Manipulation of American Life*, New York: Times Books.

Messaris, P. (1994) *Visual 'Literacy': Image, Mind, and Reality*, Boulder, CO: Westview Press.

Mithen, S. (1996) *The Prehistory of the Mind: The Cognitive Origins of Art, Religion and Science*, London: Thames and Hudson.

Nell, V. (1988) *Lost in a Book: The Psychology of Reading for Pleasure*, New Haven, CT: Yale University Press.

Nelson, K. (1996) *Language in Cognitive Development: The Emergence of the Mediated Mind*, Cambridge: Cambridge University Press.

Oatley, K. (1992) *Best Laid Schemes: The Psychology of Emotions*, Cambridge: Cambridge University Press.

Obler, L.K. and Gjerlow, K. (1999) *Language and the Brain*, Cambridge: Cambridge University Press.

Olson, D.R. (1994) *The World on Paper: The Conceptual and Cognitive Implications of Writing and Reading*, Cambridge: Cambridge University Press.

Paivio, A. (1986) *Mental Representations: A Dual Coding Approach*, New York: Oxford University Press.

Pinker, S. (1986, 2nd edn 1994) *The Language Instinct*, New York: William Morrow.

—— (1999) *Words and Rules: The Ingredients of Language*, New York: Basic Books.

Pinker, S. and Bloom, P. (1990) "Natural language and natural selection," *Behavioral and Brain Sciences*, 13: 707–84.

Radway, J.A. (1984, 2nd edn 1991) *Reading the Romance: Women, Patriarchy, and Popular Literature*, Chapel Hill, NC: University of North Carolina Press.

Reed, E.S. (1988) *James J. Gibson and the Psychology of Perception*, New Haven, CT: Yale University Press.

—— (1996) *Encountering the World: Toward an Ecological Psychology*, New York: Oxford University Press.

Reed, W.L. (1981) *An Exemplary History of the Novel: The Quixotic Versus the Picaresque*, Chicago, IL: University of Chicago Press.

Rosenblatt, L.M. (1938, 5th edn 1995) *Literature as Exploration*, foreword by W. Booth, New York: Modern Language Association.

—— (1978, 2nd edn 1994) *The Reader, the Text, the Poem: The Transactional Theory of the Literary Work*, Carbondale, IL: Southern Illinois University Press.

Rumelhart, D.E. (1980) "Schemata: The Building Blocks of Cognition," in Spiro, R.J., Bruce, B.C., and Brewer, W.F. (eds) *Theoretical Issues in Reading Comprehension: Perspectives from Cognitive Psychology, Linguistics, Artificial Intelligence, and Education*, Hillsdale, NH: Lawrence Erlbaum Associates, 33–58.

—— (1984) "Understanding Understanding," in Flood, J. (ed.) *Understanding Reading Comprehension: Cognition, Language, and the Structure of Prose*, Newark, NJ: International Reading Association, 1–20.

Scarry, E. (1999) *Dreaming by the Book*, New York: Farrar, Straus, Giroux.

Smith, F. (1971, 5th edn 1994) *Understanding Reading: A Psycholinguistic Analysis of Reading and Learning to Read*, Hillsdale, NJ: Lawrence Erlbaum Associates.

Smith, N. (1999) *Chomsky: Ideas and Ideals*, Cambridge: Cambridge University Press.

Solso, R.L. (1994) *Cognition and the Visual Arts*, Cambridge, MA: Bradford Book/MIT Press.

—— (2003) *The Psychology of Art and the Evolution of the Conscious Brain*, Cambridge, MA: MIT Press.

Sperber, D. and Wilson, D. (1986, 2nd edn 1995) *Relevance: Communication and Cognition*, Cambridge, MA: Harvard University Press.

Spiro, R.J. (1980) "Constructive Process in Prose Comprehension and Recall," in Spiro, R.J., Bruce, B.C., and Brewer, W.F. (eds) *Theoretical Issues in Reading Comprehension: Perspectives from Cognitive Psychology, Linguistics, Artificial Intelligence, and Education*, Hillsdale, NH: Lawrence Erlbaum Associates, 245–78.

Stafford, B.M. (1996) *Good Looking: Essays on the Virtue of Images*, Cambridge, MA: MIT Press.

—— (1999) *Visual Analogy: Consciousness as the Art of Connecting*, Cambridge, MA: MIT Press.

Tallis, R. (1988) *Not Saussure: A Critique of Post-Saussurean Literary Theory*, Houndsmills: Macmillan Press.

Tomasello, M. (1999) *The Cultural Origins of Human Cognition*, Cambridge, MA: Harvard University Press.

Toolan, M. (1996) *Total Speech: An Integrational Linguistic Approach to Language*, Durham, NC: Duke University Press.

Watt, I. (1957) *The Rise of the Novel*, Berkeley, CA: University California Press.

Weiskrantz, L. (ed.) (1988) *Thought Without Language*, Oxford: Clarendon Press.

Wilson, D. de A. (2000) *Cervantes, the Novel, and the New World*, Oxford: Oxford University Press.

Winn, M. (1977) *The Plug-In Drug*, New York: Viking Press.

Zeki, S. (1993) *A Vision of the Brain*, Oxford: Blackwell Scientific Publications.

—— (1999) *Inner Vision: An Exploration of Art and the Brain*, Oxford: Oxford University Press.

9 Categories and catcalls

Cognitive dissonance in *The Playboy of the Western World*

Neal Swettenham

Dear Sir,
In response to your application, we enclose Voucher to be exchanged at Booking Office at Theatre, or at Messers Cramer's, Westmoreland Street for Numbered Ticket. Should it be impossible to hear the play the night you select we will send you another Voucher on receiving your application. Yours faithfully,
W.A. Henderson,
Secretary

(Hunt 1979: 72)

We played it under police protection, seventy police in the theatre the last night, and five hundred, some newspaper said, keeping order in the streets outside. It is never played before any Irish audience for the first time without something or other being flung at the players.

(Yeats in Ayling 1992: 139)

[A] cognitive model may function to allow a salient example to stand metonymically for a whole category.

(Lakoff 1987: 90)

At their worst, the disturbances that accompanied the first performances of J.M. Synge's *The Playboy of the Western World* were so overpoweringly noisy that to offer a second opportunity to attend the play seemed to be the only recourse left open to the Abbey Theatre in Dublin. The extent of the problem was further noted in some satirical verses, penned at the time by one frustrated audience member: "Our own opinion, we admit,/Is rather – well – uncertain,/Because we couldn't hear one bit/From rise to fall of curtain" (quoted by Berrow in Harmon 1972: 81).

The play generated a prodigious sense of outrage in its first-night audience, and critics and apologists ever since have endeavoured to provide satisfying explanations for the enormity of the reaction. Lady Gregory, one of the founders of the Abbey Theatre and herself a dramatist, identified the language of the play as a principal catalyst. Having dispatched an enthusiastic telegram to Yeats (who was lecturing in Scotland at the time) at the end of the first act, which read simply: "Play great success," she later felt obliged to follow it up with a second message: "Audience broke up in disorder at the word shift" (Ibid.: 76). A report in the *Irish Times* of 30 January 1907 cited the play's narrative as a source of trouble: "The charges made against the play in defense of this rowdy conduct are that its plot and characters are an outrageous insult to the West of Ireland and its people, and that some of its language is vulgar, and even indelicate" (quoted in Kilroy 1971: 35). A more recent study by Nicholas Grene provides a detailed account of the political, ideological and historical backgrounds of the performance, and suggests that the cause of the rioting was a composite one, generated by a combination of the fateful word "shift," the view of criminality offered in the text, the play's setting in County Mayo, and its carnivalesque perspective on the Catholic faith (Grene 1999: 77–109). Still more recently, Nelson O'Ceallaigh Ritschel has insisted that it was the play's fierce indictment of empty words and empty actions implied by the behaviour of Christy Mahon and its results that roused the nationalists to such fury (Ritschel 2002: 47).

All of these different explanations, though, share one thing in common: they leave us with the sense that having once identified the significant cultural, political, or linguistic triggers for the disturbances, we will have fully solved the mystery of the Playboy riots. However, insights gleaned from second-generation cognitive science open up new and intriguing ways of reading these events. From this fresh vantage point, it is possible to consider not merely what the individual triggers for the violence might have been but also *how they may have acted upon* the assembly of "embodied minds" gathered to watch that first performance. And from an examination of this singular moment of theatre history, it is also possible to enhance our understanding in more general terms of the ways in which audiences will tend to read narrative in performance.

The prototype effect

The assertion that narrative is an interactive process is unlikely nowadays to be a contentious one. It is a given that stories are not merely told; they are also perceived and interpreted by their audiences. Theatre audiences reconstruct a narrative as it is delivered to them and come to their own conclusions about many different aspects of the story, its characters, and meanings. The primary tool that is brought to bear on a vast array of verbal, visual, and aural information during this narrative reading process is, of course, the embodied mind. As Lakoff and Johnson have expressed it, "Meaning has to do with the ways in which we function meaningfully in the world and make sense of it via bodily and imaginative structures" (Lakoff and Johnson 1999: 78).

A significant discovery within second-generation cognitive science has been a heightened awareness of the importance of categories in codifying meaning. The ability to categorise the huge quantity of "input data," with which we are constantly bombarded, has been a vital evolutionary development: without it we would simply not have survived. Consider, to take two very basic examples, the importance of learning to distinguish between items of food and not-food, or friends and not-friends.

Categorization – the grouping together of disparate objects, experiences, perceptions, and so on according to perceptions of likeness – is first and foremost a matter of biology. As Lakoff and Johnson put it:

> We are neural beings. Our brains each have 100 billion neurons and 100 trillion synaptic connections. It is common in the brain for information to be passed from one dense ensemble of neurons to another via a relatively sparse set of connections. Whenever this happens, the pattern of activation distributed over the first set of neurons is too great to be represented in a one-to-one manner in the sparse set of connections. Therefore, the sparse set of connections necessarily groups together certain input patterns in mapping them across to the output ensemble. Whenever a neural ensemble provides the same output with different inputs, there is neural categorization.
>
> (Ibid.: 18)

Categorization, therefore, is a way of reducing or "simplifying" the information being processed. It helps us to perceive objects, people, relationships, and so on, and to group them together quickly and efficiently. The advantages of this are obvious: speed of response, ease of processing, the convenience of shorthand. The disadvantages are also plain: subtle differences are elided, snap judgments are made, and modes of perception can become rigid and inflexible.

The classical view of categories, however – that they are strictly bounded fields with objects that are either "inside" or "outside" those fixed boundaries, and that all members of a category have equal status, with no one member representing the category better than any other – has been shown to be inadequate (Lakoff 1987: *passim.*). In its place have emerged concepts of graded and radial categories, with their "fuzzy boundaries" and "best examples," or *prototypes*. As the cognitive psychologist Eleanor Rosch has demonstrated, there are actually asymmetries, or degrees of membership, within most categories, making it possible to identify what may be termed prototypical or *central* category members, which define the category more precisely than other, non-central, though definitely related category members (Rosch and Mervis 1975: *passim.*). Thus, even in relation to colors, it is possible to show that there is a particular focal *red*, a version of "redness" that is identifiable as more prototypically red than other closely related shades. This is directly tied to the physiology of the human eye, whereby pure primary colors are perceived when the color response cells in the eye are firing at their neutral base rates (Lakoff 1987: 27). More significantly for the purposes of this discussion, Rosch also realized that this *prototype effect* applied to many other kinds of categories as well. So, for example, some members of the category BIRD will tend to be perceived as more "typical" than others: sparrows, starlings, and robins are generally taken to be central members of this category, while penguins, turkeys, or ostriches are usually considered to be much less representative.

In the case of a *graded* category such as, for example, RICH, the prototype will simply be an individually determined "best fit" (just how rich is "rich"?), with degrees of "richness" extending above and below it. *Radial* categories, though, are a little more complicated: they offer a range of possible prototypes, usually variations of a central case, tied to specific aspects that are deemed to be significant. For example, while the central case of the category TEACHER might be understood to be a person, male or female, usually (though not necessarily) an adult who communicates information and skills to others, many possible subcategories of teacher might be defined in different ways by different individual subjects. In relation to the aspect of "discipline," a teacher may be conceptualized as someone who is able to keep a class under control. However, if the significant aspect is deemed to be "ability to inspire," a different prototype will be envisaged. Other factors that could influence this choice of prototype might be: knowledge of the subject taught, number of years in the teaching profession, level of qualifications, and so on. Even such determinants as physical attractiveness might be brought into the question.

We should note the significance of the *prototype effect*: it has been found that subjects will tend to make generalizations from the selected prototype to other category members. The choice of prototype is a "superficial" phenomenon, which may stem from a variety of causes, but once chosen, any given prototype in a radial category may then represent or "stand for" the rest of the category in a metonymic relation. When it comes to watching a performance of *The Playboy*, therefore, it really does matter where the audience places its sympathies and which characters are thereby deemed to be representative of a wider category.

Finally, before moving on to consider the play, it is helpful to be familiar with the range of different types of metonymic models that may operate in this way, identified by Lakoff (1987: *passim.*) as:

- social stereotypes;
- typical examples;
- ideal cases;
- paragons;
- salient examples;
- submodels; and
- generators.

Each of these metonymic category types works slightly differently. *Social stereotypes*, as the label suggests, are likely to be selective and prejudicial in their representation. They are, according to Lakoff, "usually conscious and are often the subject of public discussion. They are subject to change over time, and they may become public issues. Since they define cultural expectation, they are used in reasoning and especially in what is called 'jumping to conclusions.' However, they are usually recognized as not being accurate, and their use in reasoning may be overtly challenged" (Ibid.: 85).[1] *Typical examples*, by contrast, are generally unconscious and automatic. They are more likely to include central cases that will then be used to generalize about nontypical examples. Typical examples are unlikely to be the subject of open public debate, however, and tend not to change radically over time; whereas, *ideal cases* are neither typical nor stereotypical. They will store and organize a range of "highest" cultural expectations in relation to a category. *Paragons* are individual cases that are picked out to represent either a category ideal or sometimes its opposite. *Salient examples* will be very specific instances, selected on the basis of memorability or familiarity. *Submodels* may incorporate particular restricted ways of viewing a category, as in the cases considered above of what defines a teacher. *Generators* are used to generate members of a category on the basis of central category members in combination with a clear rule. For example, where the central case of a "teacher" is taken as "someone who communicates information to others," the generating rule that decides the question of category membership in a more specific sense might be that the individual concerned must have some kind of teaching qualification.

Prototype effects and *The Playboy*

It is fruitful to consider these different prototypes in relation to one of the central controversies of *The Playboy of the Western World*. According to W.G. Fay, the actor who played Christy Mahon (the playboy) in those first performances, Synge's fundamental misdemeanour – notwithstanding his use of the word "shift" that finally sparked the violent uproar – was to mount a "deliberate attack on the national character" (quoted in Ayling 1992: 144). That being the case, what might the various prototypes operating within the radial category of Irish "national character" have been? What, for instance, would have been the *social stereotype* of IRISHNESS at that period?

When the idea for the Irish Literary Theatre (which later became the Abbey Theatre) was first conceived in 1898, Lady Gregory, W.B. Yeats, and Edward Martyn composed an open letter sent out to interested parties that included the following statements: "We will show that Ireland is not the home of buffoonery and of easy sentiment, as it has been represented, but the home of an ancient idealism. We are confident of the support of all Irish people, who are weary of misrepresentation, in carrying out a work that is outside all the political questions that divide us" (Robinson 1951: 2). In those two expressions, "buffoonery" and "easy sentiment," is a clear sense of frustration over the "misrepresentation" of the Irish by outsiders in general and the occupying colonial forces in particular. In a similar vein Grene talks of the tradition of "the stage Irishman whose ignorance is exploited for the condescending merriment of the English" (Grene 1999: 103). This, then, gives us a perceived social stereotype of Irishness: a buffoon, an ignorant and emotionally naïve peasant, to which might be added further pejoratives such as stupid, lazy, argumentative, and cowardly. Before we consider to what extent, if any, Synge makes use of this social stereotyping in the play, let us first suggest, in summary form, possible examples of all the prototypes proposed by Lakoff, both in relation to the play and to the Dublin society for which it was performed. Such a list might read as follows:

Possible prototypes of Irish national character:
Social stereotypes – buffoon, ignorant, emotionally naïve, stupid, lazy, argumentative, cowardly.
Typical examples – garrulous, friendly, Catholic, decent, law-abiding.
Ideal cases – brave, heroic, athletic, protective of women.
Paragons – individual nationalist heroes, such as Michael Davitt (a native of County Mayo and founder of the Land League) and John MacBride (see below); Father Reilly, in his role as moral guardian of the community.
Salient examples – well-known instances, in which crimes similar to that supposedly perpetrated by Christy Mahon had been committed; the Dublin audiences would almost certainly have been aware of these (see below).
Submodels – most pertinent in relation to the play would be: inhabitants of County Mayo as representative of the wider national character.
Generators – the generating rule might range from: born in Ireland to Irish parents, through to patriot/member of Sinn Fein.

To what extent do we find these different prototypes explored in the play? Does Synge, for example, pander to the social stereotype, as he was accused of doing? A character that seems to fit the description would be Shawn Keogh, Pegeen Mike's cousin and also her intended husband at the opening of the play. Shawn is depicted throughout as a coward, a buffoon, and a naïf: "SHAWN: . . . For the love of God, Pegeen Mike, don't let on I was speaking of him. Don't tell your father and the men is coming above; for if they heard that story they'd have great blabbing this night at the wake" (Synge 1964: 77); "SHAWN: I'm afeard of Father Reilly, I'm saying ..." (Ibid.: 79); "SHAWN: I'll not fight him, Michael James. I'd liefer live a bachelor, simmering in passions to the end of time, than face a lepping savage the like of him has descended from the Lord knows where" (Ibid.: 123). But although Shawn represents the fullest embodiment of these qualities, it would also be true to say that the majority of the villagers are portrayed, to some degree, as credulous, gullible, or morally questionable.

What about the *typical example*? According to Lakoff, "an enormous amount of our knowledge about categories of things is organized in terms of typical cases" (Lakoff 1987: 86). Can we differentiate usefully in the play between a social stereotype of Irishness and a typical example? In *The Playboy*, as in most other traditional narrative-based drama, we are likely to identify the "typical" characters as those that seem most representative of a wider social group and that appear to have a certain level of psychological complexity in their portrayal. (This need not necessarily imply full psychological realism but should go beyond the simple presentation of "flat" characters.) The characters that seem to occupy this kind of focalizing position are the drunken publican, Michael James and, in a different way, his daughter, Pegeen Mike.

In his capacity as landlord, Michael James is at the geographical center of this tightly-knit community and stands as "a decent man of Ireland" (Synge 1964: 124), as he puts it. In physical appearance he is described as being fat and jovial, and on the first occasion we encounter him, he is seen evincing a casual lack of concern for his daughter's security. He plans to leave her in sole charge of the shebeen[2] for the night, while he is off elsewhere attending a drunken wake: "MICHAEL: Isn't it the same whether I go for a whole night or a part only? and I'm thinking it's a queer daughter you are if you'd have me crossing backward through the Stooks of the Dead Women, with a drop taken" (Ibid.: 78). As a typical example of County Mayo man, however, he hardly shines; his modern counterpart might, perhaps, be the prototypical Homer Simpson, as he "stands for" the average middle-American male of the late twentieth and early twenty-first centuries.[3] Rather like Homer, Michael James is opportunistic, lazy, a drunkard, and very good at rationalizing his own selfish behaviour in sentiments that are both self-serving and humorous. His response, upon learning that Pegeen is determined to marry Christy rather than Shawn Keogh, is a masterful display of religious humbuggery and easy pragmatism:

MICHAEL: It's the will of God, I'm thinking, that all should win an easy or a cruel end, and it's the will of God that all should rear up lengthy families for the nurture of the earth. What's a single man, I ask you, eating a bit in one house and drinking a sup in another, and he with no place of his own, like an old braying jackass strayed upon the rocks? [*To Christy*] It's many would be in dread to bring your like into the house for to end them, maybe, with a sudden end; but I'm a decent man of Ireland, and I liefer face the grave untimely and I seeing a score of grandsons growing up little gallant swearers by the name of God, than go peopling my bedside with puny weeds the like of what you'd breed, I'm thinking, out of Shaneen Keogh.

(Ibid.: 124)

To this particular "decent man," a fine strapping lad like Christy Mahon is definitely peferable to the feeble Shawn as a son-in-law, even given the "small" detail that he is, by his own account, a murderer. Pegeen Mike, while emerging as a much more complex and subtle figure than her father, nevertheless also views herself as "typical" and in no way out-of-the-ordinary ("PEGEEN: I'm not odd, and I'm my whole life with my father only" (Ibid.: 101)), and while Christy wishes to paint her in terms of a saintly ideal, Synge is quick to remind us, via the Widow Quin, that she is, in fact, a very ordinary Mayo girl:

CHRISTY: Amn't I after seeing the love-light of the star of knowledge shining from her brow, and hearing words would put you thinking on the holy Brigid speaking to the infant saints, and now she'll be turning again, and speaking hard words to me, like an old woman with a spavindy ass she'd have, urging on a hill.
WIDOW QUIN: There's poetry talk for a girl you'd see itching and scratching, and she with a stale stink of poteen on her from selling in the shop.

(Ibid.: 109)

While Pegeen Mike is certainly pictured as an *ideal case* in Christy's exuberant imagination, it is Christy himself who fulfils this particular role most consistently in the play, becoming the focal point of admiration for the entire community from the moment when they first learn of his "crime." Philly Cullen, described in the stage directions as "thin and mistrusting" (Ibid.: 78), is, nevertheless, very quick to pronounce Christy "a daring fellow" (Ibid.: 83). Michael James immediately starts to treat him "with deference" (Ibid.: 85), Jimmy Farrell similarly commends his "bravery" (Ibid.: 84), and Pegeen credits him with "the sense of Solomon" (Ibid.: 84). Only Shawn, from mainly personal motives, is rather more suspicious at this first encounter. News spreads quickly in the little community, and very soon the Widow Quin has also arrived to appraise the newcomer. She is more pragmatic in her response ("Well, aren't you a little smiling fellow?" (Ibid.: 90)), but she too is happy to overlook the small matter of a murder committed (partly, perhaps, because she is under a similar suspicion herself).

The following morning (Act 2), Christy is the object of further uncritical adoration when village girls Susan Brady, Honor Blake, and Sara Tansey turn up to listen to him tell his story, and soon he is basking in the admiration of the entire community, to the point where even he is beginning to believe his own publicity: "CHRISTY: From this out I'll have no want of company when all sorts is bringing me their food and clothing [*he swaggers to the door, tightening his belt*], the way they'd set their eyes upon a gallant orphan cleft his father with one blow to the breeches belt" (Ibid.: 106).

As this idealized, overblown image is cumulatively punctured by events, however, the villagers turn angrily on Christy for being an all-too-normal specimen of imperfect humanity: "CROWD: [*jeeringly*] There's the playboy! There's the lad thought he'd rule the roost in Mayo!" (Ibid.: 125). Ideal cases are psychologically necessary, perhaps, but few of us, it seems, can actually sustain the image. And this too was a potential source of offence to those first Dublin audiences: Synge, like Widow Quin, is too pragmatic in his view of human behaviour to allow Christy, or indeed any of the other characters, to be positioned in the narrative as the romanticized hero.

The use of *paragons* within the play is also interesting. The dialogue is littered with references and comparisons to local, as well as national, and even mythical exemplars. When Jimmy Farrell wants to comment favourably on Christy's status as an object of curiosity, for instance, he evokes the most noteworthy models he can come up with from his own experience: "JIMMY: He'd beat Dan Davies' circus, or the holy missionaries making sermons on the villainy of man" (Ibid.: 82). (This unblinking pairing of secular and sacred entertainments in one phrase is typical of Synge's ironic attitude toward religion in general.) Pegeen, noting Christy's lyrical way with words, compares him to "Owen Roe O'Sullivan or the poets of the Dingle Bay" (Ibid.: 87). And in a wonderfully extravagant example of just such a kind of poetic bravura, Christy in his turn pictures Pegeen as an object of pagan[4] temptation to the very saints in heaven:

CHRISTY: If the mitred bishops seen you that time, they'd be the like of the holy prophets, I'm thinking, do be straining the bars of Paradise to lay eyes on the Lady Helen of Troy, and she abroad, pacing back and forward, with a nosegay in her golden shawl.

(Ibid.: 119–20)

Focusing more closely upon those paragons that are linked to the notion of Irish character, it is helpful to remember that Lakoff identifies paragons as individual cases that can be representative *either* of the ideal *or* its opposite. Certainly both types can be found in Synge's text although the emphasis is usually placed on the negative, as in Pegeen Mike's early disdainful comments about the petty criminal behaviour and braggart tendencies of most of the locals:

PEGEEN: [*with scorn*] . . . Where now will you meet the like of Daneen Sullivan knocked the eye from a peeler; or Marcus Quin, God rest him, got six months for maiming ewes, and he a great warrant to tell stories of holy Ireland till he'd have the old women shedding down tears about their feet. Where will you find the like of them, I'm saying?

(Ibid.: 76)

(This, of course, ironically prefigures just the kind of awestruck hearing that she and others will give to Christy later in the scene.) Widow Quin similarly functions, in Pegeen's imagination at least, as a paragon of wickedness:

PEGEEN: Doesn't the world know you reared a black ram at your own breast, so that the Lord Bishop of Connaught felt the elements of a Christian, and he eating it after in a kidney stew? Doesn't the world know you've been seen shaving the foxy skipper from France for a threepenny-bit and a sop of grass tobacco would wring the liver from a mountain goat you'd meet leaping the hills?[5]

(Ibid.: 92)

When the villagers are trying to elicit from Christy the precise nature of the crime he has committed, they invoke a more positive local hero, "the man beyond," who went "fighting bloody wars for Kruger and the freedom of the Boers" (Ibid.: 82) and is now in fear for his own safety. This rather obscure reference was made much more explicit in an earlier draft of the play: "Maybe [Christy] went fighting for the Boers the like of Major MacBride, God shield him, who's afeard to put the tip of his nose into Ireland, fearing he'd be hanged, quartered and drawn" (quoted in Grene 1999: 97). John MacBride was a County Mayo man who had "contested a parliamentary by-election ... *in absentia* while fighting in South Africa for the Boers against the British" (Ibid.: 97). The decision to remove the name in the final version, interestingly, makes the villagers just that little bit less bothered about the details and correspondingly less connected with the reality of concrete political action as well.

But the paragon who casts the longest shadow over the play, perhaps, while never actually appearing in person, is the local Catholic priest, Father Reilly, who operates as a touchstone of moral rectitude for the other characters:

SHAWN: ... [*with peculiar emphasis on the words*] Father Reilly has small conceit to have that kind walking around and talking to the girls.
PEGEEN: Stop tormenting me with Father Reilly....

(Ibid.: / /)

As in this instance, however, although Shawn attempts to hold him up as a paragon of virtue, for Synge he is representative of a repressive and emasculating form of religion, and his symbolic function throughout the play is almost always a negative one.

Synge also makes provocative use of *salient examples* in the play: specific instances that are either memorable or familiar. Although he singles out one anecdote told to him while he was visiting the isle of Inishmaan as the source of the narrative (Synge 1910: 64), Synge almost certainly constructed the central events of the play around a number of fairly well-known cases, in which either a similar crime was committed or there was some kind of comparable local protection offered to the perpetrator. Hence: William Malley from Galway, who, in 1873, attacked his father with a spade and subsequently escaped to America; Michael Connell from County Kerry, who murdered his father in a violent rage in 1898 (but who gave himself up to the police shortly afterwards); and a third rather different but very significant case, that of James Lynchehaun, who, in 1894, assaulted an Englishwoman by biting off her nose and gouging out one eye and was then hidden by sympathizers within the local community before also escaping to America. As Nicholas Grene points out (1999: 88–91), this incident was notorious for a number of reasons, not least because what seems to have been a personally motivated act of violence was later presented at his trial as a political action and a blow for national freedom; and Synge makes specific reference to it in the text of *The Playboy*, when he has Susan Brady comment on Sara Tansey's voyeuristic interest in crime by saying, "and you the one yoked the ass cart and drove ten miles to set your eyes on the man bit the yellow lady's nostril" (Ibid.: 95).[6] These salient examples, thus, have specific, and quite disruptive, resonances both within the world of the play and in the extra-theatrical environment of its Dublin audiences.

As indicated above, it is the inhabitants of this remote part of County Mayo taken collectively who can be seen to act as *submodels* of the Irish national character within the world of the play. And for the nationalist sympathizers watching the performance in Dublin, such unflattering portraits were deemed to be particularly offensive as well since, as Grene points out:

> the West of Ireland represented a contested site in the colonial/national-
> ist struggle. If the British represented the Irish as inherently crime-
> loving and lawless, the West of Ireland, the most remote and least
> Anglicised part of the country, was thought of as the most endemically
> anarchic. For the nationalists, exactly reversing this cultural geography,
> the West became the preserve of uncontaminated Gaelic purity where,
> setting aside the necessary resistance to colonial power, a naturally high
> respect for law and order was maintained.
>
> (Ibid.: 97)

Members of the audience apparently grew so incensed at Synge's portrayal of the Mayo characters that they shouted out repeatedly, "That's not the West of Ireland" (Kilroy 1971: 43).

Finally, when considering *generators*, we may usefully ask, what is the rule to be applied in this instance? What is the criterion by which certain charac-ters, if not others, can be said most truly to represent or "stand for" the Irish national character? This, it turns out, is a difficult question to answer. As Lakoff observes: "Most categorization is automatic and unconscious, and if we become aware of it at all, it is only in problematic cases" (1987: 6). Here, if anywhere, the Dublin audiences were encountering a plethora of "prob-lematic cases," served up for them by Synge.

The classifications suggested above could doubtless be picked over and redistributed in alternative groupings, but the central point is clear: Synge was examining the issue of national character from a variety of different perspectives in *The Playboy*, but in no way was he making the process easy for his audience. The cognitive dilemma that he presented them could be summed up in this way: How to determine the central prototype of IRISHNESS? Which of the many different radial category members considered above should be considered a "best example," metonymically standing for the wider grouping?

> Again and again necessary distinctions, differences and the ideological labelling that went with them were jumbled in unsorted contiguity. Such contamination of confused categories was a deeply disturbing affront to the middle-class nationalist community whose self-image depended on just such moral classification.

(Grene 1999: 86)

Cognitive models and basic-level categorization

We have identified, perhaps, the essential cognitive difficulty of the play for its first audiences but still not why the reactions should have been *so extreme.* Why did this confusion of categories evoke such a violent response to the point at which, on successive nights, audiences were unwilling even to listen to the words of the play being spoken in front of them?

Naturally, it is possible to address these questions solely on the basis of political and social context, as the commentaries provided by Murray (1997), Grene (1999), and Ritschel (2002) seek to do. However, for a better understanding of the full cognitive shock underlying these socio-political factors, it is necessary to consider precisely how the embodied mind organizes, stores, and communicates information about the world.

To understand the potential impact of the various prototypes presented in *The Playboy*, we need to bring to the discussion the notion of *basic-level categorization*, as first developed by Roger Brown. In his account of this, Lakoff (1987: 31–8) speaks of a "psychologically relevant" level at which we interact with the world around us, both in terms of our physical bodies and our embodied minds. It is at this level that the "*categories of the mind fit the categories of the world*" (Ibid.: 34, emphasis in original).

To illustrate this, let us consider the word CAT. This is a good example of a basic-level descriptor, and as such it is the type of word that would be found in a children's primer or in the earliest language exchanges between adult and infant. But there are other levels to be identified above and below this one. At the superordinate level would be the wider category of ANIMAL, and below would be subordinate categories such as SIAMESE, MANX, AMERICAN SHORTHAIR, etc.

The fact that a word like CAT features so early in the process of language-acquisition is no coincidence. Earliest physical encounters between a child and the world around her/him typically involve interactions with a wide range of objects, among these various kinds of animals; and parents and other adults will be quick to name these fleeting objects of attention in an effort to establish mental connections between the objects themselves and the simplest words used to describe them (few parents are likely to exclaim, "Look, Johnny, a three-year-old Japanese Bobtail!"). These encounters will later be reinforced, both by repeat occurrences and by the use of picture-books and other visual images.

The superordinate and subordinate levels are learned at a later stage of development and are what Brown described as "achievements of the imagination" in that they move beyond the immediate physical perceptions we have of an object to aspects that are more abstract, less directly graspable. By considering a variety of such examples, Brown was led to the conclusion that basic-level categorization has the following properties:

- It is the level of distinctive action.
- It is the level which is learned earliest and at which things are first named.
- It is the level at which names are shortest and used most frequently.
- It is a natural level of categorization, as opposed to a level created by "achievements of the imagination."

(Lakoff 1987: 32)

To this, Brent Berlin added the insight that the basic level also tends to be that at which things can be "perceived holistically, as a single gestalt" (Ibid.: 33). (It is for this reason that the parent pointing out a cat would be equally unlikely to say, "Look, Johnny, an animal!" – ANIMAL being too broad and diffuse a concept to be grasped at the basic level.) Finally, Rosch came to the highly significant conclusion that it is at this basic level that most of our cultural information about category members is perceived, organized, and stored.

Perhaps the best way of thinking about basic-level categories is that they are "human-sized." They depend not on objects themselves, independent of people, but on the way people interact with objects: the way they perceive them, image them, organize information about them, and behave towards them with their bodies. The relevant properties clustering together to define such categories are not inherent to the objects, but are interactional properties, having to do with the way people interact with objects.

(Ibid.: 51)

The point, in relation to the Playboy riots, is this: in just the same way that it is an "achievement of the imagination" to conceive of the superordinate level of ANIMAL, so too is it a comparable mental achievement to conceptualize the notion of IRISHNESS in any broad sense. This is actually an abstraction, a disembodied ideal, and all the evidence suggests that we do not mentally organize key information about the world in terms of disembodied models but rather as concrete examples, drawn from our physical interactions with specific objects, people, and environments. As Crane and Richardson have put it, "cognitive theory posits concepts that are not simply determined by the symbolic order in which they exist; instead, meanings are formed by an interaction of the physical world, culture, and human cognitive systems" (Crane and Richardson 1999: 128).

The theatre is a privileged space for physical embodiment and physical interaction. We do not merely read about characters, as in a novel or poem; we see and hear them as they occupy spatial co-ordinates directly in our line of vision. The first audiences of *The Playboy* correctly intuited that the narrative they were experiencing constituted a profoundly disturbing assault upon their own idealized views in relation to the Irish national character. Synge did not provide a rhetorical debate taking place on the aesthetic margins of reality, however, nor an intellectual speculation on idealism in action, but a "physical" encounter with a large number of far-from-ideal category members, any one of which might be taken to represent the category as a whole. The narrative force was a direct result of the cognitive dissonance generated by the clash of categories, operating at the most basic, and therefore most significant, level of knowledge organization.

The mental models we have of nationhood are not simply pre-existing, symbolic concepts: They are formed out of the "human-sized" encounters that we have with specific, material exemplars. In this particular encounter, audiences were being forced into an unwelcome re-evaluation of the category of IRISHNESS, during the course of which Synge would not allow any of the characters to stand metonymically as *ideal cases* or *paragons*. If he did posit such (Christy, Pegeen Mike), it was only to deflate them later.

Ritschel recalls the comment of Thomas MacDonagh, a playwright, theatre director, and also rebel commandant in the Easter uprising of 1916, who said in 1911 that the "fact of the matter is that the son was quite right to strike down the father under the circumstances" (quoted in Ritschel 2002: 49). In this reading, Christy's first act of attempted patricide is taken to be a justified, even heroic action in the cause of freedom (while the second is an empty copy, undertaken merely for Christy's own personal advantage), and Christy is understood as a revolutionary figure, albeit one who fails to follow through on his potential. But the inherent weakness of this view is the fact that the first attempt is not actually embodied in physical stage action and thus remains an abstraction, while the second is played out in real time and space. And that is the crucial difference, both for the characters within the play and for the audience watching it. We arrive, unsurprisingly perhaps, at Pegeen Mike's much-quoted observation that "there's a great gap between a gallous story and a dirty deed" (Synge 1964: 129), and yet we have a fresh perspective also on the underlying cognitive processes at work.

To some extent, it could be argued that this effect is in operation whenever we watch a piece of narrative theatre. Wherever there is material embodiment, there is also a heightened sense of physical interaction and an increased possibility of category disruption: this is the so-called "magic" of live performance. Synge, however, intensifies the force of this impact in *The Playboy* by his concentrated use of carefully selected radial categories and his refusal to identify any one of them as a "best example."

Our cognitive models are constructed directly from the raw material of physical existence, and as Mary Thomas Crane expresses it, they "seem to be 'material' in three ways: (1) they emerge from and consist in the neural matter of the brain; (2) they are shaped by perceptions of physical 'reality' and by the experience of living in the body; and (3) they use metaphor to extend concepts derived from material experience to immaterial abstractions" (Crane 2001: 17). We cannot now experience the same shock felt by the first audiences of *The Playboy*, in part because we do not inhabit the same cultural space but equally because we have different neural patterns in place: our cognitive models have been shaped by quite different physical interactions. Nevertheless, whenever we, as individual embodied minds, encounter any piece of theatre that is capable of disrupting our own category boundaries to a similar degree, we are likely to experience an analagous sense of cognitive dissonance and physical shock (though we may not resort to catcalls and violent protest in response).

The final word may be left to one of the more perceptive members of the play's original audience, who, on Thursday, 31 January 1907, wrote thus to the editor of the *Evening Mail* newspaper in Dublin:

> SIR – If Mr. Synge wishes to turn the "Sinn Fein" howlers into an applauding claque, he need only write a play portraying the Irish peasant as a flawless demi-god. . . .
>
> (quoted in Kilroy 1971: 54)

Notes

1 I quote Lakoff in full here since the notion of *social stereotype* is particularly relevant to the wider discussion. However, I am, of course, indebted to his descriptions for each of the prototypes that follow. (See especially Lakoff 1987: 84–90.)
2 Unlicensed drinking-house.
3 Of Fox Television's popular cartoon family, *The Simpsons*.
4 The lexical proximity of Pegeen/pagan is surely no coincidence (see also Ritschel 2002: 34).
5 These impassioned insults, intended to paint Widow Quin in the darkest of colors, are obscure, to say the least. Interestingly, *Cassell's Dictionary of Slang* (Green 1998) defines "shave" as a term meaning to defraud, rob, or overcharge, and says that "skipper" was nineteenth-century slang for the devil. Thus it may be that Widow Quin stands accused here of overcharging the devil himself by threepence.
6 James Carney glosses "yellow" as denoting "English" or "Protestant" (see note 29 in Grene 1999: 277).

References

Ayling, R. (1992) *J.M. Synge, Four Plays: A Casebook*, Basingstoke: Macmillan.
Crane, M.T. and Richardson, A. (1999) "Literary studies and cognitive science: toward a new interdisciplinarity," *Mosaic – A Journal for the Interdisciplinary Study of Literature*, 32(2): 123–40.

Crane, M.T. (2001) *Shakespeare's Brain: Reading with Cognitive Theory*, Princeton, NJ and Oxford: Princeton University Press.

Green, J. (1998) *Cassell's Dictionary of Slang*, London: Cassell, 1056, 1083.

Grene, N. (1999) *The Politics of Irish Drama: Plays in Context from Boucicault to Friel*, Cambridge and New York: Cambridge University Press.

Harmon, M. (1972) *J.M. Synge: Centenary Papers, 1971*, Dublin: Dolmen Press.

Hunt, H. (1979) *The Abbey: Ireland's National Theatre, 1904–1979*, Dublin and New York: Gill and Macmillan.

Kilroy, J. (1971) *The 'Playboy' Riots*, Dublin: Dolmen Press.

Lakoff, G. (1987) *Women, Fire, and Dangerous Things: What Categories Reveal about the Mind*, Chicago, IL: University of Chicago Press.

Lakoff, G. and Johnson, M. (1999) *Philosophy in the Flesh: The Embodied Mind and its Challenge to Western Thought*, New York: Basic Books.

Murray, C. (1997) *Twentieth-Century Irish Drama: Mirror Up to Nation*, Manchester: Manchester University Press.

Ritschel, N.O. (2002) *Synge and Irish Nationalism: The Precursor to Revolution*, Westport, CT: Greenwood Press.

Robinson, L. (1951) *Ireland's Abbey Theatre: A History, 1899–1951*, London: Sidgwick and Jackson.

Rosch, E. and Mervis, C.B. (1975) "Family resemblances – studies in internal structure of categories," *Cognitive Psychology*, 7(4): 573–605.

Synge, J.M. (1910) *The Aran Islands*, London: George Allen and Unwin.

—— (1964) "The Playboy of the Western World," in Armstrong, W.A. (ed.) *Classic Irish Drama*, Harmondsworth: Penguin Books.

Glossary

Compiled by Jennifer Ewing Pierce

Advisory Projection One of two forms of metaphoric projection named by Lakoff and Johnson (1999), in which the values of one subject are projected onto the values of another in a hypothetical situation. In this form, the subject projects her values onto another so that the first subject experiences the second subject's life with the first's values. Example "If I were you, I'd punch him in the nose." See also **Empathic Projection**.

Affective Cognition A general term referring to a model of cognition that integrates the role of feelings and emotions into a comprehensive model of cognition.

Associative Memory A term specific to the **Connectionist** or **Neural Network** model of cognition, referring to a system of recall in which, when one token (or representation) is encountered through sensory perception, the other token can be reliably and/or predictably recalled. The practical problems of locating a reliable correlation between the mapping of input tokens to output tokens has proven to be a stumbling block for connectionist models of cognition.

Autonomic Nervous System (ANS) Also known as the involuntary nervous system, the autonomic nervous system is the part of the peripheral nervous system that regulates the viscera (heart, belly, and bowel). The ANS operates involuntarily and reflexively, and usually occurs below the cognitive level and therefore has been traditionally categorized as "subcognitive" or "precognitive," and was the usual suspect for "fight or flight behavior." However, it is possible to bring autonomic processes into awareness and for some under conscious control. Several researchers (Antonio Damasio and Joseph LeDoux, for example) have recently called this idea of the precognitive or the subcognitive into question, maintaining that all emotion is represented in cognition.

Body Schemas A term referring to the representation of the body in the brain, which then appears as implicit knowledge about the body in space. First introduced in clinical neurology in 1912 by English neurologists Head and Holmes, the theory of body schemas has been more recently validated through the study of the "phantom limb" phenomenon. Body schemas are thought to be implicated in both acting and the observation of action in others and are apparently stored in the parietal lobes.

Broca's Area   Named for Paul Broca (1824–1880), who discovered this neuroanatomical site in the brains of patients who suffered from nonfluent aphasia (the inability to understand and produce grammatically complicated language), Broca's Area works in conjunction with **Wernicke's Area** to allow for the processing and analysis of language in both reception and production. Wernicke's Area processes the content of words, while Broca's Area is responsible for analyzing syntax. Thus, patients suffering injury to Broca's Area but not Wernicke's are unable to speak or understand grammatically but may still produce and comprehend the content of words. See also **Wernicke's Area**.

Cerebellum   Derived from the Latin for "little brain," the cerebellum is located posterior to the brain stem, is divided into hemispheres, and is surrounded by the cortex. The cerebellum controls movement, balance, and posture.

Cognitive Psychology   As a branch of psychology, cognitive psychology distinguishes itself from others by focusing on the nexus between stimulus and response. Cognitive psychology examines the mental processes and states that underlie behavior and relies on empiricist methods more than introspection or theory. Though cognitive approaches began as early as the 1950s, the term is generally understood to have come into usage when the first textbook on "cognitive psychology" was published by Ulric Neisser in 1967. See also **Cognitive Science**.

Cognitive Science   A broad-sweeping field that concerns itself with the architecture of artificial, human, and animal minds. It is widely interdisciplinary, with philosophy, psychology, neuroscience, computer science, and linguistics at its core; and it may cover an even broader spectrum of scientific and philosophic inquiry, including anthropology, sociology, and evolutionary biology. There are two branches of cognitive science, classical cognitivism (sometimes called "first-generation cognitive science") and **Second-Generation Cognitive Science**, which share basic and overlapping tenets but which also present radically divergent models of the mind/brain.

Conceptual Blending   Also called "conceptual integration theory," cognitive blending is a dynamic process of mental integration of information that, according to the theory's originators, Gilles Fauconnier and Mark Turner, is common to and even pervasive within both everyday life and art. Building on the "mental space" theory of Fauconnier's earlier work, cognitive blend theory proposes that the mind working "online" (i.e., using working memory) gathers information from at least three (although there can be multiple) "input spaces," the combination of which results in the selective projection of information into a new "space" (the blend), where new meaning emerges and may itself serve as "input" for further conceptualization.

Connectionism   A term from Artificial Intelligence research that proposes a computational paradigm modeling the computer after the neurological organization of the brain. This model utilizes networks of simple processing elements, which gain their ability to perform complex tasks through their interconnectedness rather than by relying on a centralized processing agent. For the nonspecialist, connectionism may be seen as synonymous with **Neural Networks**. Connectionism and neural networks, while applying to information-processing in computers, both draw their paradigms from biology; i.e., the biological models precede the computational ones.

Convergence Zone   An anatomical locus in the brain that categorizes memories. It does not store memories but aids in reconstructing them. Information passes through such zonos before an idea can be represented or an articulation of an idea can be manifested.

Core Consciousness   A concept introduced by the neuroscientist Antonio Damasio to describe an aspect of consciousness that gives the subject knowledge of herself in the here and now. Core consciousness has no sense of other places and other times (past, present, or future). Damasio defines core consciousness as simple and in contrast to the more complex **Extended Consciousness**.

Emotion/Feeling   Although the vernacular allows us to use these words interchangeably, **Second-Generation Cognitive Science** generally posits a distinction between emotions and feelings. Antonio Damasio, drawing heavily upon a model first proposed by William James (1884) and later enforced by Paul Ekman's influential cross-cultural studies of human facial expressions (1969), has recently suggested that emotion is the embodied response to an **Emotionally Competent Stimulus**, while feeling is the conscious awareness of the emotion. Thus, the emotion is a necessary but not sufficient condition for the feeling; that is, an emotion can exist without a feeling, but a feeling cannot exist without an emotion.

Emotionally Competent Stimulus (ECS)   The emotionally competent stimulus is a stimulus that triggers emotional response in the brain when represented across networks. The stimulus can be actual or remembered.

Empathic Projection   One of two forms of metaphoric projection named by Lakoff and Johnson (1999), in which the values of one subject are projected onto the values of another in a hypothetical situation. In this form, the first subject experiences the second subject's values by imagining what it is like to experience the world through the second subject's values. Example: "If I were you, I'd feel just awful, too." See also **Advisory Projection**.

Episodic Memory   A small part of the larger category of **Explicit Memory**, episodic memory refers to the ability to remember past events. Episodic memory is related to **Semantic Memory** but functions differently in that episodic memory is concerned with remembering that which is anchored in a past moment and later re-experienced.

Essentialism   Also known as "typology," this concept from cognitive psychology and evolutionary biology identifies the human capacity to categorize artifacts and living things in terms of basic categories called **Natural Kinds**. Unlike its use (and reputation) in philosophy and literary theory, essentialism in psychology and biology is not a metaphysical claim but an aspect of necessary human reasoning processes. See also **Natural Kinds**.

Explicit Memory   Memories that involve a conscious recall of the moment in which an idea or event was first encoded in memory. See also **Implicit Memory**.

Extended Consciousness   This is the aspect of consciousness that gives the subject her identity and sense of self in a place and time and includes the capacity for notions of past, present, and possible futures. Unlike core consciousness, extended consciousness has many grades and levels.

Folk Theories   Folk theories – sometimes referred to as "folk psychology" – view everyday understandings of the mind as constitutive of a valid theory of mind in their own right. Derived from people's observed ability to predict accurately and intuit the behavior and mental states of other human beings, folk theories can be understood as having both an extrinsic function (predicting behavior and mental states in others) and an intrinsic representation (folk theories actually represent a data structure in the mind).

Graded Categories   Referring to the psychological and biological maxim which states that minds function by categorizing information (see also **Essentialism** and **Natural Kinds**), graded categories are theorized types of categories whose relations between internal features are asymmetrically positioned along a gradient of salience or relevance. The classic example comes from an experiment by the psychologist Eleanor Rosch, who measured the response times of subjects categorizing BIRDS. In her experiment, response times were shorter for categorizing ROBIN as a BIRD and longer for categorizing CHICKEN as a BIRD, presumably because a robin was judged to be a "better" example of a bird than a chicken. Though the value judgments regarding features within a category inevitably differ from culture to culture (for instance, in a country where there are no robins, a different species will likely serve as the "better" example of BIRD), the cognitive capacity to categorize along asymmetrical gradients exists across cultures. See also other important types of categories identified by **Second-Generation Cognitive Science: Subordinate Categories, Superordinate Categories,** and especially **Prototypes**.

Implicit Memory   First defined by Graf and Schacter in 1985, implicit memory refers to a nonconscious form of memory that bears no reference to the initial encoding episode. Implicit memory was identified in experiments when subjects improved their performance of a task based on a previous performance, despite the fact that there had been no reported memory of the initial performance of the task. It is different from explicit memory, which necessarily refers to and evokes the original encoding episode. See **Explicit Memory**.

Lateralization Refers to the neuroanatomical fact that the brain has two separate halves as well as to the theory that these halves have discrete and specialized functions.

Lexical Representation A term that refers to the way in which the brain represents words to itself. Lexical representation differs from the representations of real-world events, things, people, or ideas that words are supposed to represent. An open question is whether lexical representations also contain information about the syntactic properties of words, i.e., the part of speech (noun, adjective, adverb, etc.) to which they belong.

Multiple-Selves Metaphor The process by which, according to Lakoff and Johnson (1999), the mind conceptualizes multiple values as multiple selves. This process is associated with the tendency for people to project a social role onto an individual self, such as referring to a "professional" self or a "religious" self.

Natural Kinds A term employed in evolutionary biology and philosophy of science to refer to a category of mind that presupposes an unchanging essence and that defines rather than describes. The definition gives the artifact its unique quality and seems unaltered by more superficial details. For instance, a cat has fur, whiskers, four legs, and a tail, but one could still identify its "cat-ness" if an accident were to cause the cat to lose its tail and two of its legs.

Neocortex The most sophisticated section of the cerebral cortex, this part of the brain is called "neo" because it is thought to be the latest development in the brain's evolution. The neocortex controls planning, reasoning, and language.

Neural Memory This refers to the total integrated system of data in a given neural network, including relationships between datum and evolutionarily stored processes. The term can refer to literal neuronal networks in the brain or to the analogs of such networks created in computers. See also **Neural Networks**.

Neural Networks Systems of programs and data that emulate the functioning of organic neurons using gradient-based training, fuzzy logic, genetic algorithms, and Bayesian methods. They are currently being used to model signal processing and time-series analyses, predict the weather, and even model organic thinking. Neural networks are primed with large amounts of data and rules about data relationships that enable the networks to evolve into more complex knowledge layers.

Neurons Brain cells with specialized structures called axons and dendrites, which allow information to be delivered to and from the cell body. Neurons communicate with each other electrochemically.

Prototypes   Also known as "cognitive reference points" or "basic-level categories," prototypes are categorical examples that have a special cognitive status and provide an empirically verifiable point of reference for subjects (using the techniques of response-time testing). A prototype determines the structure of a particular category, and those category types labeled **Subordinate Categories**, **Superordinate Categories**, and **Graded Categories** are so called because of this "prototype effect."

Schemas   Highly abstract mental constructions that serve as templates for understanding more concrete mental experience, schemas are the mind's way of characterizing concepts through a collection of identifiable attributes. They allow the mind to encode propositional and perceptual categories and to generalize based on a repeating pattern of perceived attributes. Schemas apply to a broad spectrum of situations, experiences, and sensations, enabling basic forms of cognition.

Second-Generation Cognitive Science   A term differentiating post-1980 cognitive-scientific theory (based on the notion of "embodied" cognition) from classical cognitivism ("first-generation cognitive science"), the latter represented by such earlier twentieth-century figures as Gottlob Frege, Noam Chomsky, Jerry Fodor, and others. Second-generation cognitive science finds its most convincing and widely read proponents in the neuroscientists Gerald Edelman and Antonio Damasio, the psychologists Evan Thompson, Francisco Varela, Eleanor Rosch, John Donahoe, and David Palmer, the linguists George Lakoff, Ronald Langacker, and Raymond W. Gibbs, and the philosopher Mark Johnson. Although there are wide-ranging theories within second-generation cognitive science that sometimes contradict each other, the consistent and unifying ideas include assertions that behavior, emotions, language, and decision-making are all predicated upon our sensorimotor experience, which is processed through embodied cognitive apparatuses.

Semantic Categories   A concept in linguistics suggesting that there are a finite number of semantic categories that organize all lexical representations. Semantic categories are descriptive of the syntactical functions of the words they organize; examples include "agents" (do-ers of an action such as "*She* wrote the essay"), "possession" ("*my* book"), and "demonstratives" (these, them, that, those, this, etc.). The semantic category as a linguistic concept has been wedded to **Second-Generation Cognitive Science** through the research on prototypes and other category types by cognitive psychologists such as Elenaor Rosch and others. See also **Prototype, Subordinate, Superordinate**, and **Graded Categories**.

Semantic Memory   Memory that is not tied to the recall of a particular event but that reflects general knowledge pertaining to the world. Semantic memory is related to, but ultimately differs from, **Episodic Memory**. Semantic memory involves the retrieval of information pertaining to the present moment and precludes a re-experiencing of the original memory. See also **Explicit Memory**.

Sensorimotor Schemas   First identified by Piaget in childhood-development studies, sensorimotor schemas are structured schemas of perception that allow for physical action in the material world.

Somatic-Marker Hypothesis   Theory put forth by the cognitive psychologist Antonio Damasio to explain how visceral and somatic states, traditionally considered "precognitive," actually become constitutive of cognition, primarily in attention-selection and decision-making. Quite literally, a "gut feeling" can allow us to make decisions quickly by allowing us to reject or accept an alternative based on negative or positive "somatic markers" (emotional responses), leading to pleasant or unpleasant feeling states.

Subordinate Categories   Referring to the way the mind orders and stores information, a subordinate category is a category containing sufficiently specialized traits to set it at an abstract distance from the prototype of that category. So, for instance, while a prototype of CAR might be the generic FOUR-DOOR SEDAN, the subordinate category might be something like a SPORTS CAR (which is distinct again from the superordinate category for CAR, a VEHICLE). See also **Superordinate Categories**, **Graded Categories**, and **Prototypes**.

Superordinate Categories   Referring to the way the mind orders and stores information relative to basic-level or prototype features, a superordinate category would be a widely encompassing descriptor of members of a category, less salient or "basic" than its prototype member. The example of VEHICLE in the entry for **Subordinate Categories** (above) shows this difference in abstraction level between the superordinate VEHICLE and the prototype FOUR-DOOR SEDAN (and the subordinate SPORTS CAR). See also **Subordinate Categories, Graded Categories,** and **Prototypes**.

Synesthesia   Although also a term used in literary criticism to denote a figure of speech, synesthesia is a scientific concept describing the phenomenon whereby input from one sensory modality is experienced through another sensory modality.

Syntax   A term in linguistics referring to the patterns governing the arrangement of semantic units into sentence structures. Syntax is controlled by **Broca's Area** and appears to be a separate function from those governing production and reception of speech (although syntax is also obviously interactive with these functions).

Wernicke's Area   First discovered in 1874 by Carl Wernicke, Wernicke's Area is a material locus in the brain hypothesized to be central to language comprehension because neuropathology in this area causes "fluent aphasia" (speech impairment). This type of aphasia impairs the patient's ability to construct meaning through listening or by producing sentences. However, the patient's ability to analyze and employ grammar and syntax remains intact as long as the adjacent Broca's Area remains intact (see **Broca's Area**). The discovery of these two neuroanatomical structures allowed cognitive scientists to identify semantics and syntax as materially discrete (though also functionally interactive) activities within the brain.

Bibliography

Afifi, A. and Bergman, R. (1997) *Functional Neuroanatomy Text and Atlas*, New York: McGraw-Hill.

Clark, A. (1998) *Being There: Putting Brain, Body, and World Back Together Again*, Cambridge, MA: MIT Press.

Damasio, A. (1994) *Descartes' Error: Emotion, Reason, and the Human Brain*, New York: Putnam.

—— (1999) *The Feeling of What Happens: Body and Emotion in the Making of Consciousness*, New York, San Diego, London: Harcourt Brace and Co.

Fauconnier, G. and Turner, M. (2002) *The Way We Think: Conceptual Blending and the Mind's Hidden Complexities*, New York: Basic Books.

Greenfield, S. (2000) *The Private Life of the Brain*, New York: Wiley & Sons.

Gregory, R.L. (ed.) (2004) *The Oxford Companion to the Mind*, Oxford: Oxford University Press.

Lakoff, G. and Johnson, M. (1999) *Philosophy in the Flesh: The Embodied Mind and Its Challenge to Western Thought*, New York: Basic Books.

LeDoux, J. (1999) *The Emotional Brain*, New York: Harper Perennial.

Nadel, L. (ed.) (2003) *Encyclopedia of Cognitive Science*, London: Nature Publishing Group.

Varela, F.J., Thomspon, E., and Rosch, E. (1991) *The Embodied Mind: Cognitive Science and Human Experience*, Cambridge, MA: MIT Press.

Wilson, R.A. and Keil, F.C. (eds) (1999) *The MIT Encyclopedia of the Cognitive Sciences*, Cambridge, MA: MIT Press.

Index

LIBRARY, UNIVERSITY OF CHESTER